WJEC GCSE HISTORY

GW00362166

The Elizabethan Age
1558–1603

Depression, War and Recovery
1930–1951

R. Paul Evans
Steve May

DYNAMIC LEARNING

HODDER EDUCATION
AN HACHETTE UK COMPANY

Every effort has been made to trace all copyright holders, but if any have been inadvertently overlooked, the Publishers will be pleased to make the necessary arrangements at the first opportunity.

Although every effort has been made to ensure that website addresses are correct at time of going to press, Hodder Education cannot be held responsible for the content of any website mentioned in this book. It is sometimes possible to find a relocated web page by typing in the address of the home page for a website in the URL window of your browser.

Hachette UK's policy is to use papers that are natural, renewable and recyclable products and made from wood grown in sustainable forests. The logging and manufacturing processes are expected to conform to the environmental regulations of the country of origin.

Orders: please contact Bookpoint Ltd, 130 Milton Park, Abingdon, Oxon OX14 4SB. Telephone: +44 (0)1235 827720. Fax: +44 (0)1235 400454. Email education@bookpoint.co.uk Lines are open from 9 a.m. to 5 p.m., Monday to Saturday, with a 24-hour message answering service. You can also order through our website: www.hoddereducation.co.uk

ISBN: 978 1 5104 0318 5

© R. Paul Evans, Steve May 2017

First published in 2017 by
Hodder Education,
An Hachette UK Company
Carmelite House
50 Victoria Embankment
London EC4Y 0DZ

www.hoddereducation.co.uk

Impression number 10 9 8 7 6 5 4 3 2 1

Year   2021 2020 2019 2018 2017

Cover photo © Morphart Creation - Shutterstock, © World History Archive / TopFoto

Typeset in India by Aptara Inc.

Printed in Italy

A catalogue record for this title is available from the British Library.

CONTENTS

Introduction   2

The Elizabethan Age, 1558–1603

1   Elizabethan government   4

2   Lifestyles of the rich and poor   23

3   Popular entertainment   44

4   The problem of religion   55

5   The Catholic threat   66

6   The Spanish Armada   82

7   The Puritan threat   95

Examination guidance   106

Depression, War and Recovery, 1930–1951

1   The coming of the Depression   116

2   Life during the Depression   120

3   The coming of war   137

4   Life during wartime   148

5   Keeping up morale   160

6   Life after war   170

7   Rebuilding the country after 1945   178

Examination guidance   189

Glossary   198

Index   201

Acknowledgements   203

Introduction

About the course

During this course you must study **four** units, each contributing a different weighting to the GCSE qualification:

- **Unit 1** Studies in Depth (Wales and the wider perspective) – weighting of 25 per cent of GCSE qualification
- **Unit 2** Studies in Depth (History with a European/World focus) – weighting of 25 per cent of the GCSE qualification
- **Unit 3** Thematic Study, which includes the study of a historical site – weighting of 30 per cent of the GCSE qualification
- **Unit 4** Working as an historian – Non-Examination Assessment – weighting of 20 per cent of the GCSE qualification.

These studies will be assessed through three examination papers and a non-examination unit.

Units 1 and 2 each consist of a one-hour examination made up of a series of compulsory questions. These will focus upon the analysis and evaluation of historical sources and interpretations, as well as testing second-order historical concepts.

Unit 3 consists of a 1-hour-and-15-minute examination made up a series of compulsory questions. These will focus upon second order historical concepts such as continuity, change, cause, consequence, significance, similarity and difference.

Unit 4 will consist of a non-examination assessment. It will involve the completion of two tasks, one focusing on source evaluation and one on the formation of different historical interpretations of history.

About the book

This book covers two options within the Unit 1 Studies in Depth – Wales and the wider perspective:

- Option 1A: The Elizabethan Age, 1558
- Option 1C: Depression, War and Recovery, 1930–1951

You will only need to study **one** of these options.

How this book will help you in WJEC GCSE History

It will help you learn the content

Many students worry that they won't know enough to answer the questions in the exam. The **author text** explains the key content clearly and helps you understand each of the topics. Each chapter equips you with the right level of knowledge and detail needed to help provide detailed answers for the exam.

The book is full of **sources**. History is at its best when you can see what real people said, did, felt and watched. Sources can help you really understand the story better and remember it because they help you see what the issues meant to people at the time.

The **activities** direct you to the things you should be noticing or thinking about in the sources and text. They also help you practise the kind of analytical skills that you need to improve in history.

Each chapter includes **key terms** to help you understand what these words mean so you can understand them and use them confidently when writing about the subject. They are all defined in the Glossary on pages 198–200.

It will help you prepare for your exam

The practice questions on the book are exam-style questions that give you the opportunity to practise exam skills.

The exam guidance at the end of the unit (pages 106–114 for The Elizabethan Age, 1558–1603, and pages 189–197 for Depression, War and Recovery, 1930–51) contain a model exam paper as well as step-by-step-guidance, model answers and advice on how to answer particular question types in the Studies in Depth – Wales and the wider perspective paper.

The Elizabethan Age, 1558—1603

1 Elizabethan government

Introduction: Elizabeth's life before she became queen

When Elizabeth I came to the throne in 1558 she was the fifth Tudor monarch to reign. The Tudor dynasty had been established by Elizabeth's grandfather, Henry Tudor, who had come to the throne in 1485 following his victory over Richard III at the Battle of Bosworth, the battle that ended the Wars of the Roses. As Henry VII, he ruled until his death in 1509 when he was succeeded by his son, Henry VIII, who in turn was succeeded by his son, Edward VI, followed by his two daughters, Mary and Elizabeth (see Figure 1.1).

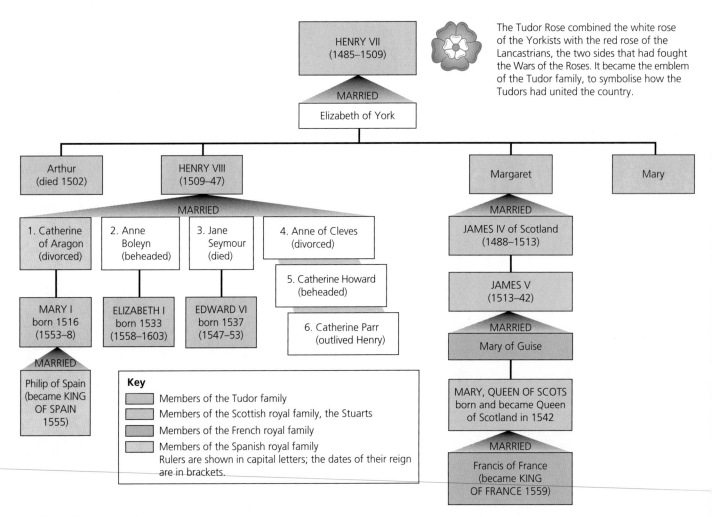

The Tudor Rose combined the white rose of the Yorkists with the red rose of the Lancastrians, the two sides that had fought the Wars of the Roses. It became the emblem of the Tudor family, to symbolise how the Tudors had united the country.

▲ Figure 1.1: The Tudor family tree

Henry VIII and his wives

Henry VIII is famous for having been married six times, the driving force behind these marriages being a desperate attempt to secure a male heir to the throne. By his first marriage to a Spanish princess, Catherine of Aragon, he had one daughter, Mary. In 1527 Henry fell in love with Anne Boleyn, a young noblewoman. In order to marry her he needed to divorce Catherine. Henry therefore petitioned the Pope, as head of the Roman Catholic Church, to grant him a divorce. This was refused. In 1533 when unmarried Anne became pregnant, Henry decided to break away from the Roman Catholic Church and create a new Church of England with himself as head. This enabled him to grant himself a divorce and marry Anne.

On 7 September 1533 Anne gave birth to a daughter. She was called Elizabeth after Henry's mother, Elizabeth of York. In 1536 Anne gave birth to a second child, a boy, but he died at birth. When Henry found out that Anne was very friendly with some of the male courtiers he sent her to the Tower of London and dissolved the marriage. After an investigation she was declared guilty of adultery and treason and Henry ordered her execution. Following the death of her mother, Elizabeth, aged just two, was declared illegitimate. This meant she now had no claim to the throne.

In 1537 Henry married Jane Seymour, his third wife. In October of that year she gave birth to a son, named Edward, but Jane did not long survive the birth, dying a few days later. Henry was to marry a further three times, his sixth wife being Catherine Parr, the daughter of Sir Thomas Parr, a wealthy nobleman from the north of England.

Having spent most of her life being moved from house to house, Elizabeth, now aged ten, went to live with her father and his new queen, Catherine, together with her half-brother Edward. Both children were brought up as Protestants.

Edward VI

In 1547 Henry died and was succeeded by his nine-year-old son who became King Edward VI. As Edward was too young to rule alone his advisers made the important decisions, which included making the Church of England more Protestant. This worried some loyal Catholics. Elizabeth, now aged fifteen, was living with her Protestant step-mother, Catherine Parr, but when Catherine died a year later, in 1548, the young princess found herself alone.

Mary I

In 1553 Edward, who had always been a sickly child, died at the age of just fifteen. The throne now passed to his elder half-sister, Mary, who was a strict Roman Catholic. Queen Mary I soon began to undo the religious changes made during Edward's reign and made the Catholic religion the main faith of the country. Protestants who refused to convert to the Catholic faith were punished and some prominent protestors were burnt at the stake. They included Archbishop Cranmer and the Protestant bishops Latimer and Ridley. In 1554 Mary announced that she planned to marry her cousin, King Philip II of Spain, one of the strongest Catholic rulers of Europe. She also began the Marian Persecution, which forced people to keep the Roman Catholic faith or face severe penalties. Her actions quickly became very unpopular with many Protestants.

▲ Henry VIII, painted by a follower of Hans Holbein the Younger in the sixteenth century

▲ Edward VI, painted by Hans Holbein, 1543

▲ Mary I, painted by Master John, c.1554

Elizabeth's position under Mary

As a Protestant, this was a difficult time for Elizabeth, especially after the outbreak of a Protestant rebellion in 1554 led by Sir Thomas Wyatt. Elizabeth was suspected of being involved in the plot and Mary ordered her arrest and imprisonment in the Tower of London. She was charged with treason, the punishment for which was death.

As there was not enough evidence to link Elizabeth with the Wyatt Plot she was released from the Tower and moved to Woodstock House in Oxfordshire where she was closely watched. She was later moved to Hatfield House in Hertfordshire, where she was advised by Sir William Cecil. It was there, on 17 November 1558, that she was brought the news that Mary had died and she was now queen of Wales and England. She was 25 years of age.

▲ Source A: A portrait of princess Elizabeth as a young girl, painted in 1545. She is shown holding her Protestant prayer book

---

Interpretation 1: J. E. Neale, an historian who specialised in Tudor history, writing in his biography, *Queen Elizabeth*, published in 1934

Mary had no doubts about Elizabeth's involvement in the plot, and if this could be proved there was small hope of mercy. Wyatt and others were examined and re-examined for evidence to convict her. It was discovered that Wyatt had twice written to her and received answers, but they were verbal only and amounted to nothing. They may not even have been hers, for some of her servants had been involved in the conspiracy, and there is no saying what use they had made of her name.

ACTIVITIES ?

1. Using the information on pages 5–8 construct a time line covering the period from 1533 to 1603.
   a) Mark the key events in Elizabeth's life up to November 1558.
   b) As you advance through the chapters of this book you can add extra events to this timeline.
2. Study Source A. What image of Elizabeth do you think the artist is trying to portray?

Practice question

Study Interpretation 1. How far do you agree with the interpretation that Elizabeth had little connection to the Wyatt Plot? *(For guidance, see pages 113–114.)*

The coronation and popularity of Elizabeth

The death of Queen Mary was greeted with a sense of relief by many, especially Protestants. During the short reign of 'Bloody Mary', the Marian Persecution had resulted in over 300 Protestants being put to death because they refused to change their religion. They included Archbishop Cranmer and the Protestant Bishops Latimer and Ridley. Many people now hoped that Elizabeth would prove to be a more just and popular monarch.

Elizabeth's coronation

Elizabeth's coronation was deliberately designed to be a splendid and colourful event to show off the power of the new monarch, with ceremonies lasting several days. On 12 January 1559 Elizabeth travelled from Whitehall to the Tower in a ceremonial barge along the Thames. Two days later she undertook a triumphal coronation procession through the streets of central London (see Source B). At intervals in the coronation procession pageants were performed and musical instruments played.

The coronation itself took place in Westminster Abbey on Sunday 15 January. Elizabeth was crowned and anointed by Owen Oglethorpe, the Catholic Bishop of Carlisle, and she came out of the Abbey to the sound of loud instruments and cheers from the crowd. Dressed in her full state regalia which included the sceptre and orb (see Source C), she walked the short distance to Westminster Hall for a state banquet.

▲ Source C: Portrait of Elizabeth painted in 1559 showing her dressed in her coronation robes, patterned with Tudor roses

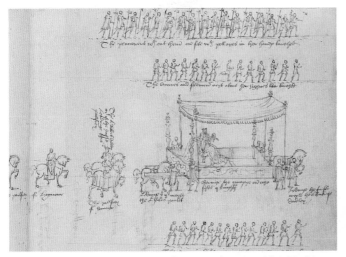

▲ Source B: A contemporary drawing showing Elizabeth's coronation procession in 1559

ACTIVITIES

1 Explain why Elizabeth wanted her coronation to be a 'splendid and colourful' event.

2 Use Source B and your own knowledge to describe Elizabeth's coronation.

Practice question

What can be learnt from Sources B and C about Elizabeth's coronation? (For guidance, see pages 107–108.)

Elizabeth's popularity

Elizabeth received a good education and by the time of her coronation she could converse in Greek, Latin, French and Italian. She was well read, particularly in the arts and literature. She loved dancing, riding and music, and was keen on archery and needlework. She also studied theology, favoured the Bible in English and was keen to avoid the religious divides that had dominated the reigns of her half-brother and half-sister.

It was said that her quick temper was a characteristic she inherited from her father, and her unwillingness to spend money copied the miserliness of her grandfather, Henry VII. However, inheriting a nation in debt, Elizabeth had little choice but to control the purse strings wisely, and with the help of her advisers on the Privy Council (see page 11), she managed to balance the nation's finances.

One item she did spend lavishly on was her appearance, taking great pride in her clothes, which were adorned in fine jewels and ornaments. She realised the importance of projecting an image of majesty and power, and this pride in her appearance remained with her throughout her long reign.

The use of portraits

One method through which Elizabeth could project her image of royal authority was through portraits. Elizabeth had many official portraits painted during her reign but as she grew older the images became less and less accurate in showing what the queen actually looked like. After catching smallpox in 1562 the queen's face was left badly scarred, prompting her to paint her face with white powder. By the 1590s her thinning hair caused her to wear a wig and her teeth had turned black. Yet her portraits did not show this and they were used as a means of propaganda, creating an image of a monarch who was ageless, strong and powerful; a wise and successful ruler. To show their loyalty many nobles displayed portraits of the queen in their great houses.

ACTIVITIES ?

1   Use Source D and your own knowledge to show how portraits were used to project an image of royal authority.

2   Why did Elizabeth consider royal progresses to be important?

Source D: The Pelican ▶ Portrait, painted by Nicholas Hilliard in 1574. It is named after the pelican brooch that she is wearing on her bodice. According to legend the mother pelican pecks at her own breast and feeds her young on her own blood so that they might live. This image therefore shows Elizabeth as the mother of her people, ready to sacrifice her life to protect them

Royal progresses

Another method used by the queen to court popularity was to undertake regular royal progresses, touring the countryside, staying in the houses of her nobles and receiving free accommodation, food, drink and entertainment. These annual royal progresses took place during the summer months when travelling was easier and involved visits to houses in the south-east and the midlands. Elizabeth never ventured as far as northern England, the south-west or Wales. For about 10 weeks each year the whole Court went on tour. It was a propaganda exercise, the chief purpose being to ensure that Elizabeth was seen by her subjects. To a noble it was a great privilege to receive her majesty, but it was also a very costly experience, since the queen travelled with an army of advisers, officials, servants and guards, all of whom had to be accommodated, fed and entertained for however long Elizabeth decided to stay. The host was also expected to present the queen with expensive gifts. This was one method by which Elizabeth was seen by her subjects and it also served to keep a watchful eye over the powerful noble families.

Source F: One of Elizabeth's royal progress journeys in 1568 described by an eye-witness

She was received with great applause and signs of joy … At which she was extremely pleased … She ordered her carriage sometimes to be taken where the crowd seemed thickest and stood up and thanked the people.

Practice questions

1 What can be learnt from Sources E and F about royal progresses? *(For guidance, see pages 107–108.)*
2 Explain the connections between any THREE of the following:
   - royal portraits
   - royal progresses
   - Elizabeth I's character
   - Elizabeth I's appearance.
   (For guidance, see page 112.)

▲ **Source E:** A painting, dated 1601, showing Elizabeth on one of her annual royal progresses

The Royal Court

Interpretation 2: An evaluation of Elizabeth's control over the Royal Court made by the writer Barbara Mervyn who was commissioned to write the book *The Reign of Elizabeth: England 1558–1603*, published in 2001

Elizabeth can be credited with maintaining a politically stable central government by creating a Court where she exercised control by awarding offices and favours. In this way she could control rival factions.

The Royal Court was the centre of all political power during the Elizabethan period. The main residence of the queen was Whitehall Palace in London where she had her ladies-in-waiting and servants living with her, together with her chief advisers and government officials. All these people made up the Royal Court and they travelled with the queen when she went on her progresses. Having her courtiers close by enabled Elizabeth to consult, seek advice and challenge her councillors, as well as keeping an eye on their activities and check upon their rivalries. Among her chief courtiers were William Cecil, Sir Christopher Hatton, Sir Walter Raleigh, Sir Francis Walsingham and Robert Dudley, Earl of Leicester, many of whom also served the queen as Privy Councillors (see pages 12–13).

The queen exercised her power and maintained the loyalty of her ministers and officials through the granting of patronage. Ambitious nobles would try to get access to the queen's court in the hope of being noticed by Elizabeth and possibly being granted an important position in central or local government. Elizabeth quickly realised the importance of using the system of royal patronage to her advantage. Knowing that the queen had the power to make or break them kept her nobles loyal and supportive. For the ambitious courtiers everything depended upon keeping the continued support of the queen.

Factions in the Royal Court

Source G: A comment upon Elizabeth's method of ruling made in the 1630s by Sir Robert Naunton who had previously been a member of the queen's court

She ruled much by factions and parties, which she made, upheld and weakened as her own great judgement advised.

By operating such a system of patronage, Elizabeth naturally generated rivalry between her courtiers and this resulted in the development of court factions. Until the 1590s, when her advancing years and the loss of many of her older ministers began to have an impact, Elizabeth was generally successful in playing off one faction against the other, using her ultimate power of dismissal to control and check her courtiers and Privy Councillors.

One of the chief rivalries in the earlier part of Elizabeth's reign was between two of her most important advisers, William Cecil and Robert Dudley. Cecil was hard working and cautious in decision making, particularly when it came to managing government expenditure. This meant he was reluctant to let the country get involved in costly wars on the continent. This was in contrast to the bolder approach of Dudley, who favoured intervention in the wars in Europe. They also contrasted in their religious views, Cecil being a moderate Protestant, whereas Dudley was a Puritan. (For differences between Protestants and Puritans, see page 55.) Other courtiers were dragged into such rivalries and were sometimes forced to support one faction against another.

Practice question

Study Interpretation 2. How far do you agree with this interpretation that Elizabeth maintained control over her ministers through awarding offices and favours? *(For guidance, see pages 113–114.)*

ACTIVITIES

1   Copy out and complete this table using the information in this section together with your own knowledge of this topic.

	How did Elizabeth use this feature to maintain control and authority over her councillors and advisers?
The Royal Court	
The use of patronage	
The development of factions	

2   What information does Source G provide about Elizabeth's method of ruling?

3   Explain why rival factions emerged round William Cecil and Robert Dudley.

The Privy Council and councillors

One of the most important means by which the country was governed during Elizabeth's reign was through the Privy Council. This was a body of advisers and ministers, appointed by the queen, to help her rule. Privy Councillors were chosen from members of the noble and gentry classes, and occasionally archbishops. Within the first few months of becoming queen, Elizabeth had appointed nineteen men to her Privy Council and, to help provide some continuity, over one-half had been members of the Privy Council of Mary I, such as Sir Thomas Cheney and Sir William Petre.

The Council met regularly, generally two or three times a week during the early part of Elizabeth's reign, but more frequently later in the reign and during occasions when it was necessary to deal with a specific issue. One such occasion occurred in 1562 when the queen's life was threatened by catching smallpox and the Council had to discuss possible succession issues. Another crisis followed Mary Queen of Scot's flight from Scotland to England in 1568, raising concerns over a possible Catholic plot to replace Elizabeth with her Catholic cousin (see page 61).

Elizabeth seldom attended Council meetings and she was not compelled to accept the advice that the Council offered her, although she seldom disregarded it completely. The council had a number of main functions and its duties were carried out by individual Privy Councillors (see Figure 1.2).

Interpretation 3: A view of the role of the Privy Council given by the historian John Warren in his book *Elizabeth I: Meeting the Challenge: England 1541–1603*, published in 2001

Its main functions were to advise the Queen, to administer the realm and to implement decisions taken by the Queen and Council. Since its leading Councillors headed departments of state, and were responsible for the royal finances, courts of law and national security, it is not surprising that they exercised considerable influence. … However, the Council was neither a unified nor an unchanging body. Although there was much continuity among some key office holders, factional rivalry may have lessened its importance.

ACTIVITY ?

How important was the Privy Council to Elizabeth in governing the country?

Practice question

Study Interpretation 3. How far would you agree with this interpretation that factional rivalry within the Privy Council may have lessened its importance? *(For guidance, see pages 113–114.)*

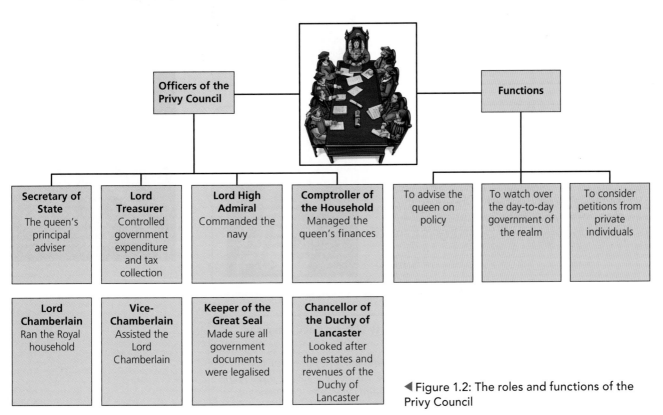

◀ Figure 1.2: The roles and functions of the Privy Council

Officers of the Privy Council

Functions

Secretary of State	Lord Treasurer	Lord High Admiral	Comptroller of the Household
The queen's principal adviser	Controlled government expenditure and tax collection	Commanded the navy	Managed the queen's finances

Lord Chamberlain	Vice-Chamberlain	Keeper of the Great Seal	Chancellor of the Duchy of Lancaster
Ran the Royal household	Assisted the Lord Chamberlain	Made sure all government documents were legalised	Looked after the estates and revenues of the Duchy of Lancaster

- To advise the queen on policy
- To watch over the day-to-day government of the realm
- To consider petitions from private individuals

Important Privy Councillors during Elizabeth's reign

Sir William Cecil
(1520–98, created Lord Burghley in 1571)

A moderate Protestant, Cecil had been a Privy Councillor during the reign of Edward VI and during Mary's reign he was appointed by Princess Elizabeth to look after her affairs. Upon becoming queen in 1558 Elizabeth appointed Cecil her secretary of state. As her principal adviser, it was Cecil who managed the meetings of parliament (see page 18) and he served as the link between the monarch and parliament. In 1572 he was appointed lord treasurer and was placed in charge of government finances. He served Elizabeth as a loyal adviser and office holder for over 40 years until his death in 1598.

Robert Dudley
(1537–88, created Earl of Leicester in 1564)

A Puritan, Dudley had been a close childhood friend of Elizabeth's. During Mary's reign he had fought against the French and in 1558 entered the new queen's Royal Court; he was appointed to the Privy Council in 1562. His close friendship with Elizabeth gave rise to rumours of an affair between them. In 1564 Elizabeth appointed him Earl of Leicester and in 1585 he was made commander of the army and sent to the Netherlands. Failing to get along with his generals he returned to England, where he soon after died in 1588. He did not get on with Cecil and was his rival as adviser to the queen.

Sir Christopher Hatton (1540–91)

A moderate Protestant, Hatton was appointed vice-chamberlain of the household and a member of the Privy Council in 1557. He entered Elizabeth's court in 1561 and became responsible for organising the queen's progresses. In 1587 he was given the post of lord chancellor, a position he held until his death in 1591.

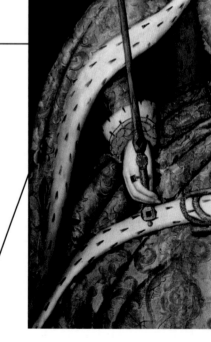

▲ **Source H:** Part of the instructions given by Elizabeth to William Cecil when she appointed him a Privy Councillor in November 1558

I have this judgement of you, that you will not be corrupted with any gift, you will be faithful to the state, and without respect of my private will, you will give me the best advice; if you know anything to be declared to me in secret, you will tell only me and I will keep it confidential.

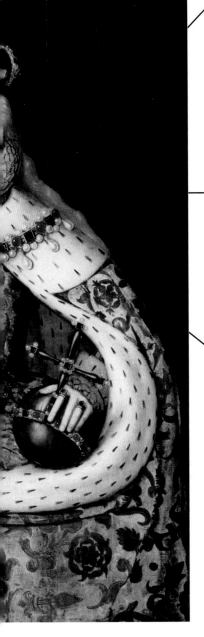

Sir Francis Walsingham (1532–90, knighted in 1577)

A devout Puritan, Walsingham was well-educated, having attended the universities of Cambridge and Padua, in Italy. In 1568 he began working for the government and in 1570, because of his command of European languages, he was appointed ambassador to Paris. In 1573 he was made secretary of state with special responsibility for foreign affairs. He was placed in charge of Elizabeth's secret service and organised a network of government spies placed all over Europe. In 1586 he uncovered a plot to murder Elizabeth that involved her cousin, Mary, Queen of Scots (see page 73).

Robert Devereux, 2nd Earl of Essex (1567–1601)

A Puritan, Essex first entered the royal court in 1584 and was appointed a Privy Councillor in 1593. He gained military knowledge fighting in France, Spain and the Netherlands. Elizabeth later put him in command of attacks on Spain and Ireland. He often quarrelled with Elizabeth and in 1601 was executed for treason due to his involvement in a plot to dismiss some of the queen's councillors.

Robert Cecil (1563–1612)

A Protestant, Robert was the younger son of William Cecil, Lord Burghley. With the help of his father's influence, he took over Walsingham's duties after his death in 1590. He was appointed to the Privy Council in 1591. He became responsible for supervising the arrangements for the succession of James VI of Scotland as king following the death of Elizabeth in 1603.

ACTIVITIES

1   Copy out and complete the table below using the information on pages 12–13 together with your own knowledge of this topic.

	Title	Religion	Date when appointed to the Privy Council	Position(s) held within the Privy Council	Example of work undertaken while a Privy Councillor
William Cecil					
Robert Dudley					
Christopher Hatton					
Francis Walsingham					
Robert Devereux					
Robert Cecil					

2   Using your completed table explain how important Privy Councillors were in helping Elizabeth govern England.

3   Study Source H. What qualities did Elizabeth expect to see in her Privy Councillors?

Practice question

Why was William Cecil, Lord Burghley, significant during the reign of Elizabeth? *(For guidance, see page 111.)*

Local government in Wales

During the sixteenth century, travel and communications were slow. It could take many days for messages from London to reach distant parts of the realm. The queen did not travel too far from London and she therefore had to rely upon a trusted body of officials to ensure that her rule was respected and that law and order was maintained. Without such officials Elizabeth would not have been able to rule the country effectively.

The Council of Wales and the Marches

The administration of local government in Wales was slightly different to what it was in England. The body responsible for exercising royal power in Wales was the Council of Wales and the Marches which was headed by a Lord President who had his headquarters in Ludlow (see Figure 1.3). The two most prominent Lord Presidents during Elizabeth's reign were:

- Sir Henry Sidney (who held office between 1560–86)
- Henry Herbert, the second Earl of Pembroke (who held office between 1586–1601).

The President was assisted by a Deputy Lieutenant and a council of 20 members nominated by the crown. They included members of the royal household, some bishops of Welsh dioceses and some justices from the Court of Great Sessions.

The Council's authority spread over the thirteen counties of Wales and the border counties of Hereford, Gloucester, Worcester, Shropshire and Cheshire. It was responsible for two areas of local government – administration and justice.

The Council served as the local representative of the Crown, ensuring that the instructions of the monarch and Privy Council were carried out in the localities and that law and order was imposed and justice administered. It served as the highest court in Wales and the Marches, hearing both civil and criminal cases, including all cases relating to murder, felony, piracy, wrecking and actions likely to disturb the peace.

> **Source I:** The Royal 'Instructions' of 1574 quoted in *A History of Wales, 1485–1660* by Hugh Thomas
>
> *They recognised the importance of the Council for:*
>
> *... the continuance of quietness and good government of the people and inhabitants within the Dominion and Principality of Wales and the Marches of the same.*

The Court of Great Sessions

The Acts of Union of 1536 and 1543 resulted in Wales formally coming under the political control of England. The English legal system was imposed upon Wales and, adapting the model of the English Assize Courts, a new Court of Great Sessions was introduced across the Principality. Twelve of the thirteen Welsh shires (excluding Monmouthshire) were divided into four court circuits:

- Chester Circuit (comprising the counties of Flint, Denbigh and Montgomery)
- North Wales Circuit (the counties of Anglesey, Caernarvon and Merioneth)
- Brecon Circuit (the counties of Brecon, Glamorgan and Radnor)
- Carmarthen Circuit (the counties of Carmarthen, Cardigan and Pembroke)

Circuit judges would tour each circuit, holding sessions twice a year in each county. They dealt with all serious crimes, including treason, murder, robbery, felony, riot and extortion. The courts operated almost unchanged until their abolition in 1830.

> **Source J:** The Welsh gentleman and historian Rice Merrick commented upon the improvement in government and justice following the Acts of Union in his book *A Booke of Glamorganshire Antiquities*, which he completed in 1578
>
> *Now, since Wales was thus, by gracious King Henry VIII, enabled with the laws of England, and thereby united to the same, and so brought to a monarchy, which is the most sure, stable and best form of government they are exempted from the dangers before remembered; for now life and death, lands and goods rest in this monarchy, and not in the pleasure of the subject.*

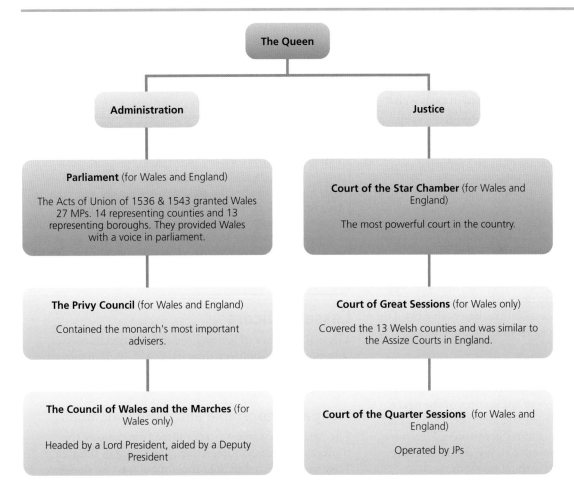

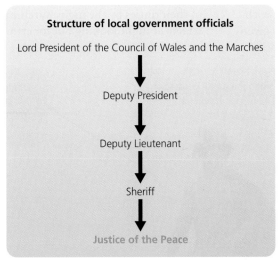

▲ Figure 1.3: How Wales was governed during Elizabethan times

ACTIVITIES

1 How important was the Council of Wales and the Marches in the government of Wales?
2 Study Sources I and J. Did the Acts of Union help establish royal authority over Wales?

The Deputy Lieutenant

The President of the Council also served as Lord Lieutenant of all the Welsh shires and working under his authority was the Deputy Lieutenant. It was a post held by a wealthy landowner and at least one was appointed in each Welsh county. They were responsible for controlling the local militia and ensuring that their area was well defended, and that volunteers were properly trained. They also supervised the work of justices of the peace (JPs) and reported on events in their area to the Lord President.

The sheriff

Each county had a sheriff and they were chiefly concerned with legal affairs, such as appointing and swear in juries, delivering prisoners to court and helping with the collection of taxes. The post of sheriff had medieval origins but by the sixteenth century the position had declined in its importance and many responsibilities had been passed on to other officials, such as the **Deputy** Lieutenant and JPs.

Justices of the peace

The real work of maintaining law and order at the local level fell upon the shoulders of the justices of the peace (JPs). They numbered between 30 and 60 per county and they were usually wealthy country gentlemen. They were unpaid but did their job because they viewed it as their duty and also because it gave them power and status within their community. During Elizabeth's reign their workload increased significantly. As well as sitting as justices in the quarter session courts, which dealt with administering justice for minor crimes, they were given

the additional tasks of overseeing the maintenance of the highways and administering poor law relief to the unemployed (see Figure 1.4). They were supported by junior officials such as the parish constable and the overseer of the poor.

> **Source K:** Examples of the work of JPs taken from the records of the Quarter Session Courts held in the West-Riding of Yorkshire during 1597–98
>
> *It is ordered that no brewers in this area shall brew any ale or beer to be sold at a greater price than a penny per quart, unless they have a special licence from a Justice of the Peace. The highway leading from Leeds to Wikebrigg is in great decay to the great hindrance of all her Majesty's subjects who travel that way. Therefore the Justices here present do order every person occupying land in Leeds to send labourers to repair the highway before August 25.*

Lesser officers

The maintenance of law and order depended upon community self-policing directed by the JP. To help with the day-to-day policing duties the JP appointed a number of lesser officials.

The parish constable and night watchman

The parish constable was appointed from among the tradesmen or husbandmen (farmers) living in the area. They were expected to hold the unpaid post for one year and were given a range of duties under the close supervision of the JP (see Figure 1.5). In the towns they were helped in their duties by the night watchman who patrolled the streets at night looking out for criminals.

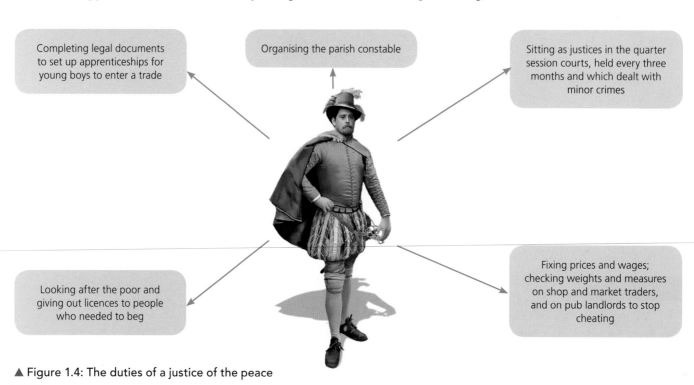

Completing legal documents to set up apprenticeships for young boys to enter a trade

Organising the parish constable

Sitting as justices in the quarter session courts, held every three months and which dealt with minor crimes

Looking after the poor and giving out licences to people who needed to beg

Fixing prices and wages; checking weights and measures on shop and market traders, and on pub landlords to stop cheating

▲ Figure 1.4: The duties of a justice of the peace

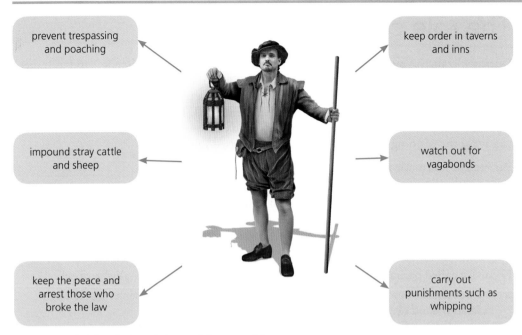

prevent trespassing and poaching

keep order in taverns and inns

impound stray cattle and sheep

watch out for vagabonds

keep the peace and arrest those who broke the law

carry out punishments such as whipping

▲ Figure 1.5: The duties of the parish constable

The overseer of the poor

To help administer relief to the poor, JPs appointed an overseer of the poor whose job it was to organise and collect a local tax (called the poor rate), from everyone in the parish, and distribute this money to those most in need of support and charity. This job increased in importance during Elizabeth's reign as the number of unemployed also increased. Without this body of mostly unpaid amateur officials local government would not have been able to operate effectively during Elizabethan times.

ACTIVITIES

1   Explain the differences between the roles and responsibilities of the justice of the peace and the parish constable.
2   'Without a body of mostly unpaid officials local government could not have operated effectively during Elizabethan times.' How far do you agree with this statement?
3   How useful is Source K to an historian studying the work of JPs during this period?

Practice question

Explain the connections between any THREE of the following:
● Sheriff
● Justice of the peace
● Parish constable
● Overseer of the poor.
(For guidance, see page 112.)

The role of parliament

During Elizabeth's reign parliament was a much less powerful body than it is today. It met only when the queen called it and it ceased to meet when she told it to close down. During Elizabeth's long reign there were just ten parliaments which met on thirteen occasions, and for 26 years there were no sessions of parliament at all. The main motive for calling parliament was usually financial, Elizabeth needed parliament to grant money from taxes to pay for the running of or defence of the country (see Table 1.1).

Parliament was made up of two bodies:

- the House of Lords: a non-elected body of about 100 lords, bishops and judges
- the House of Commons: contained about 450 members of parliament (MPs) who were elected by wealthy landowners; its members were mostly gentlemen, burgesses (merchants) and some lawyers; there were two MPs from each county and two from each important town within the county.

Elizabeth called parliament only when she needed to and this was usually because:

- she was short of money and only parliament had the power to raise money through taxes and hand over revenue to the Crown
- she needed to pass Acts of Parliament
- she desired the support and advice of her MPs and lords on important issues.

Use the information in Table 1.1 to help answer the following questions.

1 What was the most popular reason for the calling of a parliament during Elizabeth's reign?
2 What were the main problems faced by Elizabeth's government?
3 What evidence is there to suggest that wars were expensive?

Parliament	Dates of sessions	Reasons for calling parliament
1559	25 January – 8 May	• To discuss the Religious Settlement which set up the Protestant Church • To grant taxes
1563–67	12 January – 10 April 1563 30 September 1566 – 2 January 1567	• To discuss a rebellion in Scotland • To grant taxes • To decide whether to support a Protestant rebellion in France • To grant additional taxes
1571	2 April – 29 May	• To decide what to do with Mary, Queen of Scots, who had fled from Scotland to England in 1568 • To grant taxes
1572–82	8 May – 30 June 1572 8 February – 15 March 1576 16 January – 18 March 1581	• To pass laws to deal with Catholic plots against Elizabeth • To grant taxes
1584–85	23 November 1584 – 29 March 1585	• To pass laws to deal with plots against the queen • To grant taxes
1586–87	29 October 1586 – 23 March 1587	• To pass laws against Catholics • To grant taxes
1589	4 February – 29 March	• To discuss the war against Spain • To grant double taxes
1593	19 February – 10 April	• To discuss the war in Ireland • To grant triple taxes
1597–98	24 October 1597 – 9 February 1598	• To discuss the war in Ireland • To grant triple taxes
1601	27 October – 19 December	• To consider the succession • To grant triple taxes

▲ Table 1.1: Elizabethan parliaments, 1559–1601

Freedom of speech

The queen appointed the Speaker of the House of Commons and decided what topics were to be debated. While MPs had in theory freedom of speech to allow them to discuss what they wanted, Elizabeth made it clear that certain topics such as foreign policy and religion were issues to be discussed by the Privy Council not parliament. When in 1571 MPs asked the queen to consider marriage she told them that they had no right to discuss issues that were personal to her. She was furious when, in 1587, parliament discussed changes to the Church of England. She demanded MPs stop discussing the issue and ordered the arrest of five MPs. In such instances Elizabeth was prepared to limit freedom of speech within parliament.

Taxation and finance

During the Tudor period monarchs were expected to pay for the cost of running the country from their own finances. This income came from rents from the royal estates and property, and from customs duties on exports and imports. Tudor monarchs often found themselves short of money and when this was the case they had to ask parliament to grant them additional funds from taxes. Only parliament had the power to raise money through taxation. The situation was made worse during Elizabeth's reign because of high inflation, which caused prices to rise, and the country's involvement in costly foreign wars, such as the conflict with Philip II and Spain (see page 83).

When Elizabeth became queen in 1558 she inherited a government heavily in debt. The debt from Queen Mary's reign stood at the high figure of £227,000 and in an attempt to balance the books Elizabeth worked with one of her chief ministers, William Cecil, to begin a programme of economic savings. Court salaries were capped and the spending on the royal household was cut. By imposing a variety of savings the Marian debt was paid off, but the Crown was still short of money and parliament had to be recalled periodically to release funds.

The burden of local taxation increased sharply during Elizabeth's reign. The sheriff was responsible for collecting the taxes locally and this money was used to fund poor relief, which became an increasing problem during the late sixteenth century (see page 36). Money was also needed to pay for the maintenance of roads and bridges, the upkeep of all fortifications and the local militia.

QUEEN ELIZABETH IN PARLIAMENT
A L Chancellor B Marquises Earles & C Barons D Bishops E Iudges F Masters of Chancery G Clerks H Speaker of ye Commons
I Black Rod K Sergeant at Armes L Members of the Commons house M Sr Francis Walsingham Secretary of State.

▲ **Source M:** A contemporary print showing Queen Elizabeth sitting in the House of Lords, with MPs from the House of Commons also present

ACTIVITIES

1   Use Source M and your own knowledge to explain the function of parliament during this period.

2   'The power to release funds from taxes gave parliament power over the monarch.' How far do you agree with this statement?

Source L: The Lord Keeper's reply to a petition from Parliament for freedom of speech, 1593

For freedom of speech her Majesty commands me to say that no man should be afraid to say yes or no to bills. But he is not there to speak of all things that come into his mind or to suggest new religions and governments. She said that no monarch fit to rule would allow anything so stupid.

Practice question

To what extent does Source L accurately reflect the view that MPs did not have total freedom of speech? (For guidance, see pages 109–110.)

The Welsh gentry

The Elizabethan Age saw the emergence of the gentry class as the dominant force in the social and political life in Wales. The landowning gentry promoted their family fortunes and built up their estates through careful marriages, the purchase of lands and through occupying important positions in local government such as the posts of Deputy Lieutenant, sheriff and Justice of the Peace. This made them respected and powerful figures within their communities.

The following two examples will serve to illustrate the importance of the Welsh gentry class during this period.

Sir John Wynn of Gwydir (1553–1626)

Born in 1553, the son of Morus Wynn of Gwydir, a house in Llanrwst in the Conwy valley, John was proud of his rich family history. Having studied law at the Inner Temple in London, he succeeded to the Gwydir estate upon the death of his father in 1580. Under his careful direction the Wynn family was to become one of the most powerful and influential families in North Wales.

As a leading member of the gentry class, John was able to use his social standing to occupy important positions in local government:

- 1588 and 1603 – he served as sheriff for Caernarvonshire
- 1589 and 1601 – he served as sheriff for Merionethshire
- 1586–87 – he served as MP for Caernarvon
- 1587 – served as Deputy Lieutenant for Caernarvonshire
- 1608 – he was knighted and became 'Sir' John Wynn
- 1608 – he was appointed a member of the Council of Wales and the Marches
- 1611 – he was created a baronet.

John Wynn was also an educated scholar who traced his ancestry back to Owain Gwynedd, king of Gwynedd (d.1170), glorifying his line of decent in his book 'The History of the Gwydir Family' which he had completed by c.1614. He patronised local bards, built up a library of valuable manuscripts, and was the leader of taste and fashion in his area. He remodelled Gwydir Castle into a fashionable Renaissance house and upon his death in 1626, left money for the founding of a school and hospital in Llanrwst.

> **Source N:** George Owen of Henllys, a Welsh gentleman and historian, writing in his book *A Dialogue of the Government of Wales* (1594)
>
> *Whereby the people are grown to be of great wealth, the gentlemen of great livings, so that in a country, when it come first to be shire-ground [following the Act of Union, 1536] where there was scarce two gentlemen that could in lands dispend twenty pounds apiece, there are now in the said shire to be found some that doth receive yearly five hundred pounds, some three hundred pounds, and many one hundred pounds good lands, so that now there is no shire in Wales but is able to yield sufficient numbers of gentlemen that may dispend 100 pounds a year good land.*

▲ Source O: A portrait of Sir John Wynn of Gwydir painted in 1619

▲ Source P: Gwydir Castle in Llanrwst, the ancestral home of the Wynn family

Katheryn of Berain (1534/5–1591)

The life of Katheryn (or Catrin) of Berain provides one of the best examples of how careful marriages were used to enhance wealth and social status. Born into a family in the Welsh gentry, Katheryn was the daughter of Tudur ap Robert Vychan of Berain in Denbighshire. Through her mother she was the granddaughter of Sir Roland Velville, an illegitimate son of King Henry VII. She was blessed with a good pedigree which she later used to her own advantage. She married four times into some of the best gentry families in North Wales.

- Her first marriage was to John Salusbury (d.1566) who owned the wealthy Lleweni estate outside Denbigh.

- Her second marriage was to Sir Richard Clough of Denbigh (d.1570), a successful and wealthy merchant whose business interests took him to Antwerp and Hamburg where he worked for Sir Thomas Gresham, a prosperous banker. The two men later established the London Stock Exchange. Clough used his wealth to build Bachygraig near Denbigh, the first brick built house in Wales.

- Her third marriage was to Morus Wynn of Gwydir near Llanrwst (d.1580), the father of Sir John Wynn of Gwydir. The Wynn's were emerging as the most powerful family in North Wales.

- Her fourth marriage was to Edward Thelwell of Plas y Ward in Vale of Clwyd (d.1610).

Through these marriages Katheryn gave birth to six children, two by each of the first three husbands. Many of the older families in Wales claim descent from her and which is why she is sometimes referred to as 'Mam Cymru' (the Mother of Wales).

▲ Source R: Portrait of Katheryn of Berain painted in 1568. She is dressed in black and has her hand on a skull, suggesting she is in mourning for the death of a husband

Practice question

What can be learnt from Sources N and Q about the Welsh gentry during Elizabethan times? (For guidance, see pages 107–108.)

◀ Source Q: An eighteenth century painting showing Bachygraig, the house built by Richard Clough in 1567, the year he married Katheryn. It aimed to show off the wealth, power and status of the Welsh gentry

ACTIVITIES

1. What does Source N tell you about the development of the Welsh gentry by the end of the sixteenth century?

2. Study the career of Sir John Wynn of Gwydir, which was typical of many of the gentry in Tudor Wales. Use the information about Wynn's life and your own knowledge to create a mind map spelling out the importance of the gentry in Welsh society.

3. Write an obituary notice for Katheryn of Berain who died in 1591. Use the heading:
THE DEATH OF MAM CYMRU – THE EXTRAORDINARY LIFE OF KATHERYN OF BERAIN

Conclusion: How successful was the government of Elizabeth I?

The Tudor system of government was personal and was based upon the monarch. A strong monarch ensured strong government. For much of her reign Elizabeth was that strong monarch, particularly during the 1570s and 1580s, when she ruled at the height of her powers and was served by an able body of Privy Councillors and advisers within the Royal Court. Her popularity also helped to ensure loyalty and obedience from her officials.

Central government was most effective when Elizabeth used her power of patronage to keep her ambitious councillors, advisers and nobles in check. She grew skilful in handling difficult nobles and her volatile temper was often enough to ensure her officials did what was expected of them. She maintained a relatively firm control of her parliaments and exercised her power of calling and dismissing parliament to her advantage.

At the local level Elizabeth's control was dependent upon the operations of a loyal body of unpaid amateur officials in the form of the lord lieutenant and his deputy, justices of the peace, the parish constable and other officials such as the overseers of the poor. Without the co-operation of these officials working in the queen's name in the provinces the decisions made by central government could not have been carried out. As long as these officials performed their duties effectively then law and order was maintained. At this level government worked well during Elizabeth's reign, despite an ever increasing workload for many of these officers.

Summary question

Now that you have completed this chapter, use the knowledge you have acquired to answer the following synoptic question.

'Elizabeth was a popular monarch who exercised firm control in governing the country.' How far do you agree with this statement?

In your answer you might like to consider the following factors:
1. the popularity of the queen
2. the Royal Court
3. the Privy Council
4. parliament
5. and any other relevant factors you can think of.

Key question: How did life differ for the rich and poor in Elizabethan times?

Contrasting lifestyles of the rich and poor

Elizabethan society was deeply divided and there was a very structured class system that kept everybody in their place. There were enormous differences in the standards of living between those at the top of the social ladder, such as the wealthy lords who owned about 17 per cent of all cultivated land, and the hardship and poverty experienced by those at the opposite end of the ladder, the landless and unskilled labourers who often lived on the edge of starvation. While the rich led a privileged and prosperous lifestyle the opposite was true for the labouring poor, who were reliant upon low wages and often struggled to find money to pay their rent. Having no savings to help them survive through bad times, the possibility of homelessness and poverty was a constant threat.

The monarch – Queen Elizabeth I

Nobles and Lords – great landowners (about 50 families) with an income of up to £6000 per year

Gentry – lesser landowners (about 10,000 families) with an income of up to £200 per year

Wealthy merchants – successful in the business of buying and selling goods (about 30,000 families)
Professionals – the emerging middle class; e.g. lawyers, physicians, apothecaries, clergy, schoolmasters

Yeomen – owned their own property, had a few servants, and farmed some land
Tenant farmers – they rented between 10 and 30 acres from a landowner (about 100,000 families)

Cottagers – had small gardens to farm and also carried out some small-scale industry in the home such as spinning
Skilled artisans – men with a trade; craftsmen

Landless unskilled labourers – seasonal workers; unemployed during certain times of the year
The poor and unemployed

▲ Figure 2.1: Social structure in Elizabethan Wales and England

Elizabethan social structure

Those families occupying the lower levels of the social structure struggled to survive and it has been estimated that between 20 per cent and 30 per cent of the population lived on the edge of starvation. Events such as bad harvests, rising prices and changes resulting from seasonal employment were often sufficient triggers to tip these groups over into poverty. This then caused them to become beggars, an issue which became a major concern during Elizabeth's reign.

One source of information for historians of the Elizabethan age is the writings of contemporaries, people who lived at that time and who wrote down accounts of everyday life in the second half of the sixteenth century. One such writer was William Harrison, a clergyman from Essex, who toured the southern half of England during the 1570s, presenting his findings in a book which he called *The Description of England* and which was published in 1577 (see Source A). Another social commentator was Thomas Nashe who wrote about how society was structured in Elizabethan England (see Source B).

> **Source A: An account of the social structure given by William Harrison in his book *The Description of England*, 1577**
>
> *We in England divide our people into four sorts, gentlemen, citizens or burgesses (townspeople), yeomen (farmers) and labourers (farm workers).*

> **Source B: In 1593 the satirist Thomas Nashe wrote an amusing comment about how society was ordered**
>
> *In London the rich look down on the poor. The Courtier the townsman. The townsman the countryman. The merchant the retailer. The shopkeeper the craftsman. The better sort of craftsman the poorer. The shoemaker the cobbler. The cobbler the cartman.*

ACTIVITIES

1 Explain why the lower levels of Elizabethan society were in constant danger of falling into poverty.
2 Study Figure 2.1 on page 23 and Source A. Use this information to describe how society was divided during Elizabethan times.

The lifestyle of the rich

During the long reign of Elizabeth many of the landowning classes increased their wealth. Some had bought land in the 1530s following the dissolution of the monasteries by Henry VIII, land they now rented out. Some had adjusted to the new agricultural changes and abandoned the cultivation of the land in favour of more profitable sheep farming. Others had begun to exploit the mineral resources on their land by mining for coal, lead and iron ore. As well as these means, there continued to be the traditional method of increasing landholding by marrying the daughter of a wealthy landowner. Such a bride would come with a large dowry which might also include land.

Homes

Many of these landowners used their increased wealth to remodel their homes or to build new houses on a grand scale. Such houses were filled with the latest fashions in furniture and fittings, and the walls were covered in fine paintings and hung with expensive tapestries. The large number of new houses built during this period has caused some historians to label this period as the age of 'The Great Rebuilding'. These social developments were fuelled to some extent by Elizabeth's annual progresses (see page 9) which caused her courtiers to remodel or rebuild their homes so that they could entertain the queen in style when she visited them.

Many of the homes of the great lords had been defensive structures built to protect them against attack and they had survived since medieval times with very few changes. They were often large, with rooms poorly lit by small narrow windows, which had wooden shutters and no glass, and narrow winding staircases designed for defence. The centre of the house was the communal great hall where people ate, worked, entertained and slept.

Practice question

To what extent does Source B accurately reflect the social structure of Elizabethan society? *(For guidance, see pages 109–110.)*

New building styles

The new homes were designed to enable a clear divide between owner and servant. The houses were symmetrical in design, the ground plan of many being styled in the shape of the letter 'E' or 'H' (see Figure 2.2). Some were constructed of stone while others had a timber framework with wattle and daub or, increasingly, brick infill between the beams. Windows were large and glazed with leaded glass and placed symmetrically across the building. The introduction of new building materials, such as bricks, enabled the construction of chimneys, which were often grouped together in stacks of two, three or more, and decorated with a twisting pattern of bricks. Increased light, large fireplaces, lower ceilings finely plastered in geometric patterns, and wood panelled or tapestry lined walls improved living conditions.

The great hall was now used as the servants' dining room, or as a venue for formal events such as banquets, or even converted into a grand entrance hall.

The long gallery

One new feature of these houses was the building of a long gallery, which ran the whole length of the house on the upper floor. It was a wide passage with windows all along one side, one or more fireplaces to provide warmth, the long wall opposite the windows lined with family portraits, some stools, small tables and chests, and window seats to provide views of the formal garden below. The floor was strewn with rushes. The principal function of the gallery was for recreation, providing a place for the owners to exercise in bad weather, to walk, listen to music and dance, and to provide an area for the children to play games.

Family and servant wings

Within the family wing of the house there were a series of rooms, which included the parlour. This was used as a sitting room and took its name from the French word *parler*, meaning to speak. It was decorated with tapestries, carved panelling, a decorated plaster ceiling and a large fire place.

There were also a series of bedrooms, one opening onto the other without a corridor. The master bedchamber had a 'withdrawing room' next door where servants slept within call of their master or mistress. To provide some privacy and warmth the four poster beds had heavy curtains around them. Also included in the bedroom were a chest, chair, bowl and wash stand.

The other wing of the house contained the servants' quarters, including the kitchen and bedrooms.

Elizabethan mansion houses

Some of the finest houses built in the Elizabethan style were:

- **Burghley House**, Lincolnshire – constructed by Elizabeth's chief minister, William Cecil and completed by 1587
- **Longleat House**, Wiltshire – built for Sir John Thynne and completed in 1580
- **Holdenby House**, Northamptonshire – built for Elizabeth's Lord Chancellor, Sir Christopher Hatton and completed in 1583
- **Hardwick Hall**, Derbyshire.

> **Source C:** An account of the changes in buildings and lifestyle identified by the clergyman William Harrison in his book *Description of England* (1577)
>
> *The ancient manors and houses of our gentlemen are of strong timber … Such as be built lately are either of brick or stone, or both; their rooms large and comfortable. Those of the nobility are … so magnificent and stately that a dog today has the same comforts as a prince of olden times … There are old men in the village where I live which have noted three things to be marvellously altered in England …*
>
> *One is the multitude of chimneys, whereas in their younger days there were not more than two or three … The second is the great improvement in lodging [homes]. The third thing they tell is of the change from wooden platters [plates] into pewter, and wooden spoons into silver and tin.*

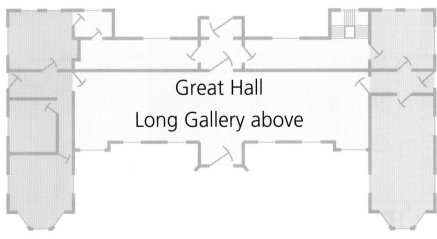

Servants' wing – divided into a series of rooms, including the kitchen

Family wing – divided into a number of rooms

◀ Figure 2.2: Plan of a typical Elizabethan mansion built in the shape of the letter E

Hardwick Hall

Hardwick Hall was built for Elizabeth Talbot, Countess of Shrewsbury (commonly refered to as Bess of Hardwick–see box) and was completed in 1597. It was described as having 'more glass than wall'.

Landscaped gardens

Remodelling the grounds immediately around the house was just as important as the changes to the main building itself. Until the sixteenth century gardens had served the purely practical function of providing food for the table, but by Elizabethan times gardens were being designed and developed for pleasure purposes. A formal garden was laid out by Bess to show off the view in front of Hardwick Hall. Many of these new designs took the form of a knot garden and were made up of a series of geometric beds of flowers with paths spaced between them. The edges of each bed were marked with low box or lavender hedges. Owing to the problems of cutting the grass without a lawnmower, there were few lawns. Herb beds and beds to grow vegetables continued to be important, both as a valuable source of food but also to be viewed for pleasure.

▼ **Source D:** A photograph of Hardwick Hall in Derbyshire which was built in the 1590s by Elizabeth, Countess of Shrewsbury

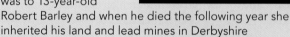

Bess of Hardwick

Elizabeth Hardwick married four times, rising from minor gentry stock to the top ranks of English society and becoming one of the wealthiest women in Elizabethan England.

1527: born around 1527, she was the daughter of John Hardwick, a Derbyshire gentleman

1543: her first marriage was to 13-year-old Robert Barley and when he died the following year she inherited his land and lead mines in Derbyshire

1547: her second marriage was to Sir William Cavendish, a wealthy landowner, with whom she had eight children; William died in 1557

1559: her third marriage was to Sir William St Loe and his death in 1565 left Bess one of the wealthiest women in England with an annual income of £60,000

1568: her fourth marriage was to George Talbot, 6th Earl of Shrewsbury; he died in 1590

1590–97: construction of Hardwick Hall

1597: Bess moved in to Hardwick Hall

1608: she died on 13 February 1608, aged 81

▲ **Source E:** A view of the long gallery at Hardwick Hall in Derbyshire

ACTIVITIES

1 Copy out and complete the table below, using the information in this section to compare and contrast medieval and Tudor building styles.

	Pre-Tudor homes for the lords and nobles	Changes made to the homes of lords and nobles during Elizabethan times
What the house looked like from the outside		
Building materials		
Function of the Great Hall		
The Long Gallery		
Changes in style: • windows • chimneys • staircases		
Function and design of the garden		

2 Study Sources D and E. Explain why Hardwick Hall is regarded as one of the best examples of a late sixteenth-century house built in the 'Elizabethan style'.

3 'Elizabeth Hardwick was one of the wealthiest women in Elizabethan England.' Explain how she became so wealthy.

Practice question

What can be learnt from Sources C and D about the houses for the rich during Elizabethan times? *(For guidance, see pages 107–108.)*

Fashion

A fashionable Elizabethan nobleman would wear the latest fashion made of the finest materials, such as silk, linen and velvet (see Figure 2.3). His outfit would consist of a plain vest on top of which would be placed a doublet or shirt with long sleeves and small ruffs around the cuffs. Below the doublet a trunk hose was worn (type of breeches down to knee height) and silk or woollen stockings. A coloured and embroidered jerkin or jacket was worn over the doublet, topped with a stiffened ruff around the neck. Leather shoes with a heel and buckle completed the outfit, although some jewellery such as pearl earring was becoming popular. When outdoors the noblemen would put on a cloak made of satin, velvet and cloth, a hat, together with a sword and dagger.

Figure 2.3: A fashionable ▶ Elizabethan nobleman, **c.**1580

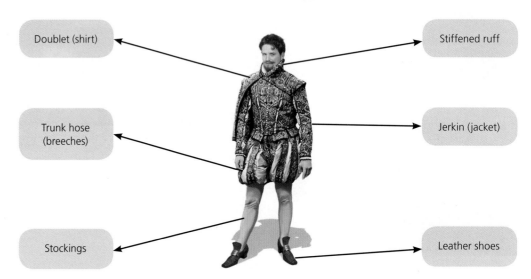

An Elizabethan lady of fashion would wear a long shift and knitted stockings, over which would be placed a farthingale or petticoat, sewn into which were wooden hoops to help keep the under-gown splayed out (see Figure 2.4). This was normally patterned or embroidered and had wide sleeves which ended with small ruffs. A gown of satin or velvet topped these layers and this was generally worn without sleeves. Leather shoes with buckles were worn and jewellery such as bracelets, brooches, strings of pearls, earrings and rings helped to advertise wealth and status. When venturing out the lady would wear a cape and hat.

Figure 2.4: A fashionable ▶ Elizabethan lady, **c.**1580

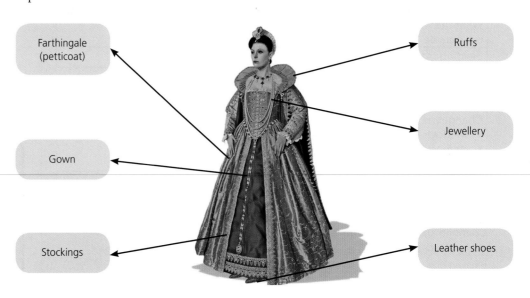

Education

The sons of the wealthy nobles and lords were tutored at home, most receiving education in the classics as well as providing them with a good knowledge of French, Latin and Greek. Teaching social etiquette, such as table manners was deemed important, as was a grounding in the fashionable pursuits of hunting, hawking and dancing. Daughters would be tutored by a governess and would be taught the practicalities of running a large house and its staff.

The household

The wife of a nobleman was expected to supervise the day-to-day running of the household, which included the production of everyday items such as bread, ale, the salting of the meats and fish, the making of jams and preserves, and the making of soap, candles, medicines and ointments.

▲ Source F: A scene from Sir Henry Unton's memorial picture, painted in 1596, which shows life in an Elizabethan household

ACTIVITIES ?

1 How did the Elizabethan noble class dress to display their wealth and status within society?

Study Source F.

2 Identify what activity is taking place in each of the following rooms in the home of Sir Henry Unton: (a) great hall, (b) parlour, (c) private rooms, (d) grand staircase.

3 How useful is this source to an historian studying the lifestyle of the rich during Elizabethan times?

Practice question

Explain the connections between any THREE of the following:
- new building styles
- landscaped gardens
- fashion
- education.

(For guidance, see page 112.)

Lifestyles of the gentry in Wales

While not as wealthy as the noble class, the gentry and yeoman class did attempt to copy the changes in home and living accommodation, fashion and education, although not on such a grand scale.

Homes

The gentry owned more land than they could farm and rented out a large part of their estate to tenant farmers in order to secure a regular income of several hundred pounds a year. They copied the trend among the richer nobles to modernise and re-fashion their homes from medieval, often fortified dwellings, into more fashionable domesticated living accommodation.

The new houses they built were of stone, brick or half-timbered, had at least eight rooms as well as additional servants' quarters. In terms of remodelling, ceilings were inserted to replace the high open roofs of the medieval hall, the walls were panelled with oak or covered with plaster, and decorated with tapestries rather than paintings of family members. Such changes enabled an upper floor to be added, which were used as bedrooms and storerooms. The former great hall was converted into a private dining room for the master of the house and his family and a living room, while the servants were relegated to the kitchen and ancillary rooms. Oak staircases were installed to connect the hall with the upper rooms, windows were widened, lengthened and mullions were added, and glass was inserted to replace the former wooden shutters. Large open fireplaces were installed with brick-built chimneys.

As in England, the gentry class in Wales were active in bringing about improvements to their homes. The emerging middle class in Wales – the lawyers, bankers, merchants and court officials – were keen to show off their newly acquired wealth and status by building themselves new fashionable houses. These reflected the latest styles of architecture, the new tastes in internal decoration and garden design. Two Elizabethan houses which display this new style and wealth are St Fagan's in Cardiff and Plas Mawr in Conwy, both built by men who had created their own wealth rather than inherited it.

St Fagan's Castle, Cardiff

St Fagan's house in Cardiff has been described as one of the finest Elizabethan houses in Wales. It was built over a twenty-year period between 1560 and 1580 by a lawyer, Dr John Gibbon. The house had three floors and was designed in the shape of the typical Elizabethan 'E' style. The ground floor contained a hall, drawing room, buttery and kitchen. A grand staircase led up to the first floor which contained a series of reception rooms, a Great Hall and a Long Gallery which ran along the rear of the house. The rooms were lit by large glazed mullioned windows and heated by large fireplaces. Tapestries and paintings adorned the walls, the ceilings and chimney breasts being of finely decorated plasterwork. The outside walls were constructed of stone which were faced with whitewashed cladding and the roof was of slate (see Source G). It served to demonstrate the wealth and status if its owner.

▼ Source G: St Fagan's in Cardiff – a fine example of an Elizabethan house built between 1560 and 1580 by Dr John Gibbon, a Tudor gentleman

Plas Mawr townhouse, Conwy

Built by Robert Wynn, a court official and successful merchant who was an uncle to Sir John Wynn of Gwydir in Llanrwst, Plas Mawr in Conwy is the finest example of an Elizabethan townhouse in Wales. Wynn had made his wealth serving as a court official in London in the service of Sir Walter Stone (d.1550) and Sir Philip Hoby (d.1558). Upon returning to Wales at the start of Elizabeth's reign, he commenced a career as a successful merchant and between 1576 and 1585 he built for himself the fine townhouse of Plas Mawr (the Great Hall). The inside of the house was finely decorated by ornamental plasterwork, fine wooden screens and specially commissioned furniture and silver plate. The initials 'R.W.' appeared in the plasterwork together with coats of arms and family crests (see Sources H and I).

◀ **Source H:** Plas Mawr in Conwy – a fine example of an Elizabethan townhouse built between 1576 and 1585 by Robert Wynn, a wealthy Tudor gentleman

ACTIVITY ?

Using Sources H and I, as well as your own knowledge, explain how Robert Wynn was able to demonstrate his wealth and status as a member of the Welsh gentry class.

◀ **Source I:** The Great Chamber in Plas Mawr, Conwy, with its finely decorated plasterwork and rich furnishings. It displays the wealth of some of the enterprising Tudor gentry in Wales

Fashion

In terms of fashion the gentry class followed the style adopted by their social superiors, the nobles and lords. Their outfits, while modern and stylish, lacked the expensive fine threads of gold and silver or the jewellery embroidered into the doublets and gowns of the very wealthy. Fashion was taken seriously as it was a demonstration of personal power, status and social standing.

The Welsh gentry were also the protectors of Welsh custom and tradition. They were the patrons of the wandering poets and bards who visited the gentry houses to praise their sponsor, and some employed their own harpist to provide evening entertainment. They built up libraries of valuable books and manuscripts and they became patrons to the revived Eisteddfod, sponsoring the competitions in music, poetry and dance. Many of them also took great pride in their ancestry. Gentlemen like Sir John Wynn of Gwydir and Sir Edward Stradling of St Donat's in Glamorganshire, compiled their family trees to proudly trace their ancestors back to the age of the medieval Welsh princes.

Education

The sons of the gentry class often attended grammar school, so called because they concentrated upon the teaching of Greek and Latin grammar. The number of grammar schools increased during Elizabeth's reign and by the end of the century there were around 360 schools across Wales and England with one in virtually every large town. The foundation of the famous grammar schools in Rugby and Harrow date from this period.

Tudor education aimed to produce the 'perfect' gentleman and the teaching was very strict, with flogging being a common punishment. The school day was long, lasting from 6 or 7 a.m. in the morning to around 5 p.m. in the afternoon, with a break for lunch. From such schools some boys would go on at the age of fifteen or sixteen to one of two universities, either Oxford or Cambridge, where their degree would include compulsory lectures in mathematics, music, theology, astronomy and geometry. An alternative was to go to the Inns of Court in London to study law.

After university some would commence careers as lawyers, clerics or enter royal employment, serving in either central or local government departments. Gentlemen were also expected to be educated in social etiquette and have good table manners. They were also required to be good at gentlemanly pursuits such as hunting, fencing, music and dancing. They might even engage in some of the newer pastimes such as tennis and bowls.

> **Source J:** In his *Book of Nurture, or School of Good Manners* (1577), the Tudor gentleman Hugh Rhodes offered advice to parents and teachers
>
> *There are few things more necessary than to teach and govern children in learning and good manners, for it is a high service to God … [Parents should] cause their children and servants to use fair and gentle speech, with reverence and courtesy to their Elders and Betters [and tell them off] for idle talk and stammering, also clumsy gestures in going or standing … Keep them from reading fables, fantasies and songs of love which cause much mischief.*

Source K: In his book, *The Description of England* (1577), William Harrison commented upon the expansion of university education during Elizabeth's reign

In my time there are three noble universities in England … Oxford … Cambridge … London [Inns of Court] … of which the first two are the most famous … In most of our colleges there are also great numbers of students, of which many are found by the revenues of the houses and other by the purveyances [money] of their rich friends … They were built by their founders at the first only for poor men's sons, whose parents were not able to bring them up unto learning, but now they have the least benefit of them, by reason the rich do so encroach upon them.

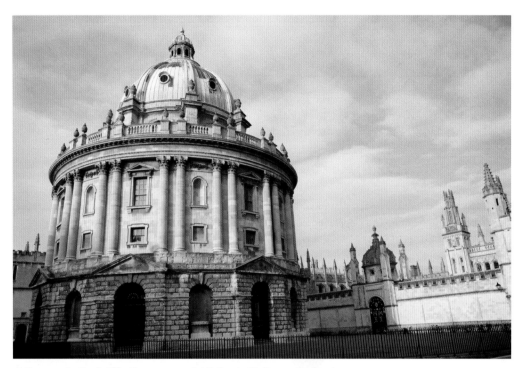

▲ **Source L:** Radcliffe Camera and All Souls College, Oxford

ACTIVITY ?

Compare and contrast the lifestyle of the noble and gentry classes during Elizabethan times. In your comparison you should refer to (a) homes, (b) fashion and (c) education.

Practice questions

1 To what extent does Source J accurately reflect the importance of education in the lives of Elizabethan gentry families? *(For guidance, see pages 109–110.)*
2 What can be learnt from Sources I and K about the lifestyle of the gentry in Elizabethan times? *(For guidance, see pages 107–108.)*

Lifestyle of the lower classes

The lower classes followed a lifestyle that was distinctly different from that enjoyed by their social superiors.

Homes

The lower classes lived in much smaller homes, a poor man's cottage usually having only one room, which in some instances was shared with animals. It had an earth floor and walls made of a timber frame with wattle and mud infill and a thatched roof. The room was furnished with few pieces of furniture or possessions, the norm being just a bed, a table and some stools. Some who acquired a little money, such as craftsmen or small farmers, were able to build a new house with glazed windows, separate bedrooms, brick chimneys, a parlour and a kitchen (see Source M).

The working day

Tenant farmers and labourers worked long hours, from around 5 a.m. in the morning to about 5 p.m. in the evening. They would have breaks at 7 and 11 a.m. for bread, ale and cheese. The main meal would be around 6 p.m. and would usually be vegetable stew since the lower classes could seldom afford to buy meat.

Life expectancy was low and only a few infants survived beyond the age of five, many of them dying from diseases such as smallpox, typhus and influenza.

▼ Source M: Originally built in the 1490s, this timber-framed home of a yeoman farmer was modernised during Elizabeth's reign through the addition of a brick-built chimney and glass windows

> **Source N:** In his book, *The Description of England* (1577), William Harrison comments upon the diet of the lower classes
>
> *Poore neighbours are inforced to content themselves with rie [rye], or barleie [barley], yea, and in times of dearth, with bread made … of peason, beans or otes [oats].*

Fashion

The tenant farmer or labourer would normally possess a pair of leather shoes, knitted woollen stockings, leather breeches, a doublet and jerkin (jacket and waistcoat) made of fustian (course twilled cloth or corduroy) or canvas, and a felt hat or cap. Women wore a petticoat, mantle, doublet, kerchief, ruffs, a net or cap on the head, and leather shoes. Such was their poverty that they possessed few changes of clothes.

Education and leisure

With little or no education, the lower classes spent what little leisure time they had on visits to the inn and tavern (see Source O), gambling in the cock or bear baiting rings, playing cards and dice or betting on the racing (see pages 44–45). Fishing and archery were common pastimes throughout the Tudor period, as was the watching of strolling players performing a new play. The poor could generally not afford to educate their children but for those lucky enough to attend the local parish school, they were taught basic reading and writing in English. Most were forced to leave well before their teenage years in order to work.

▲ Source O: A contemporary painting depicting a drinking scene at an inn

ACTIVITIES

1   Explain why most members of the lower classes received little education.
2   Compare and contrast the lifestyle of a rich Elizabethan nobleman and his lady with that of a tenant farmer and his wife. Your account should contain reference to (a) homes, (b) fashion, (c) education and (d) pastimes.

Practice questions

1   What can be learnt from Sources M and N about the lifestyle of the lower classes during Elizabethan times? *(For guidance, see pages 107–108.)*
2   To what extent does Source O accurately reflect everyday life of the lower classes? *(For guidance, see pages 109–110.)*

Poverty in Elizabethan times

Society has always had a proportion of the population classified as poor and in need of help and support from others. Throughout the medieval period the church had played a key role in looking after the poor and destitute, providing shelter and relief in alms-houses or in the monasteries. The rich and better off had also made donations to help relieve the poor. During the Tudor period, however, attitudes towards the poor and how they should be dealt with hardened, partly resulting from changes within society, together with a sharply rising population and the pressures this brought, and the effects of increasing economic hardship.

Tudor governments came to classify the poor and destitute into one of two categories:

1 the 'impotent poor' – those who were genuinely unable to work due to age, hardship or some other infirmity; it was recognised that these individuals were in need of poor relief

2 the 'able-bodied poor' – those considered capable of work but who were either unable or unwilling to find employment; it was thought these individuals needed to be encouraged or even forced to find work in order to prevent them from resorting to begging.

During Elizabeth's reign the sharp rise in poverty together with a charitable system of support that could no longer cope with the increasing number of people in need of relief, forced her governments to pass a series of acts to help regulate, administer and control the relief of the poor. It introduced a system of poor relief which remained relatively unchanged for the next two hundred years.

Source P: Poverty was on the rise during Elizabeth's reign. This contemporary woodcut of 1569 shows a wealthy gentleman rejecting requests for help from a beggar

The causes of poverty

There was a sharp rise in poverty during the sixteenth century, especially during the reign of Elizabeth. Historians have suggested a number of reasons to help explain why this increase occurred (see Figure 2.5).

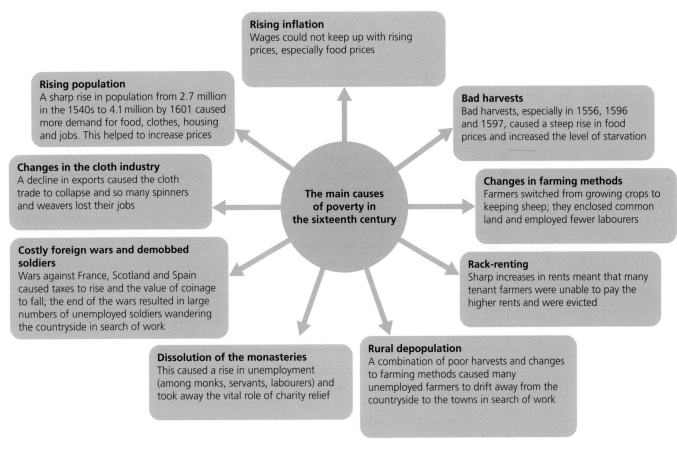

Rising inflation
Wages could not keep up with rising prices, especially food prices

Rising population
A sharp rise in population from 2.7 million in the 1540s to 4.1 million by 1601 caused more demand for food, clothes, housing and jobs. This helped to increase prices

Bad harvests
Bad harvests, especially in 1556, 1596 and 1597, caused a steep rise in food prices and increased the level of starvation

Changes in the cloth industry
A decline in exports caused the cloth trade to collapse and so many spinners and weavers lost their jobs

The main causes of poverty in the sixteenth century

Changes in farming methods
Farmers switched from growing crops to keeping sheep; they enclosed common land and employed fewer labourers

Costly foreign wars and demobbed soldiers
Wars against France, Scotland and Spain caused taxes to rise and the value of coinage to fall; the end of the wars resulted in large numbers of unemployed soldiers wandering the countryside in search of work

Rack-renting
Sharp increases in rents meant that many tenant farmers were unable to pay the higher rents and were evicted

Dissolution of the monasteries
This caused a rise in unemployment (among monks, servants, labourers) and took away the vital role of charity relief

Rural depopulation
A combination of poor harvests and changes to farming methods caused many unemployed farmers to drift away from the countryside to the towns in search of work

▲ Figure 2.5: The main causes of poverty in the sixteenth century

ACTIVITIES ?

1 Explain the difference between 'impotent poor' and 'able-bodied' poor.

2 Study Figure 2.5. Identify and explain THREE factors which you consider to be the most important reasons for causing an increase in poverty during the sixteenth century.

Practice question

Why were changes in farming methods a significant cause of the increase of poverty during Elizabethan times? *(For guidance, see page 111.)*

The issue of unemployment and vagrancy

Rising unemployment combined with economic hardship resulted in an increase in homeless beggars who toured the country in wandering bands or gathered in towns, causing problems for the authorities. Contemporaries referred to them as 'sturdy beggars' or vagabonds and sometimes as rogues, the latter being a person who survived through a life of crime.

As their numbers increased during Elizabeth's reign, society felt threatened, particularly as the lifestyle and activities of these vagabonds were blamed for the increase in crime, especially theft and burglary. This fear was based upon a number of assumptions:

- vagabonds were seen to be idle and too lazy to find a job
- they were too prepared to turn to crime as a way of life
- by wandering from place to place they helped to spread disease, especially the plague
- they increased the fear of rebellion, especially as many vagabonds were ex-soldiers
- the burden of looking after the poor was increasing, causing poor rates to rise and fuelling resentment from those having to pay this relief.

> **Source Q:** Concern over rising crime rates caused Edward Hext, a justice of the peace in Somerset, to write to Lord Burghley on 25 September 1596
>
> *And this year there assembled 80 rogues ... and took a whole load of cheese from one countryman and ... shared it out amongst themselves ... They say that the rich men have got it all in their own hands and will starve the poor ... I say that the large numbers of idle, wandering people and robbers of the land are the chief cause of the food shortage, for they do not work but lie idly in ale-houses day and night eating and drinking excessively ... And when they are put in jail, the poor country people they have robbed are forced to feed them.*

> **Source R:** William Harrison commented on the increase in begging in his book *The Description of England* (1577)
>
> *It is not yet threescore years since this trade of begging began. But how is has increased since then. They are now supposed, of one sex and another, to number 10,000 people as I have heard reported.*

Types of vagrants

The Tudor clergyman William Harrison estimated that there were about 10,000 vagabonds wandering around the countryside, causing concern to the authorities and plaguing towns and villages, especially when they resorted to crime. In 1566 Thomas Harman published a study of vagabond life, which he called *A Caveat or Warning for Common Cursitors, vulgarly called vagabonds*, in which he identified 23 different categories of vagabonds, described according to the methods they used to seek out a living. The most common types were:

- **Clapper dudgeon (a)** – tied arsenic on their skin to make it bleed, hoping to attract sympathy while begging.
- **Hooker or angler (b)** – carry a long wooden stick and knock on the doors of houses seeking charity during the day to see what may be stolen. After dark they return and use the hooked stick to reach in through windows to steal clothes and valuables, which they later try to sell.
- **Doxy (c)** – a devious female beggar who would carry a large bag on her back and at the same time she would be knitting to make it look like what she was knitting was going into her bag, but what she was really doing was walking around and picking up anything that would be worth money, putting it into her bag and running off with it. One of her common tricks was to steal chickens by feeding them bread tied to a hook, carrying the birds away in the large sack on her back.

- **Abraham man (d)** – pretended to be mad, hoping that their threatening behaviour would result in charity donations through pity.
- **Ruffler (e)** – former soldiers who have become vagabonds and who survive by robbing, using threats or by begging, as opportunity arises.
- **Dummerers (f)** – they pretended to be dumb in order to beg for charity from passers by.
- **Counterfeit crank (g)** – dressed in tatty clothes and pretended to suffer from 'falling sickness' (epilepsy), sucking soap to fake foaming at the mouth; this was commonly used by the counterfeit crank Nicholas Blunt (alias Nicholas Jennings) who was interviewed by Harman.

Local responses to vagrancy

Some areas attempted to introduce their own solutions to the problem. London used St Bartholomew's Hospital and St Thomas' Hospital, which it had obtained following the Dissolution of the Monasteries, for the sick and also Christ's Hospital, which it opened as an orphanage. The cities of Norwich, Ipswich, Cambridge and Exeter experimented with the introduction of taxes on wealthy locals as a way to reduce the number of poor. However, what was needed was direction from central government and this came in stages through the introduction of the Poor Law Acts.

> **Interpretation 1:** G. R. Elton, a leading historian who specialised in Tudor history, writing in his book *England under the Tudors*, published in 1974
>
> *The real problem of the poor was twofold. There were those who could not work and those who would not work and there is little evidence that those who wanted to work but could not find it ever made up a sizable proportion of the wandering poor.*

ACTIVITIES

1 Explain the problems caused by the increase in the number of vagabonds during Elizabeth's reign.
2 Giving examples from the listing of Thomas Harman, describe the methods used by vagabonds to obtain money and food.

Practice questions

1 To what extent does Source Q accurately reflect the problems caused by an increase in the number of wandering beggars? *(For guidance, see pages 109–110.)*
2 Study Interpretation 1. How far do you agree with this interpretation that the unemployed who were able to work but could not find suitable work made up little of the wandering poor? *(For guidance, see pages 113–114.)*

Government legislation

Elizabeth inherited a problem of increasing poverty and she attempted to deal with it by passing a series of Acts of Parliament, some of which built upon earlier laws. This policy culminated in the Elizabethan Poor Law of 1601.

Previous legislation

Previous Tudor monarchs had attempted to pass laws to punish vagrants but they had had only limited impact. Henry VIII's law of 1536 ordered vagabonds to be whipped, while an act passed by Edward VI in 1547 sentenced them to be branded with the letter 'V' and to receive two years' hard labour. Despite such punishments the number of beggars and vagrants continued to rise.

Elizabeth's legislation

The reign of Elizabeth, however, proved to be a turning point and while vagabonds were still punished, for the first time the government came to accept responsibility for dealing with the poor. It came to distinguish between the 'deserving' and 'undeserving' poor and it put in place systems to help those in genuine need of support and to deal with the idle and lazy by finding them work.

What brought about this change in attitude were the effects of a rapidly rising population and the pressure this put on jobs and supplies, the fear of social unrest and possible rebellion, and sustained periods of economic hardship during the 1570s and 1590s which increased poverty levels. The result was the passing of a series of Acts which collectively made up the Elizabethan Poor Laws and which created a nationwide compulsory system of poor relief (see Table 2.1).

Source S: A section from the Vagabonds Act of 1572

Where all the parts of the realm of England and Wales be presently exceedingly pestered with rogues, vagabonds and sturdy beggars, by means whereof daily happeneth horrible murders, thefts and other outrages, be it enacted that all persons above the age of fourteen years, being rogues, vagabonds or sturdy beggars ... shall be grievously whipped and burnt through the gristle of the right ear with a hot iron.

And forasmuch as charity would that poor aged and impotent persons should necessarily be provided for [and] have habitations and abiding places to the end that they nor any of them should hereafter beg or wander about; it is therefore enacted that the Justice of the Peace shall make a register book of the names and surnames of all aged poor, impotent and decayed persons ... and shall tax all and every the inhabitants to such weekly charge as they and every of them shall weekly contribute towards the relief of the said poor people.

Source T: An account of the workings of the 1572 Vagabonds Act given by William Harrison in his book *A Description of England* (1577)

A rogue being apprehended, committed to prison, and tried in the next assises [court session] ... if he happen to be convicted for a vagabond ... he is then immediately adjudged to be grievously whipped and burned through the gristle of the right eare, with a hot iron of the compass of an inch about.

Practice question

To what extent does Source S accurately reflect the seriousness of the problems caused by increased vagrancy? *(For guidance, see pages 109–110.)*

Year	Act	Key details of act	Impact upon vagrancy
1563	Statute of Artificers	• Compulsory for boys to serve a seven-year apprenticeship in a craft or trade • Maximum wage limit set	• Attempted to create employment and reduce vagrancy • Tied men down to one area
1572	Vagabonds Act	• Severe penalties to be used against vagrants • JP's to keep a register of the poor of their parish • Local people must pay a poor rate and provide shelter for the elderly and sick • Overseers of the Poor were to be appointed to help JP's carry out this work	• Punishments were harsh to deter vagrancy – whipping, boring through the ear with hot iron, death penalty for third offence • Government accepted that some people were in need of support • The Act did nothing to remove the causes of poverty
1576	Act for the Relief of the Poor	• JP's were to build two Houses of Correction in each county • JP's were to keep materials in every town to provide work for those unable to find a job • Those who refused were to be sent to the House of Correction	• Help given to provide work for able-bodied vagrants • Vagrants were to be punished for not finding work • The Act did nothing to remove the causes of poverty
1598	Act for the Relief of the Poor	• Four Overseers were appointed to each parish to collect and supervise the administration of poor relief • Work was to be found for able-bodied men and women • Poor children were to learn a craft or trade • Introduction of a compulsory poor rate to be paid by all inhabitants	• The Act did help those in need of support • It did attempt to provide jobs • The Act was to remain in force until 1834
1598	Act for the Punishment of Rogues	• JP's to establish Houses of Correction for rogues and vagabonds • Begging was strictly forbidden and anyone found begging was to be whipped and returned to place of birth; if this was not known they were to enter the House of Correction	• The Act helped to contain poverty and vagrancy • It reduced the risk of social unrest
1601	Act for the Relief of the Poor	• The 1598 Poor Law, which had been temporary, was now made permanent • This became known as the Elizabethan Poor Law	• A realisation that government had responsibility towards helping the poor • Set up a legal framework to tackle poverty

▲ Table 2.1: Government legislation to deal with poverty and vagrancy during Elizabeth's reign

How successful were the Elizabethan poor laws?

The Elizabethan poor laws did not end poverty but they did introduce an organised system of monitoring and administering poor relief. In reality their impact was mixed:

- the poor laws did not end poverty and it continued to rise
- the laws did help thousands of people in need of support
- the threat of social unrest and possible rebellion was reduced
- the laws reflected a change of attitude – the government now recognised that it did have some responsibility to look after the poor
- the system of poor relief set up by Elizabeth's government remained in place for the next 200 years.

ACTIVITIES

1 Explain how the Acts of 1572, 1576 and 1598:
   a) helped the impotent poor
   b) punished the able-bodied beggars
   c) helped to pay for the relief of the poor.
2 Why did government attitudes towards helping the poor change during Elizabeth's reign?
3 Copy out and complete the following table to enable you to make a judgement about how successful Elizabeth's government was in dealing with poverty.

Areas where government action was successful	Less successful areas

▼ Source U: A woodcut from Holinshed's *Chronicle* of 1577 which shows a vagabond being whipped through the streets. On the left is another vagabond being hanged, the final penalty for begging

Practice question

What can be learnt from Sources T (page 40) and U about the punishment given to vagabonds? *(For guidance, see pages 107–108.)*

Conclusion: How did life differ for the rich and poor in Elizabethan times?

The reign of Elizabeth was a time of considerable social change. The noble and gentry classes experienced improvements in their lifestyles, some of the most significant being the building of fashionable houses to replace the medieval defensive structures which they had inherited from their ancestors. These houses included new design features such as large glazed windows, private quarters to separate the lord and lady from the servants, the abandonment of the Great Hall and the introduction of the Long Gallery. The rooms were furnished with rich tapestries, paintings and fine furniture. Such grand houses demanded the wearing of fine clothes and shoes by their owners, as the nobles dressed to impress. Surrounding these new style houses were landscaped gardens.

Although on a lesser scale, the gentry copied these changes. They funded these improvements through their newly acquired wealth gained from such means as professional careers, land purchases and advantageous marriages. They built themselves new houses, dressed in fashionable clothes and ensured their children received a suitable education to set them up for a professional career or a good marriage.

In contrast, the lifestyle of the lower classes changed little during this period. Their income did not increase and with the effects of rising prices, more and more of them struggled to make ends meet. As job opportunities declined due to changes in agricultural patterns such as the shift away from crop farming to sheep farming which was less labour intensive, many peasants were forced to abandon their rented homes and wander the countryside in search of work. They only added to the existing burden of the unemployed, putting additional strain upon the system of poor relief.

Elizabeth's reign witnessed a sharp increase in the number of wandering beggars, some genuinely unemployed, others preferring to beg rather than search for work. In an attempt to deal with the increased pressure for alms relief, the government introduced laws to help those in genuine need and punish those cheating the system. These developments highlighted how the gap between rich and poor had widened during Elizabeth's reign.

Summary question

Now that you have completed this chapter, use the knowledge you have acquired to answer the following question.

Did the differences in the lifestyles of the rich and poor become more or less pronounced during the reign of Elizabeth I?

In your answer you may wish to consider the following factors:

1 homes of the rich and poor
2 fashion
3 education
4 poverty
5 and any other relevant factors you can think of.

3 Popular entertainment

The importance of popular entertainment

During the Elizabethan Age the majority of people had little time off work. The only break from their day job were Sundays, which was a day of worship, and the few religious festivals scattered through the year, together with other special days such as May Day, harvest, new year and Shrove Tuesday which were occasions for celebrations and entertainment. Life was hard, mortality rates were high due to frequent outbreaks of the plague, and life expectancy was low. Entertainment was therefore popular whenever a time and appropriate occasion permitted.

The rich would attend feasts, jousts, banquets and sporting events such as horse-racing, while the poorer sections of the population would be entertained by occasional visits from travelling fairs with puppet shows, conjurors, trained animals and hawkers. They might also be visited by wandering bands of players who would perform short plays. Dancing, music and singing were common to all sections of society, as were gambling, observing cruel sports like bear-baiting and some sports such as archery and bowls. Perhaps because they led a hard life, people living during the Elizabethan Age were keen to be entertained and to participate in a range of activities.

Cruel sports

One pastime enjoyed by all sections of society was the watching of blood sports. The most popular were bear-baiting, bull-baiting and cockfighting. Such events attracted large audiences, many of whom placed bets on the outcome of the contests.

Bear- and bull-baiting

Many towns had arenas where bears or bulls were attacked by dogs. In the case of bears they would be chained to a wooden stake by one hind leg or chained by the neck. Dogs would be released around the bear to make it angry. The dogs would attack the bear, attempting to kill it by biting its throat, and the spectators would place bets on which dog would survive the longest before being killed by the angry bear. Another variant of this activity was for the bear to be blindfolded and for it to be attacked by five or six men with whips.

One of the most popular bear baiting arenas was called the 'Bear Garden' and was located in Paris Garden in Southwark in London. It could accommodate up to a thousand people and was a circular building with a central pit around which was staged seating protected under a thatched roof. This design was copied by the builders of the first theatres to appear in London during the 1570s. Queen Elizabeth enjoyed this type of entertainment a great deal and when she went on her royal progresses towns put on bear-baiting shows for her. When MPs attempted to pass a law in 1585 to ban bear-baiting on a Sunday, Elizabeth overruled them.

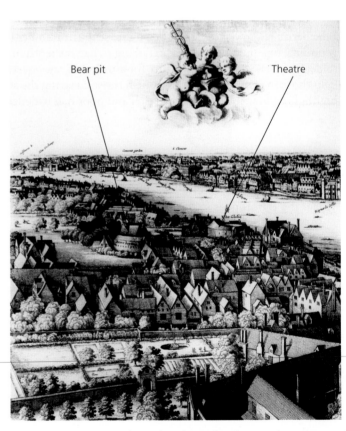

▲ Source A: A view of London drawn by the Dutch artist Wenceslaus Hollar in 1647 showing the Bear Garden and the nearby Globe theatre. Notice the similarity in style between the two buildings

In the case of bull-baiting, the bull would have a rope tied around the base of its horns and the other end of rope would be attached to a stake in the centre of the ring. In a contest lasting about an hour, trained bulldogs would then be set free one by one by their owners in order to attack the bull. During the contest the audience would place bets on the outcome of the baiting match. Owing to the difficulty of obtaining bears, bull-baiting was a far more common activity across Wales and England.

> **Source B:** In 1598, Paul Hentzner, a German visiting England, reported seeing a blinded bear being attacked by a group of six men for popular entertainment
>
> *The bear cannot escape from them because of the chain; he defends himself with all his force and skill, throwing down all who come within his reach ... and tearing the whips out of their hands and breaking them.*

◄ Source C: A woodcut showing bear-baiting in action, **c.**1620

Cockfighting

Cockfighting was another popular entertainment and most towns had a cockfighting pit. Most often it was a fight between a single pair of birds, but sometimes as many as twenty gamecocks could be put into the ring at the same time and allowed to fight it out until only one bird was left. Spectators would bet on which bird they thought would win.

ACTIVITIES ?

1   Copy out this table and use the information on pages 44–45 together with your own knowledge to complete it.

The popularity of cruel sports during Elizabethan times

Cause	Description of the cruel sport	Reasons for its popularity
Bear-baiting		
Bull-baiting		
Cockfighting		

2   What does Source A suggest about the popularity of cruel sports as a form of entertainment during this period?

> ### Practice question
>
> What can be learnt from Sources B and C about cruel sports during Elizabethan times? *(For guidance, see pages 107–108.)*

Entertainment enjoyed by the rich

Having more leisure time than the rest of society, the rich classes could afford to enjoy a range of entertainments. Some of the most popular included hunting, hawking, archery, dancing, music and ball games.

Hunting

Hunting remained a very popular pastime among the rich throughout Tudor times. Deer hunting was very much an upper-class sport and wealthy Elizabethan nobles had their own deer parks which also provided them with venison for their table. Great hunt picnics were often arranged, the prey being stags, deer and sometimes hares, hunted either on foot or on horseback.

Hawking

Hawking was another popular pastime. It involved the use of a trained falcon or hawk to fly off a trainer's arm when the blind cap was taken off its head, kill selected prey and then return. Bells were attached to the bird's legs so that the trainer could keep track of its whereabouts.

The upper classes used peregrines and they were the only persons allowed to breed hawks, while the lower orders made use of kestrels and sparrow hawks.

> **Source D:** An extract from a letter written by Edward Vaughan of Somerset to Sir Edward Stradling of St Donats in Glamorganshire in July 1575 requesting a hawk
>
> *Right worshipful, with my humble commendations [greetings] unto you. Not forgetting your former promise unto me for a hawk of your eyrie [nest of bird of prey], it makes me the more bold with you in craving a hawk of this year, the rather for my necessity who am at this present destituted [without any] and would fain have my want supplied therein.*

Archery

Archery remained a popular activity throughout the Tudor period and men over the age of 24 were expected to practise archery on a Sunday after church. They used two types of bow – the long bow and the crossbow.

Source E: A contemporary ▶ woodcut showing an Elizabethan gentleman preparing his hawk

Dancing

Dancing was very popular among all classes. While the lower classes enjoyed traditional country dances, the upper classes could employ musicians to play popular foreign dance tunes such as the slow pavan, the galliard and the gavotte. One dance, called the volta, was considered to be too wild and disgusting by some since it involved the lady having to leap into the air. The queen liked dancing and was said to be very accomplished at it (see Source F).

Music and singing

Singing was an important home entertainment and many people could play an instrument, the key musical instruments being the recorder, the viol, the lute and virginals. The music of some English composers of the period such as Tallis, Byrd and Morley was famous across Europe.

Ball games

Tennis was a game that emerged during Tudor times and became popular among the upper classes. Played in a closed or open court, it involved two players hitting a small ball to and fro, either with the palm of the hand or with a racket.

Bowls was a fashionable game played by all classes. Skittles and kayles (an early form of bowls) were also played quite widely.

By far the roughest of all the ball games was football, a sport which was more popular amongst the lower classes. It was very different to the modern game as there was no pitch, no proper goals and no limit as to the number of players on each team. There were few rules, making it a very rough game which often resulted in many injuries as well as the occasional death. With the finishing point up to a mile apart, fights often erupted between the two sides, and the winner was the side who succeeded, by whatever means, to drive the ball across the opposite finishing line. Contemporaries were keen to point out the violence associated with the game.

Source F: A description of the game of football written by a Tudor clergyman, the Archdeacon Philip Stubbes, in his book *The Anatomy of Abuses* (1583)

Football is more a fight than a game ... Sometimes their necks are broken, sometimes their backs, sometimes their legs. ... Football encourages envy and hatred ... sometimes fighting, murder and a great loss of blood.

The Cnapan

In south-west Wales, particularly in the counties of Pembrokeshire and Carmarthenshire, the game of football was commonly referred to as 'cnapan' or sometimes 'knapan'. It was played in a very similar fashion to that in England, with the gentry being on horseback, and the common people divided into two teams of players. The game had no pitch, few rules, and was played over a wide area. To win the teams had to push forward with the cnapan (ball) until one of them crossed the finishing point, which was usually the next village. The violence associated with the game was vividly described by George Owen of Henllys, (see Source G).

Source G: George Owen of Henllys, a Welsh gentleman and historian, writing in his book *A Description of Penbrockshire* (1603) about a game in 1594

About one or two of the clock afternoon begins the play, ... after a cry made both parties draw to into some plan, all first stripped bare saving a light pair of breeches, bare-headed, bare-bodied, bare legs and feet. ... There is a round ball of wood such as box, yew or holly tree which should be boiled in tallow to make it slippery and hard to hold. This ball is called cnapan and is by one of the company hurling bold upright into the air, and at the fall he that catches it hurls it towards the country he plays for, for goal or appointed place there is none. ... The play is not given over until the cnapan be so far carried that there is no hope to return it back that night ... it is oftentimes seen the chase to follow two miles and more ... It is a strange sight to see a thousand or fifteen hundred naked men to concur together in a cluster in following the cnapan as it is hurled backward and forward.

ACTIVITIES

1 Study the information on pages 46–47 and use it to:
   a) Compose a mind map to identify the common types of entertainment enjoyed by the noble class during Elizabethan times.
   b) Identify which of the entertainments were mainly undertaken by males and which by both males and females.
2 Study Source G. How did a football match held during Elizabethan times differ from a game today?

Practice question

To what extent does Source F accurately reflect attitudes towards rough sports during this period? (For guidance, see pages 109–110.)

The development of the Elizabethan theatre

At the start of Elizabeth's reign in 1558 there were no theatres in the country, but by the time of her death in 1603 theatres had been built across London and in many provincial towns, making a visit to the theatre one of the most popular forms of entertainment. The development of the theatre was rapid and went through several phases from wandering players to the establishment of theatre companies and the creation of purpose-built theatres.

Bands of strolling players

During the reigns of the early Tudor monarchs it was common for wandering bands of players to tour the country, stopping at towns to perform their plays to audiences of townsfolk, farmers, tradesmen, women and children. The players would use the courtyard of an inn or market square where they would erect a portable stage so that they could be seen from the front and the side by the audience. The more wealthy landowners would sometimes have a private showing in their homes. Such plays were a very popular form of entertainment. A common theme for these early performances was the adventures of Robin Hood, where the poorer elements of society triumphed over the rich. However, such themes worried the authorities and there were calls for such plays to be banned.

In Wales the short plays performed by such bands of strolling players were called interludes. They were usually presented by a narrator and most plays tended to adopt themes of social injustice or immorality. Landlords, lawyers and the ineffective cleric were often the main focus of jokes, much to the amusement of the audience. As this was the only opportunity people had to see such plays, interludes became a popular form of entertainment.

> **Source H:** The Tudor scholar Richard Morrison in his book, *The Laws of England* (1535), called for the banning of many plays
>
> *Robin Hood plays should be forbidden and others devised that show the wickedness of the bishop of Rome, monks, nuns and such like … Things sooner enter by the eyes, than by the ears: remembering more when they see rather than when they hear.*

Formation of theatre companies

As the popularity of such entertainment grew the authorities began to fear that the subject matter of many plays could encourage people to rebel, a fear which only added to the concern that many of the wandering players were classed as vagrants and beggars. There was also a health issue as it was believed that the gathering of large crowds to watch performances helped to spread diseases such as the plague. As a result a law was passed in 1572 banning strolling players from touring the country unless they had been granted a licence to perform from the Lord Chamberlain. This helped to ensure that the government had some control over what was being performed and where it was performed.

The result was the formation of theatre companies who had the financial support and patronage of a wealthy nobleman. Some of the leading companies established during Elizabeth's reign were:

- The Earl of Leicester's Players, established in 1574
- The Queen's Men, established in 1583
- The Lord Admiral Howard's Company, established in 1583
- The Lord Chamberlain's Men, established in 1594.

As well as touring the countryside, such companies also performed before the queen at Court and in the stately homes of their patron. As performances by such companies grew in popularity the courtyard inns became too small and overcrowded to stage such events. The solution was the construction of permanent theatres, first in London and later in provincial towns.

Building the first theatres

By 1576 the actor-manager James Burbage had raised sufficient funds to pay for the building of Britain's first purpose-built theatre since Roman times. It was called 'The Theatre' and was built on Finsbury Fields at Shoreditch, then a suburb of London. It proved to be an instant success, attracting large audiences and it resulted in the building of other theatres across the city. The Curtain opened the following year in 1577, The Rose opened in 1587, The Swan in 1596 and The Globe in 1599. The Globe premiered most of Shakespeare's plays and was built by James Burbage's sons, Cuthbert and Richard. Concerns over public health, law and order, together with stern opposition from Puritans over the sinfulness of 'the theatre', meant that most of these theatres had to be built outside the city walls.

As a result of the construction of permanent theatres, audience figures grew and by 1595 thousands of people attended plays each week in London.

Theatre	Dates	Owner	Companies who performed there
The Theatre	1576–98	James Burbage	The Lord Chamberlain's Men
The Curtain	1577–1622	Henry Lanman	The Lord Chamberlain's Men Queen Elizabeth's Men
The Rose	1594–1600	Philip Henslowe	Lord Admiral Howard's Company
The Swan	1595–1601	Langley	
The Globe	1599–1613	Richard and Cuthbert Burbage	The Lord Chamberlain's Men
The Fortune	1600–1621	Edward Alleyn and Philip Henslowe	Lord Admiral Howard's Company

▲ Table 3.1: London theatres built during Queen Elizabeth's reign

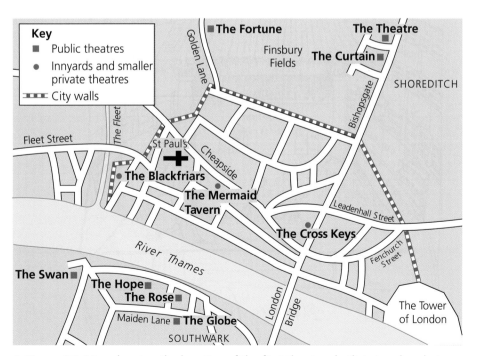

▲ Figure 3.1: Map showing the location of the first theatres built in London during Elizabeth's reign

Source I: Part of a petition sent by the inhabitants of Blackfriars in London to the Privy Council in 1596, in which they voice their opposition to the proposed building of a theatre in their area of London

A general inconvenience to all the inhabitants … by reason of the great gathering together … of all manner of vagrant and lewde persons that … will come thither and worke all manner of mischeefe.

Source J: A description of early Elizabethan theatres made by the Dutch artist Johannes de Witt who visited London in 1596

There are four theatres in London of notable beauty … In each of them a different play is daily exhibited to the populace. The two more magnificent of these are situated to the south beyond the Thames and are called the Rose and the Swan.

Source K: Thomas Platter described a visit to the theatre when he visited London from Basle in Switzerland in 1599

On September 21st after lunch, about two o'clock, I and my party crossed the water, and there in the house with the thatched roof, witnessed an excellent performance of the tragedy of the first Emperor Julius Caesar.

ACTIVITIES

1   Study Sources H and I. Explain why some Elizabethans saw the theatre as a threat to law and order.

2   Use Source K and your own knowledge to explain why a visit to the theatre became a popular form of entertainment.

Design of the theatre

The first playhouses built in London were round or octagonal in shape, with an open space in the centre, into which jutted a raised stage. While the outside of the playhouse had plain, limewashed walls and a thatched roof, the inside was ablaze with colour, especially the stage. The rear part of the stage had a roof to protect the actors during wet weather. It was supported by thick oak pillars painted to look like marble, while the back walls of the stage had finely painted panels. Apart from this decoration there was no scenery and this meant that the players had to tell the audience where they were and what time of day it was. Actors appeared on stage through doors in the back wall of the stage or through a trap-door.

To the audience the theatre mirrored the universe. Beneath the stage lay hell, out of which emerged devils or evil spirits through a trap-door. The stage was the earthly region where the actors performed their comedies or tragedies. Above the stage was the canopy which symbolised heaven and was painted with scenes showing stars, the sun, the moon and the symbols of the zodiac. The centre of the ceiling also had a trap-door from which could descend a god or goddess to hang above the actors.

As they had no means to light the theatre plays were performed in the afternoon and a flag was flown or a cannon sounded to inform Londoners that a play was about to be performed. Prices were low which helped to ensure that the poorer sections of society were able to afford the cheapest tickets in the central pit. Here the audience were open to the elements and stood around three sides of the stage. For a few pennies more a ticket could be bought for a seat in the galleries which had a roof to protect them against rain.

Source L: Drawing of The ▶ Swan theatre in London, painted by the Dutch artist, Johannes de Witt in 1596

Actors

Within the theatre companies bands of professional actors of men and boys developed. As women were not allowed to act, their parts were taken by male actors. Actors were expected to be multi-functional as they were required to take on many roles within each play and also be able to sing, dance and play musical instruments. Some of the best known of Elizabethan actors are outlined in Table 3.2.

Richard Burbage (1567–1619)	Son of theatre builder and actor James Burbage (see page 49). He established a reputation as a good tragic actor, performing leading roles in many of Shakespeare's plays. He went on to be part-owner of The Globe theatre.
Edward Alleyn (1566–1626)	A tragic actor who became a popular figure in the Elizabethan theatre. He played leading roles in Marlowe's plays including *Dr Faustus*, *Tamburlaine* and *The Jew of Malta*. He retired in 1598 at the height of his fame and went on to co-own The Fortune theatre with Philip Henslowe.
Will Kempe (d. 1603)	A popular actor and dancer who specialised in comic roles. He played many of the leading parts in Shakespeare's comedies, including that of Falstaff in the plays of *Henry IV* and in *The Merry Wives of Windsor*.
Thomas Pope (d. 1603)	He was a member of The Lord Chamberlain's Men and established a reputation as a comedian and acrobat. He was a colleague of Shakespeare's.

▲ Table 3.2: Well-known Elizabethan actors

Playwrights

The building of such theatres demanded new plays to be written to satisfy the desire of ever-growing audiences. As a consequence of this, Elizabeth's reign has come to be seen as the 'Golden Age' of English drama during which a number of important playwrights emerged whose works are still performed today in theatres across the world. Figure 3.2 at the bottom of this page provide details on some of most famous playwrights and poets in this period.

ACTIVITIES

1 Copy out this table and use the information on Elizabethan playwrights together with your own knowledge to complete it.

Leading playwrights of the Elizabethan era

Name of playwright	Style of writing they specialised in (e.g. comedy)	Most famous plays	Dates when they were active writing plays

2 Research the career of the Elizabethan playwright Ben Jonson and one other of your choice, adding the details to the table you have completed in question one above.

Practice question

Why were playwrights significant in the development of the theatre during Elizabethan times? *(For guidance, see page 111.)*

Christopher Marlowe (1564–93)
Marlowe was one of the greatest playwrights and poets of his day, playing a leading role in the development of the 'tragedy' play. His most famous work was *Doctor Faustus* (c.1589) which was set in Germany and involved the effects of a pact made between Dr Faustus and the devil. It gave Faustus magical knowledge of the world for 24 years but at a terrible price. In 1592 Marlowe completed his last play, *Edward II*. In 1593 he was stabbed to death by Ingram Frizer during a tavern brawl. Some suspect it to have been an assassination resulting from Marlowe's work as a government spy.

William Shakespeare (1564–1616)
Shakespeare is considered to be the most important playwright of Elizabethan times. Born in Stratford-Upon-Avon. Unlike Marlowe, Kyd and Dekker, who tended to concentrate upon one style of writing, Shakespeare wrote at least 37 plays – comedies, tragedies and historical dramas – writing about two plays a year. Shakespeare quickly became one of the most popular writers of the commercial theatre and his plays were well received by the queen. Among the most popular of his plays were *Richard II* (1595), *Romeo and Juliet* (1595), *The Merchant of Venice* (1597), *Hamlet* (c.1599), *King Lear* (c.1604), *Macbeth* (1606), *Anthony and Cleopatra* (1606) and *The Tempest* (1611). In 1610 Shakespeare returned to Stratford to retire and it was there that he died in 1616.

Thomas Kyd (1558–94)
Kyd is an important figure in the development of English drama, helping to pioneer the 'revenge tragedy'. He was a close friend of Marlowe and at one point in his career the two playwrights shared lodgings. Kyd's most famous work was the *Spanish Tragedy* (c.1585–92).

Thomas Dekker (c.1572–1632)
A dramatist and pamphleteer, Dekker wrote a large number of plays, particularly comedies. His *Shoemaker's Holiday* (1599) was a rowdy comedy based upon the daily lives of ordinary Londoners. Another popular play was *Old Fortunatus,* also written in 1599.

Other Elizabethan playwrights and dramatists
Francis Beaumont, John Fletcher, John Ford, Thomas Heywood, Ben Jonson, Philip Massinger, Thomas Middleton and John Webster.

◄ Figure 3.2: Prominent Elizabethan playwrights and poets

Attitudes towards the theatre

While the growth in theatre productions during Elizabeth's reign helped to make this period a 'Golden Age' for drama, with London having seven theatres by 1600, each of them attracting large audiences each day, such developments were not universally popular and the theatre aroused strong opposition from certain sections of the population. Society became bitterly divided between those who welcomed and enjoyed the growth in theatre productions and those who were vehemently opposed to such developments.

In Wales the development of the theatre was slow. This was because the Principality had few large towns to support the regular viewing of permanent theatres. What was more practical and more popular was the interlude which drew large audiences whenever bands of strolling players visited a town.

Support for the theatre

During Elizabeth's reign the theatre quickly developed into a popular form of cheap entertainment, attracting large audiences drawn from all social classes. The queen herself was a passionate lover of the theatre and became an important patron. She enjoyed the plays of Marlowe and Shakespeare, and was present at the first performance of the latter's play *Twelfth Night* in 1601. Nobles also frequented the theatre, and a visit to watch the performance of a new play became part of the social calendar, an opportunity to dress up and be noticed.

One reason for the popularity of the theatre was the actual plays performed there. Playwrights produced dramas with gripping storylines and colourful characters, tales of heroism, and plots with good triumphing over evil. Plays could be used by the authorities as propaganda. For example, *Alarum for London*, which showed Catholic Spanish soldiers killing innocent Protestant people in Antwerp, was frequently performed during the 1580s to generate anti-Spanish feeling during the time of Elizabeth's main conflict with Philip II. Shakespeare's plays delivered the strong message that obedience and loyalty to the monarch was essential in order to ensure that law and order was maintained. As Source M illustrates, many contemporaries saw the advantages of allowing people to attend the new theatres.

> **Source M:** In his book, *Pierce Penilesse* (1592), the Tudor pamphleteer and playwright Thomas Nashe wrote in support of playhouses
>
> *Plays are very necessary …. [In] the afternoon, being the idlest time of day, men … divide into gaming, drinking, or seeing a play: is it not better they should see a play? … Most plays show the ill-success of treason, the fall of hasty climbers, the wretched end of usurpers [those who seize power illegally], the misery of civil war and how God is evermore punishing murder.*

> **Source N:** Extract from a sermon attacking the theatre preached by a Puritan minister, John Stockwood, in 1578
>
> *Will not a filthy play with the blast of a trumpet sooner call thither [here] a thousand than an hour's tolling of a [church] bell bring to the sermon an hundred.*

ACTIVITY

Why do Sources M and N have differing views on the appeal of the theatre? In your answer you should refer to both their content and the authors.

Opposition to the theatre

While the theatre quickly established itself as a popular form of entertainment, it also had its critics.

Opposition from the authorities

As London's population rose sharply during the Tudor period, up from 50,000 in 1500 to over 200,000 by 1603, the authorities grew increasingly concerned about maintaining law and order. They wanted to avoid the gathering of large crowds which often resulted in some civil disturbance, and so they pressed for the new theatres to be built outside the city walls. The theatre attracted a mixed crowd of people, from those who were simply out to enjoy a play, to beggars and pickpockets, who viewed this as an opportunity to engage in crime to their advantage. This potential for lawlessness was what worried the authorities the most and it explains why they objected to the opening of theatres so close to the city centre.

> **Source O: Extract from a document written by the Council of the City of London in December 1574, expressing concern over maintaining law and order**
>
> *Great disorders and inconveniences have affected this city by the great multitudes [crowds] of people, especially youths, who go to plays and shows – especially quarrels and fights; drunkenness in inns which have open stages and galleries adjoining them; withdrawing of the Queen's subjects from church services on Sundays and holidays when plays are performed; the waste of money by poor persons; various robberies by picking and cutting of purses.*

> **Source P: A letter addressed to the Privy Council written by the Lord Mayor of London in 1597 in which he complains about the problems caused by the rise in the number of theatres in the city**
>
> *Theatres are places of vagrants, masterless men, thieves, horse-stealers, whoremongers, cheats, swindlers, traitors and other idle and dangerous persons to meet together to the great displeasure of Almighty God and the hurt and annoyance of her Majesty's people. We cannot prevent this for the theatres are outside the area of our control.*
>
> *They maintain idleness in such persons as have no work, and draw apprentices and servants from their work, and all sorts of people from attending sermons and other religious services, causing great damage to the trade and religion of this realm.*
>
> *In times of sickness many who have sores amuse themselves by hearing a play, whereby others are infected.*

Practice question

To what extent does Source O accurately reflect the criticism of the new theatres during Elizabethan times? *(For guidance, see pages 109–110.)*

Opposition from religious groups

Some of the strongest opposition to the growth of the theatre came from religious groups, chief of which were the Puritans, whose numbers grew steadily during Elizabeth's reign. They considered the theatre to be the work of the devil, encouraging people to be sinful and tempting them away from leading a pure, simple and pious life. They considered the plays to lack decency and morals, and to contain rude gestures and antics, which caused audiences to lead a sinful and corrupt lifestyle. They viewed plays as being coarse and boisterous, and the actors little more than half-lawless villains. In their opinion, such plays should be banned.

In Wales, the bad language and immoral actions of the interlude met with the disapproval of religious leaders, many of whom were the focus of the humour within the interlude plays.

> **Source Q: An extract from a sermon preached by Thomas White, a Puritan minister, outside St Paul's Cathedral in 1578**
>
> *Look upon the common plays in London, and see the multitude that flocketh to them. Look at the expensive theatre houses, a monument to London's extravagance and foolishness. I understand that they are now forbidden because of the plague. I like this well, for a disease is only patched up if the cause if not cured. The cause of plagues is sin and the cause of sin is plays – therefore the cause of plagues are plays.*

> **Source R: An attack on the theatre written by Philip Stubbes in 1583 in his book *The Anatomy of Abuses***
>
> *Do they not maintain vulgarity, foolishness and remind people of false religions? Do they not encourage prostitution and uncleanness? They are plain devourers of maidenly virginity and chastity. For proof of this, look at the flocking to theatres daily and hourly, night and day, to see plays where [there are] such suggestive gestures, bawdy [rude] speeches, laughing, kissing, winking and glancing of eyes.*

ACTIVITIES

1. Explain why interludes were popular in Wales during Elizabethan times.
2. Use the information from pages 52–53 and your own knowledge to identify the arguments put forward by Elizabethans to support and criticise the theatre, then copy and complete the table below.

Arguments put forward by those who supported the Elizabethan theatre	Arguments put forward by those who opposed the Elizabethan theatre

3. Explain why Sources M and Q have different views about the theatre as a form of popular entertainment.

Conclusion: What were the most popular types of entertainment in Elizabethan times?

Entertainment occupied an important place in the lives of people during Elizabethan times. Some forms of entertainment common in earlier periods continued to be equally popular during Elizabeth's reign, particularly the passion for cruel sports. Sports which attracted crowds such as bear- and bull-baiting, and cockfighting, together with the gambling which went along with it, remained common pastimes across the country. For richer members of society more individual activities were popular such as hunting, hawking, archery and dancing.

However, Elizabeth's reign also witnessed the development of new types of popular entertainment, one of the most significant being the theatre. Copying the design of the venues used for cruel sports, new theatres were built in many cities and large towns, usually situated just outside the town/city walls so that they fell out of the control of the mayor. The growth was so fast that London had over seven theatres by the end of the sixteenth century. In Wales, however, it was the interlude which developed as the most popular form of theatrical entertainment.

To keep the spectators attending in large numbers new plays had to be continually written and performed, leading to the growth in the number of playwrights. They wrote comedies, tragedies and historical dramas and some of the playwrights such as Shakespeare and Marlowe made it their career.

Such development, however, came at a cost and the growth of the theatre aroused opposition. The authorities became concerned about the difficulties of policing the large crowds and with the threat of spreading illness and disease which the coming together of such large numbers of people brought. By far the most bitter opposition came from religious groups, especially the Puritans, who viewed the theatre as sinful and the cause of a decline in moral standards and attitudes. Yet, despite the opposition, the theatre continued to grow in popularity, while the passion for cruel sports gradually became less attractive towards the end of Elizabeth's reign.

Summary question

Now that you have completed this chapter, use the knowledge you have acquired to answer the following question.

'A visit to the theatre was the most popular form of entertainment during Elizabethan times'. How far do you agree with this statement?

In your answer you may wish to consider the following:

1 the attractions and popularity of the theatre
2 the attraction of cruel sports
3 other forms of popular entertainment
4 and any other relevant factors you can think of.

4 The problem of religion

Key question: How successfully did Elizabeth deal with the problem of religion?

Religious problems in 1559

When Elizabeth was crowned queen in January 1559 she faced a number of problems, one of the most pressing being the fact that the country was bitterly divided by religion. Having been Roman Catholic for over 1,000 years, the twenty years prior to Elizabeth's accession had witnessed three major changes to the official religion of the land. Elizabeth had inherited a history of religious divide and dispute.

Henry VIII
- put an end to the pope's authority by making himself head of the church in Wales and England
- did not change church services but introduced an English Bible
- remained a Catholic but by the end of his reign many of his subjects had turned Protestant.

Edward VI
- was heavily influenced by his advisers the Duke of Somerset and the Duke of Northumberland, both of whom were Protestants
- introduced a new Protestant Prayer Book and communion service
- required church services to be conducted in English instead of Latin
- had decorations and all images in churches torn down
- allowed priests to marry.

Mary Tudor
- restored the authority of the pope as head of the church
- restored Latin Mass, Catholic doctrine and ritual
- separated priests and their wives
- began to persecute Protestants, a policy that earned her the title 'Bloody Mary'.

Catholic views from abroad and within England

To the pope and many foreign Catholics Elizabeth had no right to be queen. They considered her to be the illegitimate daughter of Henry VIII, whose divorce of Katherine of Aragon had not been recognised by the pope, thereby making the marriage to Anne Boleyn (Elizabeth's mother) illegal. Support for this view also came from the Catholic king of France, Francis II, who proclaimed that Mary Stuart, Queen of Scotland, was the rightful ruler of England, not Elizabeth. Many Catholic extremists living in Wales and England wanted to get rid of Elizabeth and replace her with a Catholic monarch. This was to prove a long-running problem for Elizabeth, who had to face a number of Catholic plots trying to replace her as queen (see Chapter 5).

Protestant views

Yet it was not just Catholic extremists who posed a threat to the new queen. By 1559 more than one-half the population of the country were Protestants. Some of them were extreme Protestants known as Puritans. They believed in a very simple faith and bitterly rejected the rich decoration and elaborate ceremonies of the Catholic Church. They wanted to wipe out all traces of the country's Catholic past, persecute Catholics who refused to convert and get rid of Catholicism in Wales and England once and for all (see Chapter 7).

Reaching a compromise

Elizabeth therefore faced the very difficult task of attempting to satisfy the religious desires of these contrasting groups, each of whom had their own ideas about how the Church should be run (see Table 4.1).

Catholic beliefs	Protestant beliefs	Extreme Protestant (Puritan) beliefs
• The pope was head of the Church • Cardinals, archbishops and bishops were to help the pope govern the Church • Church services and the Bible were to be in Latin as read only by priests • Churches should be highly decorated • Priests should not marry • When the bread and wine was given during Mass a miracle took place, with the priest having the power to turn the bread and wine into the actual body and blood of Jesus	• The monarch should be the head of the Church • Archbishops and bishops should help the monarch govern the church • Church services and the Bible should be in English which everyone could read • There should be little decoration in churches • They believed that spending money on elaborate church decoration was against the teaching of Jesus • Priests should be allowed to marry • The bread and wine given during Holy Communion remained bread and wine, but were also the body and blood of Jesus	• There should be no head of the Church or bishops • Churchgoers should elect committees to run their church • Church services should be simple • No need for any decoration • The bread and wine remained bread and wine during Communion, as Jesus was spiritually but not physically present during the service

▲ Table 4.1: Contrasting views on the Church

If Elizabeth was to be successful she would have to try to reach a compromise and fashion a church which was acceptable to each of these rival factions. This was a serious challenge which, if she failed, could result in a war being fought over religion as was then happening in Germany and France. Many previous rebellions had been caused by disputes over religious issues and Elizabeth wanted to avoid this from happening during her reign.

ACTIVITIES ?

1 How had the religion of England changed since the start of the reign of Henry VIII and the end of the reign of Mary I?

2 Explain the main differences in religious beliefs between Catholics and Protestants in 1559.

Practice question

Why was the settlement of the religious question a significant threat to Elizabeth? *(For guidance, see page 111.)*

▲ Figure 4.1: The religious problems facing Elizabeth

The aims of the Religious Settlement

When dealing with the problem of religion Elizabeth had to proceed carefully. She needed to weigh up the impact her choice would have on different groups – Catholics, Protestants and extremist groups, as well as the reaction of foreign powers who, if she acted unwisely, might decide to support a rival candidate to replace her as queen.

A Catholic Church?

A Puritan Church which is strongly Protestant?

A compromise?

Factors to consider

With regards to foreign powers the biggest concern was the possible reaction of England's powerful Catholic neighbours.

- France had a particular concern. In 1559 a new king, Francis II and his seventeen-year-old wife, Mary Stuart of Scotland, succeeded as the new Catholic rulers of France. Many Catholics considered Mary to be the rightful queen of England and some thought Francis might press her claim.
- King Philip II of Spain, a devout Catholic who had been the husband of Elizabeth's sister, Mary Tudor, was concerned with developments and he especially did not want to see France and Scotland gain any influence over the English Crown.
- Another concern was Scotland which was ruled over by a French regent, the Catholic widow of James V, Mary of Guise, who was the mother of Mary Stuart. While she was a strong Catholic many of the Scottish nobles were firm Protestants and did not want to see any growth in Catholic power.
- Above all these concerns stood the attitude of the pope. If he chose to excommunicate Elizabeth this would free her subjects from the bond to obey her and he could also call on the other Catholic powers to launch a religious crusade against England.

Within the country, Elizabeth also had to consider the impact any Religious Settlement would have upon her own government and her people.

- While the majority of MPs in the House of Commons were Protestant, many of the members of the House of Lords were Catholic.
- There were also the views of the Protestant Marian exiles to consider. They had fled abroad to avoid persecution during Mary Tudor's reign but now wished to return and expected to obtain key posts in government and in the church. Many of them had become influenced by the Puritan ideas of John Calvin (see page 95) and hoped Elizabeth's planned changes would reflect these beliefs and practices.
- As for the ordinary people, the majority were conservative in their religious sympathies.

Elizabeth's religious beliefs

Elizabeth understood the important place religion had in the lives of her people. She had lived in Protestant households as a child. Her mother, Anne Boleyn, had placed Elizabeth's religious education under the care of her chaplain, Matthew Parker, a cleric who Elizabeth later appointed as her first Archbishop of Canterbury. During her father's last years she had been cared for by Catherine Parr, an enthusiastic Protestant. Along with her brother, Edward, they had been taught by a Protestant tutor, Roger Ascham from Cambridge.

Owing to her Protestant upbringing Elizabeth's life had been in danger during her sister Mary's reign. She had refused to become a Roman Catholic and her name had been associated with anti-Catholic plots, for which Elizabeth had been sent to the Tower of London.

While Elizabeth disliked the authority of the pope, there were aspects of the Catholic faith that she did believe in. She thought that priests should wear vestments, and she liked ornaments and decoration in churches. She kept crucifixes and candles in her private chapel, and she was opposed to the idea of bishops and clergymen being allowed to marry.

Most of all Elizabeth wanted to unify the country and did not wish to see her subjects punished because of their religious beliefs. She desired to create a church that the majority could accept. Her personal preference was for a church with a Protestant doctrine which retained traditional structure and Catholic ritual. She hoped for a compromise settlement.

The 'middle way'

Elizabeth was aware that the majority of the population was conservative in religion and preferred the ceremonies and celebrations associated with the Catholic Church. She wanted to avoid the mistakes of Edward and Mary's reign when adopting a strict and extreme policy had offended and caused resentment in large sections of the people. Such division would only serve to weaken Elizabeth's position as queen. Her sister Mary, by enforcing a strict following of the Catholic faith, had caused people to practise their Protestant faith in secret, some had been put to death and became martyrs to their faith, while others had fled abroad, waiting for a suitable time to return and take action against Mary's extreme policies. Elizabeth hoped to avoid this situation.

Elizabeth was a moderate Protestant. She wanted to heal the religious divisions of previous reigns by creating a church which displayed tolerance; a church which belonged to everybody.

In formulating her Religious Settlement Elizabeth adopted a via media or 'middle way', creating a church which reflected both Protestant and Catholic attitudes and practices:

- she made Protestantism the official religion
- she brought back changes made in Edward's reign, introducing a new Prayer Book, a Bible in English, simpler churches and allowed priests to marry
- she refused to give way to extreme Protestant ideas
- she kept some aspects of the old Catholic church, such as archbishops, bishops and cathedrals. She allowed churches to continue using crosses and candles, and allowed priests to wear vestments
- she did not persecute Catholics, but she did fine them for not attending church.

Her policy of toleration seemed to work. Most people were prepared to accept and follow her form of Protestant church.

> **Interpretation 1: The view of the writer Barbara Mervyn who was commissioned to write a school history textbook, *The Reign of Elizabeth: England 1558–1603*, published in 2001**
>
> *Elizabeth did not want to be associated with Mary's legacy. The restoration of Roman Catholicism and the authority of the Pope were too closely associated in the minds of the English with the persecution of heretics, an unpopular Spanish consort and the loss of Calais. There was much to be gained from embarking on a new policy that would signal a break with the immediate past and enable Elizabeth to emerge as the architect of, and inspiration for, a new order.*

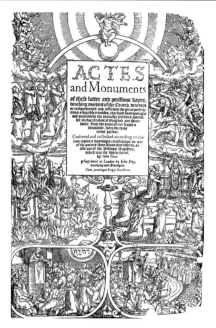

▲ Source A: The front cover of Foxe's *Book of Martyrs*, published in 1563. Foxe was a Protestant clergyman who wanted to show how bad things had been under Mary I so that people might be more willing to accept the Settlement of 1559. One of the boxes shows Protestant priests being burnt to death

Practice question

Study Interpretation 1. How far do you agree with this interpretation of the aims of Elizabeth's Religious Settlement of 1559? *(For guidance, see pages 113–114.)*

ACTIVITIES

1   Working in pairs, make a copy of the following table about the possible threats facing Elizabeth from foreign powers.
    a) One of you should complete the list of rulers and their religious beliefs.
    b) The other should identify the threats they posed to Elizabeth.

Country	Religious beliefs of the rulers	Possible threats to Elizabeth
France		
Spain		
Scotland		
The pope		

2   To what extent does the Religious Settlement of 1559 display the religious beliefs of Elizabeth I?

3   How useful is Source A to an historian studying attitudes towards religion during the reign of Mary I?

4   Explain why Elizabeth adopted a 'middle way' in her Religious Settlement of 1559.

The Acts of Supremacy and Uniformity

When Parliament met in February 1559 Elizabeth put forward plans to create a new church. She wanted MPs to approve her plans quickly but to her surprise some MPs voiced concerns and opposition was stronger in the House of Lords. Many Puritan MPs thought the Settlement did not go far enough to erase all traces of the Catholic faith. Such concerns therefore forced her to make some changes and after four months of discussion her MPs finally agreed to the creation of a new Church of England. Two important Acts of Parliament were passed which together formed the Elizabethan Church Settlement which made England a Protestant country again. The Act of Supremacy established the monarch's authority over the Church, while the Act of Uniformity spelled out the form of service to be followed.

Source B: Extract from the Act of Supremacy 1559

All and every Archbishop, Bishop and all and every other cleric, … and all and every judge, justice, mayor, and every other lay or officer and minister and every other person having Your Highness's fee or wages shall make a[n] oath …

… I … do utterly testify and declare in my conscience that the Queen's Highness is the only Supreme Governor of this realm and … that no foreign prince, person, bishop … hath or ought to have any jurisdiction, power, superiority, or [authority over religion or state matters within the realm].

Source C: Extract from the Act of Uniformity 1559

All and every person and persons inhabiting within this realm … shall diligently and faithfully, having no lawful or reasonable excuse to be absent, endeavour themselves to resort to their parish church or chapel accustomed … upon every Sunday and other [religious days] … upon pain that every person so offending shall forfeit for every such offence twelve pence to be [collected] by the church wardens of the Parish …

ACTIVITIES

1 Make a copy and complete the following table to show how Elizabeth used the Religious Settlement to take firm control over the Church.

	Key features	How it strengthened Elizabeth's control over the church
Act of Supremacy		
Royal Injunctions		
Visitations		
Act of Exchange		

2 How successful was Elizabeth in securing the support of her bishops to the Religious Settlement?

Act of Supremacy, 1559	Act of Uniformity, 1559
• Elizabeth became head of the Church of England instead of the pope • Elizabeth adopted the title of 'Supreme Governor of the Church of England' • All important officials such as judges, lawyers, JPs, MPs and the clergy, had to swear an oath of loyalty accepting Elizabeth's title • If they refused to swear the oath they could be imprisoned; if they refused three times they could be executed • Bishops would be used to govern the new church • The Marian heresy laws were repealed • A church High Commission was established to ensure the changes were implemented at parish level	• The 1552 Protestant Book of Common Prayer was to be used in all churches • The Bible was to be in English • Church services were to be conducted in English • There was compromise on the issue of real presence during Communion service – worshippers took the bread and wine, not as the body and blood of Christ, but to remember that Christ died for them on the cross • Ornaments and decorations were allowed in churches • Clergy had to wear vestments • Clergy were allowed to marry • All clergy had to take an oath to use the new Prayer Book • Everyone had to attend church on a Sunday and other holy days and to participate in the new services • Recusants (those who refused to go to church) had to pay a fine of 1 shilling (12 old pence/5 new pence) for every absence from a church service • The monasteries founded by Mary I were to be closed down and their wealth passed on to the crown

▲ Table 4.2: Key elements of the Act of Supremacy and the Act of Uniformity

Measures to enforce the Acts

In order to enforce what was laid down in the Acts of Supremacy and Uniformity a number of other measures were added to the Settlement.

The Royal Injunctions, 1559

These were intended to provide a set of instructions to the clergy on a wide range of practices, the aim being to establish a uniformity of worship and behaviour. The Royal Injunctions of 1559 ordered clergy to:

- observe and teach the royal supremacy and to denounce superstition and papal authority
- condemn Catholic practices such as processions, pilgrimages and monuments, and to ban 'fake' miracles
- identify recusants and report them to the Privy Council or to local JPs
- fine recusants a shilling for each occasion they failed to attend a church service on a Sunday and on holy days
- preach only with the permission of the bishop and to obtain a licence to preach from the authorities
- ensure that each parish church had a copy of the Bible in English
- ensure uniformity of practice during church services – the congregation was to bow at the name of Jesus and kneel when at prayer
- require all clergy to wear clerical dress which included the surplice, a white linen gown
- priests were now allowed to marry but only after they had obtained permission to do so from their bishop and two JPs.

The Visitations

To make sure that the Acts of Supremacy and Uniformity, together with the Injunctions, were enforced, a force of 125 commissioners were appointed. Their job was to tour the country, judge whether the regulations were being followed correctly and make the clergy take an Oath of Supremacy. Over 400 clergy either resigned or were sacked from their posts between 1559 and 1564, over one-half of them because they were Catholics.

Practice question

What can be learnt from Sources B and C (see page 59) about the Religious Settlement of 1559? *(For guidance, see pages 107–108.)*

The Act of Exchange, 1559

Like her father, Elizabeth realised that the Church was a wealthy institution and that some of that wealth could be used by the monarch to help fund ventures such as costly foreign wars and to reward loyal followers with land. The Act of Exchange passed in 1559 allowed Elizabeth to take land and buildings belonging to the Church, and also force bishops to rent land to her. The result was that the church lost considerable wealth and if the queen did not wish to use her own money or lands to reward her nobility and gentry, she could order her bishops to grant favourable leases to these men. It was a further example of how the monarch could exercise royal control over the Church.

The Episcopacy – the role of the bishops

While the queen held the position of supreme governor, the daily organisation and supervision of the church was the responsibility of the episcopate, the bishops. Elizabeth favoured the use of bishops to administer the church and rejected the Geneva model of control set up by Calvin which replaced bishops with ministers elected by the congregations.

Elizabeth hoped that the Catholic bishops who had been in post under Mary I would continue in office but their refusal to take the Oath of Supremacy made this impossible and they were forced to resign. However, this did allow Elizabeth the opportunity to appoint Protestants in their place. These men would be more willing to enforce the Religious Settlement of 1559, thereby ensuring uniformity of doctrine and practice.

One problem was that some of the new bishops who had returned to England from exile after 1558 held Calvinist views. They considered the Acts of Supremacy and Uniformity as only the start of the reform of the church. Elizabeth, however, regarded it as a conclusion and this was to lead to tension between the queen and some of her bishops later in her reign.

The Thirty-nine Articles, 1563

At a church convocation held at Canterbury in 1563 the delegates drew up Thirty-nine Articles of faith. These laid down the beliefs of the Church of England. They rejected many Catholic practices and confirmed the key elements of Protestant belief. They were not finally approved by the Queen until 1571, after which all clergy had to swear to follow them.

Reactions to the Settlement

Elizabeth had hoped that her Religious Settlement of 1559 would serve to calm the tension and settle the upheaval which had dominated religious life in Wales and England since the days of her father, Henry VIII's reign. She had not intended her Settlement to be too strict, in the hope that gradually people of all religious standpoints would come to accept it as a working compromise. While this proved to be the case during the early 1560s, the situation became less stable and secure during the 1570s and 1580s due to the actions of some Catholics and extreme Protestants, both of whom disliked aspects of the Settlement (see Chapters 5 and 7).

▲ Matthew Parker, Archbishop of Canterbury (1559–1575)

Reactions at home

By the mid-1560s most people in Wales and England had come to accept the new church:

- The new Archbishop of Canterbury, Matthew Parker, was a moderate Protestant and commanded respect.
- Most of the clergy took an oath of loyalty in the new church and only around 250 of the 9,000 priests (less than 3 per cent) refused to accept the changes and lost their jobs.
- The majority of the devout Catholic bishops from Mary I's reign resigned their posts and were replaced by loyal Protestants.
- Reaction amongst most Catholics and Protestants was muted.
- The fines for recusancy were not strictly enforced.
- Opposition to parts of the Settlement emerged later in the reign over issues such as what priests were to wear to conduct services (the Vestments Controversy – see page 97).

Reactions abroad

Foreign reaction to the Settlement was limited during the early 1560s:

- France was drifting towards civil war and therefore showed little interest in the Settlement.
- King Philip II of Spain initially wished to maintain a friendship with England and hoped that the changes introduced by Elizabeth would not be permanent.
- The pope voiced little criticism to events in England and, like Philip, hoped that the changes could be overturned with time.

A less tolerant attitude emerged after the ending of the Council of Trent. These meetings of leading Catholic clergy which had been called to discuss the future of the Church had been going on since 1545. When the council finally completed its discussions in 1563 it produced a series of hard line decrees against the spread of Protestant ideas. Some of the delegates had even called for the excommunication of Elizabeth. By the 1570s and 1580s attitudes had hardened and both Spain and the papacy became actively involved in plots to overthrow Elizabeth and the Protestant faith.

ACTIVITIES ?

1 How successful was Elizabeth in getting acceptance of the Religious Settlement from her people?

2 What was the reaction of foreign countries to the Religious Settlement?

Practice question

Study Interpretation 2. How far do you agree with this interpretation of the Religious Settlement of 1559? (For guidance, see pages 113–114.)

Interpretation 2: The view of writers Nicholas Fellows and Mary Dicken who were commissioned to write a school history textbook called *England 1485–1603*, published in 2015

The Settlement of 1559 has been described as a Via Media, that is a middle way, between Catholicism and Protestantism, but it clearly was far from establishing a Catholic Church. It was a Protestant Settlement, but not an extreme one and the 'wolves coming out of Geneva', against whom one of the Catholic bishops had warned Elizabeth, were dissatisfied with some of the content. They expected further revisions in a more Calvinist direction. But Elizabeth had made her Settlement with some difficulties and sacrifices and she had no intention of re-visiting or revising her decisions. It was some years before the radical Reformers came to understand that the lady was not for turning.

The Translation of the Scriptures into Welsh

To Protestants the Bible was central to their belief, which meant that it was important for ordinary men and women to be able to hear the word of God in their own language if they were to obtain salvation.

The importance of the 1563 Act of Parliament

The production of a Welsh version of the Scriptures was the work of a group of Protestant men from North Wales. The two most important persons were William Salesbury and William Morgan. Salesbury was given help and encouragement from Dr Richard Davies who, due to his Protestant beliefs, had been forced into exile during Mary's reign. Following the accession of Elizabeth he returned to Wales and was appointed Bishop of St Asaph in 1559, before moving on to become Bishop of St Davids in 1561.

It was Richard Davies who was largely responsible for persuading Parliament to pass an Act in 1563 which ordered the five Welsh bishops (they included the Bishop of Hereford in their list) to ensure that the Bible and Prayer Book were translated into Welsh by St David's Day, 1567, and put alongside the English version in every church in Wales. This Act was the reason for the start of the translation, but it was a process that was to take 25 years before it was completed.

William Salesbury and the translation of the New Testament and the Book of Common Prayer

The work of translating the New Testament into Welsh largely fell upon the shoulders of William Salesbury. Born around 1520 in Llansannan in Denbighshire, he was educated at Oxford where he became heavily influenced by Protestant beliefs. Between 1547 and 1552, he published a number of religious works but when Mary became queen he was forced into hiding at the family home of Cae Du. Following Mary's death Salesbury became friendly with Richard Davies, the new Bishop of St Asaph, who encouraged him to embark upon the work of translation.

In translating the New Testament from Greek into Welsh Salesbury was helped by Richard Davies (then Bishop of St David's), and Thomas Huet, Dean of St David's. In 1565, he moved to St David's to join them and for nearly two years they worked on the translation. As well as the New Testament, Salesbury also translated the Book of Common Prayer. Both were published in London in 1567. This meant that important religious books were now available in Welsh for the first time. However, Salesbury's unusual method of translation and his odd phrasing made the texts difficult to read and this limited their impact and usefulness.

Source D: Bishop Richard Davies, translator of the New Testament into Welsh, writing in the Preface to the *New Testament* (1567)

Awake now lovely people of Wales! I remember one excellent virtue which improved your lives namely the worship of pure Christianity. But recently you have not participated in anything of the good fortune of the world! This is because no one has written nor printed anything in your language. Therefore now you should be glad and offer your thanks to God, and to her grace the Queen. For by their authority and their command, your Bishops with the help of William Salesbury are bringing to you in Welsh and in print the Holy Scriptures.

▲ Source E: The title-page of the Welsh New Testament published in 1567

William Morgan and the translation of the Old Testament

The task of translating the Old Testament from Hebrew into Welsh was performed by William Morgan. The son of tenant farmer from Wybrnant in the Conwy valley, Morgan was educated at St John's College Cambridge where he became a brilliant Hebrew scholar. He began his translation whilst at Cambridge but undertook most of it while vicar of Llanrhaeadr-ym-Mochnant, a post he held from 1578 to 1595. Morgan received some help from Archdeacon Edmund Prys with whom he had been a student at Cambridge.

The translation was a slow process, with Morgan writing by candlelight using a goose quill pen. By the end of 1587, he had finished and he moved to London. As English printers had no knowledge of Welsh, Morgan was needed to be available to check and correct their work. The new Welsh Bible was dedicated to Queen Elizabeth who ordered that 'One Bible be put in every church throughout Wales so that all who speak Welsh can read and understand.' Morgan also produced a revised translation of the New Testament of Salesbury. As a result of his scholarship he was appointed Bishop of Llandaff in 1595 and in 1601 moved back up north to become Bishop of St Asaph. He died in 1604.

Unlike Salesbury, Morgan wrote in a fluent style which was easy to understand, adopting the prose of ordinary spoken Welsh. His translation of the Old Testament was well received and its publication in 1588 has been seen as important in the history of Wales as the defeat of the Armada that same year was in the history of England. A new edition of his work appeared in 1620, edited by Richard Parry, Morgan's successor as Bishop of St Asaph and John Davies of Mallwyd.

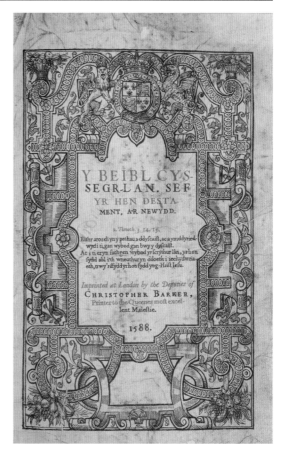

▲ Source F: The title-page of William Morgan's translation of the Bible, 1588

◀ Source G: A picture of Bishop William Morgan by Keith Bowen

The impact of the translation on the Welsh language

In the long-term the translation of 1588 had a dramatic impact upon the preservation of the Welsh language, Welsh culture and Welsh tradition. It meant that services could now be conducted in Welsh and that congregations could hear the Bible read to them in a language which they understood. The Bible became a powerful medium in keeping the Welsh language alive. In reality, however, very few could go the parish church to read the scriptures themselves.

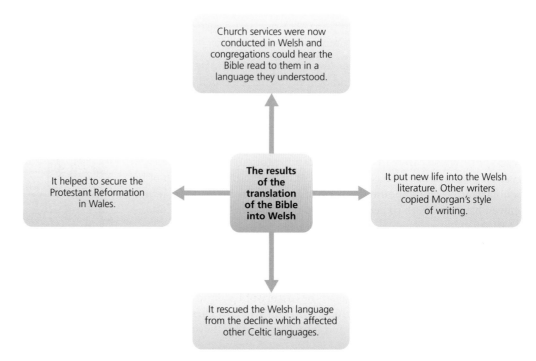

Church services were now conducted in Welsh and congregations could hear the Bible read to them in a language they understood.

The results of the translation of the Bible into Welsh

It helped to secure the Protestant Reformation in Wales.

It put new life into the Welsh literature. Other writers copied Morgan's style of writing.

It rescued the Welsh language from the decline which affected other Celtic languages.

▲ Figure 4.2: The results of the translation of the Bible into Welsh

Source H: In his book *A Dialogue of the Government of Wales* (1594), the historian George Owen of Henllys was quick to recognise the importance of the translation

We have the light of the Gospel, yea the whole Bible in our native tongue … whereas the service and sacraments in the English tongue was as strange to many or most of the simplest sort as the mass in the time of blindness was to the rest of England.

ACTIVITIES

1 Study the contributions made by Richard Davies, William Salesbury and William Morgan in making the Scriptures available in Welsh to the people of Wales. Which individual do you think played the most important part in this process? Give reasons to explain your answer.

2 Study Source D. What is the main message made by the author of this source?

Practice questions

1 What can you learn from Sources F and H about the translation of the Scriptures into Welsh? *(For guidance, see pages 107–108.)*

2 Why was the translation of the Scriptures into Welsh significant in the acceptance of Elizabeth's Religious Settlement in Wales? *(For guidance, see page 111.)*

Conclusion: How successfully did Elizabeth deal with the problem of religion?

Elizabeth had come to the throne at a time of religious uncertainty. Her sister, Mary I, had followed an active policy of persecution against those who refused to acknowledge the Catholic faith, causing a sharp divide between those who had adopted Protestantism as their faith. The country ran the risk of being torn apart by contrasting religious views.

Elizabeth had the difficult task of trying to reach a compromise settlement that would be acceptable to both Protestants and Catholics alike, and which would not lead to persecution for those who were not strict followers of the new 'middle way' she adopted. To a large extent the Religious Settlement of 1559 was a success as it was a compromise that was acceptable to the vast majority. It settled the issue of who was in charge of the church and how it was to be governed and administered. It attempted to tackle areas of religious dispute such as the issue of the meaning of bread and wine during communion service. While the Settlement was not ideal it did bring about an end to active religious persecution and discrimination, features which had so dominated the reigns of Edward and Mary.

However, as with all compromises, there were those on the extremes of the religious divide who questioned the Settlement. The Catholics wished to see the reinstatement of the pope as the head of the Church, while some Puritans wanted to see an end to the power of the archbishops and bishops in favour of a more locally regulated church. These issues were to play a more active part in Elizabeth's reign during the 1580s and 1590s.

Summary question

Now that you have completed this chapter, use the knowledge you have acquired to answer the following question.

'The Religious Settlement of 1559 solved more problems than it caused.' How far do you agree with this statement?

In your answer you might like to consider the following factors:

1   Elizabeth's wish to reach a compromise settlement
2   the key features of the 'middle way'
3   reactions of the Catholics and Puritans to the Settlement
4   reactions of foreign powers
5   and any other relevant factors you can think of.

5 The Catholic threat

Early toleration

The extent to which the majority of the population of Wales and England were either Catholic or Protestant in 1558 has been a matter of considerable debate among historians. Traditionally historians have assumed that the majority of Elizabeth's subjects were ready to accept the Protestant religion of their new queen and only a minority of staunch Catholics, the loyal supporters of the pope, were unwilling to adapt and accept the Religious Settlement of 1559. In recent decades, however, some historians have revised this view and concluded that the traditional viewpoint is too simplistic. Instead they argue that the majority of the population, especially those outside London, were Catholic and not Protestant in 1559. It was precisely for this reason that Elizabeth chose to proceed cautiously with her Religious Settlement, adopting a 'middle way' which selected features from both the Catholic and Protestant faiths, thereby reducing the alienation of her subjects regardless of their faith.

Certainly in the first decade of her reign Elizabeth adopted an attitude of toleration towards Catholics and did not vigorously impose her Protestant ideas. Several factors account for this early toleration:

- when trying to get the Religious Settlement of 1559 passed through Parliament, Elizabeth was shocked by the degree of opposition she met in the House of Lords from powerful Catholic nobles
- the fear of possible foreign intervention if she cracked down too harshly upon the Catholics
- the fear of rebellion from powerful Catholic nobles within Wales and England
- the realisation that the majority of the population were still Catholic at heart.

Elizabeth therefore wisely selected to proceed cautiously and followed a gradual approach towards the implementation of her Religious Settlement, hoping by doing so to win her subjects over rather than alienating them. Events during the late 1560s and early 1570s, however, caused her to abandon this policy of toleration in favour of a firmer policy of forced conformance. Elizabeth began to adopt a harsher policy towards those Catholics who demonstrated reluctance to follow her religious settlement as a result of the following:

- **1568**: The arrival of Mary Queen of Scots in England
- **1569**: The Rebellion of the Northern Earls
- **1570**: The issue of a Papal Bull of Excommunication against Elizabeth
- **1571**: The Ridolfi Plot
- **1574**: The first arrival of seminary priests in England from Douai in Flanders
- **1580**: The arrival of the first Jesuit priests into England
- **1583**: The Throckmorton Plot
- **1586**: The Babington Plot
- **1588**: The Spanish Armada.

Recusancy

The term recusant was used to describe those individuals who rebelled against Elizabeth's Religious Settlement by refusing to attend church services. They believed in the doctrine of the Roman Catholic Church, especially the Latin Mass, and were not prepared to compromise. This was a direct challenge which caused Elizabeth to respond in 1581 by increasing the fines for recusancy to £20 and by making it a treasonable offence to attempt to convert people to the Catholic faith. This law was especially aimed at the seminary priests who began to be smuggled into Wales and England from northern France after 1574.

In 1568, William Allen set up a college in Douai in Flanders to train English Catholics for the priesthood (see Source A). These priests were taught that it was their duty to return to England to re-establish the Catholic faith and, if necessary, seek martyrdom for their cause. Their arrival, which coincided with the uncovering of several plots by prominent Catholics against Elizabeth, fuelled growing suspicion that Catholics could not be trusted to be loyal to the Crown. In all, some 438 seminary priests were sent to England causing the government to pass an Act of Parliament in 1585 that ordered all such priests to leave the country or be put to death. It also stated that anyone found helping or hiding a priest could be put to death. In total, 98 priests were sentenced to death.

> **Source A: A report in the Spanish state papers, dated 28 December 1579, describing the growth of the Catholic training college set up in Douai in 1568**
>
> *The number of Catholics, thank God, is daily increasing here, owing to the College and seminary for Englishmen which your Majesty [Philip II] ordered to be supported in Douai, from where there has come in the last year (and from the College of Rome) a hundred Englishmen who have been ordained there, by which means a great number of people are being converted, generally persons who have never heard the truth preached before. These priests go about disguised as laymen, and although they are young men, their good life, fervency and zeal in their work are admirable.*

Jesuits

Many of these seminary priests were Jesuits, members of the Roman Catholic missionary order known as 'The Society of Jesus' which had been founded in 1534. Its chief aim was to destroy heresy (Protestantism). They swore an oath of allegiance to the pope and were prepared to die for their cause. They began to arrive in England in disguise in 1580, spreading the message that true Catholics should not accept the Elizabethan church. They claimed that they only came to hold services for Catholic families in the privacy of their own homes, but the government claimed otherwise, believing them to be missionaries with the sole purpose of converting people to the Roman Catholic Church and allegiance to the pope.

Government response to recusancy

In order to deal with recusancy the government passed a series of acts:

- **1581:** two Acts of Parliament were passed which increased the fines against recusants and made any attempt to convert people to the Catholic faith to be judged to be a treasonable offence.
- **1585:** an Act of Parliament ordered all Jesuits and seminary priests to leave the country or be killed; in addition, anybody found hiding or helping a priest in any way could also be given the death sentence.
- **1593:** an Act forbade large gatherings of Catholics and confined known Catholics to a radius of 5 miles (8 km) from their homes.

ACTIVITIES

1 What can you learn from Source A about the purpose of the Catholic college set up at Douai in 1568?

2 Why were the entry of Jesuit priests into England seen as a threat to the Religious Settlement?

Case study: Edmund Campion

One of the most famous Jesuit priests and recusants was Edmund Campion. Campion was one of the first priests to be sent to England. Following his capture he was tortured, found guilty of treason and executed in 1581.

Edmund Campion (1540–81)

- 1540 born the son of a London bookseller
- 1557–64 studied at Oxford University
- 1571–73 trained at Douai College
- 1572 went to Rome
- 1573 joined the Jesuits
- 1578 ordained as a Jesuit priest
- 1580 chosen, along with Robert Parsons, to return to England on a religious mission to spread the Catholic faith. He arrived in secret and travelled to Lancashire, an area with a high proportion of Catholic families. He then moved south to preach in the homes of rich Catholic families in London, constantly having to dodge the authorities
- 1581 arrested at Lyford in Berkshire. He was sent to the Tower and tortured. Campion was found guilty of treason and executed by hanging on 1 December 1581.

Source B: Letter written by Edmund Campion, a Jesuit priest, soon after his arrival in England in 1580

I cannot long escape the hands of the heretics [Protestant authorities]; the enemy has so many eyes … I wear ridiculous clothes … I often change my name … I read letters [newspapers] that tell news that Campion is captured, which I hear in every place … I have published the reasons why I have come. I have asked for a debate with the Queen but am told the Queen will not allow [religious] matters, already decided, to be questioned … Very many are being restored to the Church.

Source C: A report of the trial of Edmund Campion which was printed in a book by Raphael Holinshed *Chronicals of England, Scotland and Ireland* (1577)

On Monday, being the twentieth of November, Edmund Campion … [and seven others] … were brought unto the high bar at Westminster where they were severally and together indicted upon high treason. When they convicted them on these matters (which with obstinacy they still denied), they came to the intent of their secret coming into this realm, which was the death of her Majesty and the overthrow of the kingdom. 'Yea' saith Campion, 'never shall you prove this, that we came over either for this intent or purpose, but only for the saving of souls, which mere love and conscience compelled us to do, for that we did pity the miserable state of our country.'

▲ Edmund Campion, 1540–81

▲ Source D: A contemporary drawing made in Rome in 1584 showing Campion being tortured on the rack during his captivity in the Tower of London

Practice question

What can be learnt from Sources C and D about the trial and interrogation of Edward Campion in 1581? *(For guidance, see pages 107–108.)*

The arrival of Mary, Queen of Scots, in England, 1568

In May 1558 Mary, Queen of Scots, was forced to flee Scotland and seek sanctuary across the border in England. Her arrival would cause problems for Elizabeth.

Mary sent to France

Mary had a very eventful past. She had been born in 1542, the daughter of James V of Scotland and his French wife, the devout Catholic Mary of Guise. Her father died when she was just a few days old and she was crowned Queen of Scotland, with her mother acting as regent for the young monarch. In 1548, at the age of six, she was sent to be brought up and educated in Catholic France. When she was fifteen years old she was married to Prince Francis, the eldest son of the French King Henry II. In 1559 her husband became King Francis II but died the following year.

Mary returns to Scotland

In 1561 Mary returned to Scotland, but it was a very different Scotland to the one she had left in 1548. In the intervening years it had become predominantly Protestant and in 1559 the Scottish Protestant lords had rebelled against Mary of Guise's government and she had been forced to flee from Edinburgh in 1559. When France prepared to send troops to defeat the Scottish rebels, Elizabeth had been forced to conclude the Treaty of Berwick with the Scots in 1560, promising to send an army north to help defeat the French. Following the death of Mary of Guise,

French troops withdrew and Scotland returned to the rule of the Protestant lords who maintained friendly relations with England. In was into this Protestant environment that Mary, Queen of Scots, found herself in 1561.

Mary and Darnley

In 1565 Mary married Henry Stuart, Lord Darnley, and in June of the following year gave birth to a son, the future King James VI of Scotland. However, the marriage was not a happy one and Darnley became jealous that Mary was becoming very friendly with her Italian secretary, David Rizzio. On 9 March 1566 he and a group of friends murdered Rizzio at Holyrood Palace. He was stabbed to death.

Mary and Bothwell

Mary then became friendly with James Hepburn, the Earl of Bothwell. When Darnley fell ill with smallpox, Mary brought him to Kirk O'Field, a large house in Edinburgh where she nursed him daily. On the evening of 9 February 1567 she left the house to attend a wedding. That night the house was blown up and the following morning Darnley's body was found in the garden. He had been strangled (see Source F). Bothwell was accused of murdering Darnley and was put on trial. He was found 'not guilty' of the charge of murder.

Three months after Darnley's death Mary married Bothwell. This was a step too far for some of Mary's Protestant lords, who now rebelled against her. She was imprisoned at Loch Leven castle and in July 1567 was forced to abdicate in favour of her young son who had been brought up a Protestant.

▲ Source E: Portrait of Mary, Queen of Scots, painted in 1578 when she was 36 years of age. The caption in the top corner describes her as Queen of Scotland, widow of the King of France and a prisoner in England

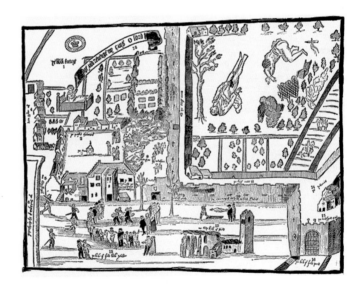

▲ Source F: A drawing sent to Elizabeth's chief adviser showing what happened at Kirk O'Field. It shows the stripped bodies of Darnley and his servant lying dead in the garden of the house

Mary arrives in England

In May 1568 Mary managed to escape from her captivity at Loch Leven and fled across the border to England. Her arrival in Protestant England presented Elizabeth with a serious problem. There were numerous options open to her but each one had its drawbacks (see Figure 5.1).

Having considered the various options, Elizabeth chose to hold Mary captive. It was a decision that had long-term consequences for dissatisfied English Catholics who saw Mary as a suitable alternative queen of England. Over the following two decades Mary remained a significant big problem, being at the centre of numerous plots to unseat Elizabeth.

> **Source G:** Letter written by Sir William Cecil to Elizabeth on 16 October 1569
>
> *The Queen of the Scots is and shall always be a dangerous person to your estate. Yet there are degrees of danger. If she is kept a prisoner ... it will be less, if at liberty, greater.*

> **Interpretation 1:** The view of the writer Barbara Mervyn who was commissioned to write a school history textbook *The Reign of Elizabeth: England 1558–1603*, published in 2001
>
> *Mary Stuart was a problem for Elizabeth because of her claim to the English throne and the fact that, as she was both half-French and Catholic, recognition of her claim might jeopardise England's future political independence and its official Protestant religion. As her reign progressed, Elizabeth's failure to marry or name her successor encouraged Mary to try to win the recognition she saw as rightfully hers.*

ACTIVITIES

1 Explain why the years 1548, 1561, 1565 and 1567 were turning points in the life of Mary, Queen of Scots.
2 Why, in 1568, did Elizabeth decide:
   a) not to send Mary back to Scotand, and
   b) to keep her captive under house arrest?
3 What does Source F suggest about the death of Lord Darnley in 1567?

Practice questions

1 To what extent does Source G accurately reflect the seriousness of the threat posed by Mary, Queen of Scots, to Elizabeth in 1568? *(For guidance, see pages 109–110.)*
2 How far do you agree with Interpretation 1 that Mary, Queen of Scots, was a major threat to Protestant England? *(For guidance, see pages 113–114.)*

Keep Mary in England
If Elizabeth kept Mary in prison, English Catholics or Spain or France might try to free her.

Send Mary back to Scotland
The Scots wanted Mary back to put her on trial. They might execute her and Elizabeth would feel responsible for handing over a fellow queen and relation.

Allow Mary to go to France
If Elizabeth let her go abroad to France or Spain, Mary might persuade those countries to invade England.

Execute Mary
If Elizabeth ordered Mary to be executed then English Catholics might rebel, and Catholic France and Spain might attack her.

What should Elizabeth do with Mary, Queen of Scots?

Acknowledge Mary as heir to the throne of England
Elizabeth could say Mary was to be her heir but as Mary was Catholic this would be hated by both English and Scottish Protestants.

Help Mary to regain her throne
If Elizabeth helped Mary regain the Scottish throne she would anger the Scottish Protestants.

◀ Figure 5.1: Options considered by Elizabeth upon the arrival of Mary in England

The rebellion of the Northern Earls, 1569

The rebellion of the Northern Earls in 1569 was the first in a series of Catholic plots which attempted to replace Queen Elizabeth with her cousin, Mary, Queen of Scots.

The causes

With the arrival of Mary in 1568 any hopes Elizabeth may have had up to this point that Catholicism in England was on the wane were now dashed. The situation was made worse by the fact that Elizabeth had refused the requests of her Privy Councillors to marry in order to produce an heir to the throne and thereby ensure the continuance of her Religious Settlement. To many English Catholics, Mary now provided hope that all was not lost.

The rebellion was led by two powerful Catholic lords, Charles Neville, Earl of Westmoreland, and Thomas Percy, Earl of Northumberland. Their plan was to depose Elizabeth and replace her with Mary who was then to be married to Northumberland's brother-in-law, Thomas Howard, Duke of Norfolk. However, Elizabeth had learnt of the planned marriage beforehand and had promptly forbidden it to take place, upon which Norfolk had begged for forgiveness and was sent to the Tower. When Elizabeth then demanded the two earls should appear before her to answer charges, they refused and started their rebellion.

The events

In November 1569, with a force of around 4,600 men, the rebels marched into Durham, held Catholic Mass in its cathedral and tore up the English Prayer Book and the Bible, as a sign of their rejection of the Religious Settlement. From Durham the rebel force marched south to Bramham Moor but upon hearing that the queen had sent forces north under the leadership of the Earl of Sussex, the President of the Council of the North, the rebel earls abandoned plans to besiege York and retreated north. Unable to stop the advance of Elizabeth's forces the rebels continued to retreat until in January 1570 the two leaders, Westmoreland and Northumberland, fled across the border into Scotland. The reasons for the failure of the rebellion are outlined in Figure 5.2.

The aftermath

Northumberland was eventually captured by James Douglas, Earl of Morton, and handed him over to Elizabeth in 1572. Northumberland was interrogated (see Source H) and after being tried for treason he was beheaded at York. Westmoreland managed to avoid capture and escaped across the Channel to Flanders where he later died in poverty. Of the others indirectly involved in the rebellion, the Duke of Norfolk was later released from prison and pardoned in 1570. However, in a deliberate attempt to re-impose royal authority in the north, over 800 rebels, mostly commoners, were executed and many leading families who demonstrated Catholic sympathy had land confiscated.

> **Source H:** Information provided by the Earl of Northumberland during his interrogation in 1572
>
> *Our first object in assembling was the reformation of religion and preservation of the person of the Queen of Scots, as next heir failing issue of Her Majesty, which causes I believed were greatly favoured by most of the noblemen of the realm.*

ACTIVITIES ?

1 What does Source H suggest were the main causes of the rebellion?

2 How serious a threat was the Northern Rebellion to Elizabeth and her government?

Poor planning and leadership
- The rebel army retreated once it heard news of a large royal army heading towards them.
- The rebel leaders lacked a coherent plan of action.

Why did the 1569 Rebellion fail?

Lack of foreign support
- The rebellion had failed before the pope issued his Bull to excommunicate Elizabeth.
- The foreign help promised by De Spes, the Spanish ambassador, did not materialise.
- Philip II of Spain was reluctant to help Mary as he thought she was more likely to support France when made Queen of England.

Popularity of Elizabeth
- There was no enthusiasm to replace Elizabeth with Catholic Mary, or for the restoration of the pope as the head of the church.

Figure 5.2: Reasons for the ▶ failure of the rebellion of the Northern Earls, 1569

The excommunication of Elizabeth, 1570

In February 1570 Pope Pius V issued a Papal Bull, *Regnans in Excelsis*, which proclaimed Elizabeth's excommunication. It referred to the queen as a 'servant of wickedness' who was not the rightful queen of Wales and England and it called upon all loyal Catholics to remove her from the throne. It also released Catholics from their oath of allegiance to the monarch. The Bull was quite a serious threat to Elizabeth as it now gave Catholics permission to plot against the queen and plan her removal from office to be replaced by Mary. It provided justification for rebellion and for foreign intervention to help Mary, Queen of Scots.

Response to the Papal Bull

Parliament responded to the Papal Bull by issuing a new Treason Act in 1571 which:

- made it treasonable to declare that Elizabeth was not the lawful queen
- made it treasonable to introduce or publish any Papal Bull
- allowed for the confiscation of the property of those Catholics who had fled abroad and did not return within twelve months of leaving.

For her part, Elizabeth took the opportunity to increase royal control over the north of England. A new Council of the North was set up, headed by a Puritan, the Earl of Huntingdon, who immediately took action to reduce the power of the earls by taking away their control and hold over the peasants living on their estates.

> **Source I:** An extract from the Papal Bull issued by Pope Pius V in February 1570, which excommunicated Elizabeth
>
> *Elizabeth ... the pretended queen of England, ... having seized on the kingdom, and monstrously usurped the place of Supreme Head of the Church in all England, and the chief authority and jurisdiction thereof, hath again reduced the said kingdom into a miserable and ruinous condition, which was so lately reclaimed to the Catholic faith and a thriving condition [during the reign of Mary I] ... declare the aforesaid Elizabeth, as being an heretic and favourer of heretics ... to have incurred the sentence of excommunication and to be cut off from the unity of the body of Christ. And moreover we do declare her to be deprived of her pretended title to the kingdom aforesaid ... and we do command and charge all and every noblemen, subjects, people, and others aforesaid, that they presume not to obey her, or her orders, mandates and laws.*

ACTIVITY ?

Explain why the issue of the bull of excommunication was a threat to Elizabeth's position as queen.

Practice question

What can be learnt from Sources I and J about the excommunication of Queen Elizabeth?
(For guidance, see pages 107–108.)

Source J: A contemporary ▶ drawing showing Pope Pius V issuing a bull of excommunication against Queen Elizabeth

Catholic plots

During the 1570s and 1580s some Catholics became more radical in their opposition to Elizabeth and took part in plots designed to overthrow her.

The Ridolfi Plot, 1571

In 1571 William Cecil (now Lord Burghley) and his spymaster Sir Francis Walsingham, uncovered a Catholic plot to overthrow the queen and replace her as ruler by Mary, Queen of Scots. The plot was organised by Roberto Ridolfi, a Florentine merchant and banker, who had settled in England. It involved Mary, the Duke of Norfolk, Philip II of Spain, De Spes the Spanish ambassador and the pope. A Spanish army would land and help English Catholics overthrow Elizabeth and make Mary queen. She would then marry the Duke of Norfolk and turn England Roman Catholic again. However, Cecil and Walsingham, through their network of informers, were able to foil the plan. The torture of some of those involved revealed the names of other members of the conspiracy and arrests followed.

Norfolk was found guilty of treason and sentenced to death. However, in the case of Mary, despite intense pressure from Parliament, Elizabeth steadfastly refused to authorise her execution and she was kept in prison. Both Ridolfi and the Spanish ambassador, De Spes, were expelled from the country.

> **Source K:** Extract from Parliament's charges against Mary, Queen of Scots, made in May 1572
>
> *She has wickedly challenged the Crown of England.*
>
> *She has sought to withdraw the Duke of Norfolk from his natural obedience, against the Queen's express prohibition.*
>
> *She has stirred the Earls of Northumberland and Westmoreland to rebel.*
>
> *She has practised [tried] to procure [get] new rebellion to be raised within this realm.*
>
> *We, your true and obedient subjects, do most humbly beseech your Majesty to punish and correct all the treasons and wicked attempts of the said Mary.*

Many MPs and most Privy Councillors wanted Elizabeth to take action against Mary in 1572 by ordering her execution. Elizabeth, however, resisted such demands for Mary to be put to death.

Why?

- Elizabeth was extremely reluctant to order the death of her cousin and heir.
- She believed that executing a queen of royal blood went against God's will.
- There was no absolute proof that Mary was directly involved in the plot.
- Mary's execution might result in possible action against England from Spain, France or by the pope.
- Mary's execution would anger many Catholics in Wales and England and might cause them to join in any future rebellions or plots.

ACTIVITY

Explain why Elizabeth refused to take action against Mary, Queen of Scots, following the failure of the Ridolfi Plot.

Practice question

To what extent does Source K accurately reflect the seriousness of the threat posed by Mary, Queen of Scots, in 1572? *(For guidance, see pages 109–110.)*

The Throckmorton Plot, 1583–84

Despite the failure of the Ridolfi Plot, Mary continued to be at the centre of plans to overthrow Elizabeth. The arrival from 1580 onwards of Jesuit priests into England (see page 67) further alarmed Elizabeth's ministers who suspected these priests to be instrumental in organising plots against the queen. Such suspicions were confirmed in 1583 when Francis Throckmorton, a young English Catholic, took the lead in organising a plot that involved French Catholic forces, backed by Spanish and papal money, to invade England and free Mary from captivity. Throckmorton acted as the go-between for Mary, Queen of Scots, and the Spanish ambassador, de Mendoza (see Source M).

However, Elizabeth's secret service uncovered the plot and arrested Throckmorton. Under torture he revealed that the Duke of Guise was planning to invade England from the Spanish Netherlands, but he was adamant that Mary knew nothing about the plan. He was condemned to death for treason and was executed. Mendoza was expelled from England and Mary was moved to Tutbury castle in Staffordshire. She was banned from receiving any visitors and her mail was checked by Walsingham's agents.

> **Source L:** Extract from a letter written by Pope Gregory XIII to his ambassador in Spain in 1580
>
> *Since that guilty woman [Elizabeth] … is the cause of so much injury to the Catholic faith … there is no doubt that whosoever sends her out of the world … not only does not sin but gains merit … And so, if those English gentlemen decide actually to undertake so glorious a work, your Lordship can assure them that they do not commit any sin.*

ACTIVITIES ?

1 Why, according to Source L, did the pope give his blessing to attempts to overthrow Elizabeth?
2 Explain why the Throckmorton Plot failed.

Practice question

Explain the connections between any THREE of the following:
● Mary, Queen of Scots
● the Ridolfi Plot
● the Throckmorton Plot
● Bull of excommunication.
(For guidance, see page 112.)

▲ **Source M:** Francisco de Mendoza, the Spanish ambassador

The increasing Catholic threat, 1584–85

As the threat from the Throckmorton plot was diminishing, news reached Elizabeth in July 1584 that the leader of the Dutch Protestants, William of Orange, had been shot dead by a Catholic assassin. The previous October Elizabeth's life had been threatened when John Somerville, an English Catholic, attempted to assassinate her with a pistol, an act which caused him to be sentenced to death for treason, although he escaped the hangman by committing suicide in his cell.

Parliament was now increasingly concerned for the queen's safety and later that year issued the 'Bond of Association', which stated that if Elizabeth was murdered, Parliament would ensure that the murderers were punished. To many it seemed as if the Catholic threat was becoming more serious, particularly after the declaration of war between England and Spain in 1585. Sir Francis Walsingham's network of agents actively hunted traitors (see Source N). King Philip II of Spain gave orders for the construction of a large fleet to invade England. In response Parliament increased the legislation against Catholics by ordering all Jesuit and seminary priests to leave the country within 40 days (see Source O).

> **Source N: A report sent to Sir Francis Walsingham in February 1585 from one of his secret agents**
>
> *I have revealed the miserable and perfidious design of the enemies of the state, who desire nothing but its total ruin, and to raise and stir up the people of England against their princess by a civil war. This they do by means of evil rumours and defamatory books, popish and contrary to religion, which are transported into England from France at the instance of those who are in flight from their country, and also of the Spanish ambassador and of others who favour them: such as Mass-books, other defamatory books written by Jesuits, book of hours and other books serving their purpose.*

> **Source O: Extracts from the Act against Jesuit and seminary priests passed by Parliament in 1585**
>
> *Whereas divers persons called or professed Jesuits, seminary priests and other priests … have of late years come and been sent … into this realm of England and other of the Queen's Majesty's dominions, of purpose … not only to withdraw her Highness' subjects from their due obedience to her Majesty but also to stir up and move sedition, rebellion and open hostility wither her Highness' realms and dominions …*
>
> *And be it further enacted … that it shall not be lawful for any Jesuit, seminary priest or other such priest, deacon or any religious or ecclesiastical person … by any authority … from the see of Rome … to come into, be or remain in any part of this realm or any other of her Highness' dominions after the end of … forty days … every person so offending shall for his offence be adjudged a traitor … and every person which … shall wittingly and willingly receive, relieve, comfort, aid or maintain any such Jesuit, seminary priest … shall also for such offence be adjudged a felon without benefit of clergy and suffer death.*

ACTIVITIES

1 Did the actions of John Somerville pose a real threat to Elizabeth?
2 Use Source O and your own knowledge to explain why the government took action against Jesuit and seminary priests.

Practice question

To what extent does Source N accurately reflect the threat posed by Catholic priests during the 1580s? *(For guidance, see pages 109–110.)*

The Babington Plot, 1586

In 1586 Walsingham (see Source T) uncovered another Catholic plot and, on this occasion, he claimed to have proof of Mary's direct involvement. Anthony Babington, a young Catholic nobleman, was at the centre of a plot to overthrow Elizabeth and place Mary, Queen of Scots, on the throne in her place. Letters written in cipher code were sent between Babington and Mary informing her about the progress of the plot (see Source P). Unbeknown to both correspondents all the letters, which were sent secretly hidden inside a beer barrel, were being intercepted and read by Walsingham's spy agents. Walsingham had the code deciphered and waited to gather enough evidence to directly implicate Mary in the plot against Elizabeth.

In June 1585 Babington wrote to Mary outlining a plot to murder Elizabeth, release Mary from her captivity and, with the help of an invasion force from Spain, place her on the throne of England.

Mary's replies to Babington's letters were intercepted and sent to Walsingham who now had the proof he needed to confirm Mary's involvement in a plot to overthrow Elizabeth.

In August 1586 Walsingham struck. Babington was arrested and confessed. In September he and six other plotters were executed.

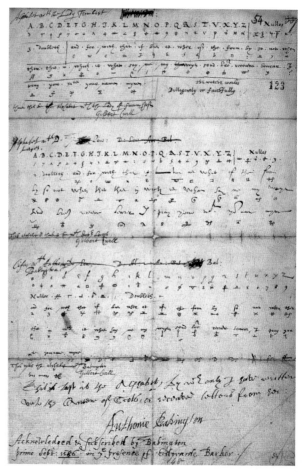

▲ Source R: The cipher code used by Mary, Queen of Scots, in her letters to Babington

> **Source P: Extract from a letter written by Babington to Mary, Queen of Scots, on 28 June 1585**
>
> *Myself with ten gentlemen and a hundred of our followers will undertake the delivery of your royal person from the hands of your enemies.*
>
> *For the dispatch of the usurper, from the obedience of whom we are by the excommunication of her made free, there by six noble gentlemen, all my private friends, who for the zeal they bear to the Catholic cause and your Majesty's service will undertake that tragical execution.*

> **Source Q: Extract from a letter sent by Mary, Queen of Scots, to Babington on 17 July 1586**
>
> *Everything being prepared, and the forces as well within as without ... then you must set the six gentlemen to work and give order that, their design accomplished, I may be in some way got away from there and that all your forces shall be simultaneously in the field to receive me while we await foreign assistance ...*
>
> *Now as no certain day can be appointed for the performance of the said gentlemen's enterprise, I desire them to have always near them ... four brave men well horsed to advertise speedily the success of their design, as soon as it is done, to those appointed to get me away from hence ...*

Practice question

What can be learnt from Sources R and P about the Babington Plot? *(For guidance, see pages 107–108.)*

? ACTIVITIES

1 Write a report to Walsingham explaining Mary's involvement in the Babington Plot.

2 Make a copy and complete the following table which examines the threats posed to Elizabeth by a series of Catholic plots.

Name of plot	Outline of the plot	Reasons why the plot failed	What happened to the plotters?	How serious was the threat posed to Elizabeth by this plot?
Ridolfi				
Throckmorton				
Babington				

The trial of Mary, Queen of Scots, October 1586

Claiming to have direct proof of Mary's involvement in the Babington Plot, Walsingham and other Privy Councillors now demanded that she be given the same treatment as the other conspirators and executed. Elizabeth was against this but she did allow Mary to be put on trial for treason. Mary was moved to Fotheringhay Castle in Northamptonshire where the trial took place in October 1586. She was found guilty of 'imagining and encompassing her Majesty's death' and sentenced to death. Elizabeth, however, refused repeated requests from her Privy Councillors to sign the death warrant and it was not until 1 February 1587 that she finally agreed.

The execution of Mary, Queen of Scots, February 1587

Even though she had signed the death warrant Elizabeth still refused to release the document. The Privy Councillors were forced to go behind her back and persuade her secretary, William Davison, to take the warrant to Fotheringhay where Mary was executed on 8 February 1587 in the great hall of the castle. It took three blows of the axe to sever her head from her body (see Source T).

When she heard the news of the execution Elizabeth was furious. She ordered Davison to be imprisoned in the Tower and banned him from court. Blaming Lord Burghley, she refused to speak to him for a month and she wrote a letter of apology to Mary's son, the young King James VI of Scotland.

Source T: A contemporary account of Mary's execution sent to Lord Burghley in February 1587

Groping for the block, she laid down her head, putting her chin over the block with both her hands, which, holding there still, would have been cut off had they not been seen. Then she, lying very still upon the block, one of the executioners holding her slightly with one of his hands, she endured two strokes of the other executioner with an axe, she making a very small noise or none at all, and not stirring any part of her from where she lay. And so the executioner cut off her head, save for one little gristle. Once cut asunder, he held up her head to the view of all the assembly and said, 'God Save The Queen'. Her lips stirred up and down a quarter of an hour after her head was cut off. Then one of the executioners, pulling off her garters, espied her little dog which had crept under her clothes. It could not be gotten away from her except by force, but afterwards came back to lay between her head and her shoulders, until it was carried away and washed.

◄ **Source S:** Sir Francis Walsingham, who was instrumental in Mary, Queen of Scots', execution

The consequences of the death of Mary: the end of the Catholic threat?

With the execution of Mary many of Elizabeth's Privy Councillors and MPs hoped that the event would signal an end to Catholic plots to undermine the queen's position. Some, like Sir Christopher Hatton, believed that while the threat had been reduced it had not been eradicated (see Source U). In reality the execution had only a limited impact.

- English Catholics – there was no backlash from English Catholics, and neither were there any further Catholic plots for the rest of Elizabeth's reign.
- Scotland – while King James VI protested at his mother's death, he took no action and blamed the Privy Councillors rather than Elizabeth herself.
- France – King Henry III did nothing, wanting to keep on friendly terms with Elizabeth as a safeguard against the growing power of Spain.
- Spain – King Philip II was already planning his invasion of England and the execution just confirmed his desire to rid England of Protestantism.

> **Source U:** Part of a speech made by Sir Christopher Hatton to Parliament in 1589, in which he warned of a continuing Catholic threat
>
> *Vile wretches, bloody priests and false traitors, here in our bosoms and beyond the seas. We have chopped off some of the enemy's branches but they will grow again.*

ACTIVITIES

1 Explain why Elizabeth did not want to sign the death warrant for Mary's execution.
2 To what extent did the Catholic threat end with the execution of Mary, Queen of Scots?

Practice question

What can be learnt from Sources S and V about the execution of Mary, Queen of Scots? *(For guidance, see pages 107–108.)*

▲ Source V: An anonymous painting of the execution of Mary, Queen of Scots, in February 1587, drawn by an eyewitness

Catholic recusancy in Wales

While the majority of Catholics in Wales accepted Elizabeth's Religious Settlement and conformed to what was expected of them, a small number chose not to and adopted various methods of defiance. Their opposition grew as Elizabeth's reign progressed.

Recusancy
Some refused to attend church services and were fined for not doing so. Edward Morgan of Llantarnam paid £7,760 in fines during Elizabeth's reign and William Griffith of Llancarfan was forced to give two-thirds of his lands in payment of fines.

Catholic martyrs
A number of Welshmen who refused to renounce their Catholic faith were put to death for their religious beliefs. They became Wales's only Catholic martyrs and they were William Davies, John Jones and Richard Gwyn.

Plots against Elizabeth
Some Welsh Catholics supported the claim of Mary, Queen of Scots and were involved in plots against Elizabeth. Hugh Davies of Plas Du was involved in the Ridolfi Plot of 1571 and was forced to flee abroad after its failure. Thomas Salusbury, heir to the Lleweni estate near Denbigh and Edward Jones of Plas Cadwgan of Wrexham were both involved in the Babington Plot. They were found guilty of planning a rising in Denbighshire in support of Mary which was to take place immediately after the success of the plot. They were arrested in August, found guilty of involvement and both were executed on Tower Hill in London in September 1586.

Exile
Some chose to leave the country and among them were a number of senior churchmen. Thomas Goldwell, Bishop of St Asaph, Morys Clynnog, Bishop elect of Bangor and Gruffydd Robert, Archdeacon of Anglesey all left Wales for Italy during the early years of Elizabeth's reign.

Catholic training college
Two Welshmen, Owen Lewis and Morgan Phillips, went across the Channel to the Catholic training college at Douai in Flanders where they helped to train the new generation of Catholic seminary priests.

How did Welsh Catholics respond to Elizabeth's Religious Settlement?

Publishing Catholic literature
Some helped to keep the Catholic faith alive by printing and distributing religious works in the Welsh language. As Catholics were forbidden from publishing books they were forced to set up secret printing presses. One of the most successful was hidden in a cave at Rhiwledyn on the Little Orme, Llandudno.

▲ Figure 5.3: How did Welsh Catholics respond to Elizabeth's Religious Settlement?

Case study: the Welsh Catholic Martyrs

Three Welshmen paid the ultimate price for refusing to renounce their Catholic views and were consequently put to death. They became Catholic martyrs; men who died because of their faith.

Richard Gwyn

He was born at Llanidloes in Mongomeryshire into a Protestant family. After finishing at St John's College in Cambridge he became a schoolmaster in the district around Wrexham where, under the influence of Father John Bennett, he was converted to Roman Catholicism. He then acted as an agent between the seminary priests and the Catholic families of north-east Wales. He was arrested and imprisoned several times for his refusal to accept Elizabeth as Head of the Church. On the last occasion he was held in prison and tortured for four years before being brought to trial. Upon being found guilty he was put to death by being hung, drawn and quartered on 15 October 1584. He was the first Welsh Catholic to die a martyr's death (see Source Y).

William Davies

A native of Croes-yn-Eirias in Caernarvonshire, Davies became a Catholic priest in 1585 and during the following year he lived in the secret cave at Rhiwledyn on the Little Orme in Llandudno. Here he helped to print Catholic literature, including *Y Drych Cristianogawl (The Christian Mirror)*, which was the first book to be printed in Wales (see Sources W and X). In 1592 he was arrested and sent to prison at Beaumaris. Refusing to renounce his Catholic faith, he was executed on 27 July 1593.

John Jones

Born at Clynnog in Caernarvonshire, he fled abroad to Rome during the middle part of Elizabeth's reign where, in 1591, he became a Franciscan Friar, taking the name Brother Godfrey Maurice. He soon after returned to England in disguise but was arrested in 1594 by the priest-hunter Richard Topcliffe. He was hanged at Southwark in London on 12 July 1598.

> **Source W:** Part of a letter written by J.P. William Griffith to Archbishop Whitgift on 19 April 1587, informing him about the discovery of a secret printing press at Rhiwledyn
>
> *There is a cave by the seaside about three fathoms deep ... and the xiii of this April there were in the cave twelve or more Jesuits, seminaries and recusants, the which were discovered by a neighbour thereby who saw at the cave mouth one or two of them with pistols. ... He went to the Justice Sir Thomas Mostyn who raised 40 people and came to the cave mouth. He did not dare enter the cave but left a watch on it overnight. ... I know not how by the next morning all were suffered to escape. ... There was found the next day in the cave weapons, food and the cave boarded and their altar carried away.*

◀ **Source X:** The title page to *Y Drych Christianogawl (The Christian Mirror)*, which was printed on the secret Catholic printing press in Rhiwledyn cave, Little Orme, Llandudno

> **Source Y: An account of the execution of the Catholic martyr Richard Gwyn in Wrexham on 15 October 1584. It was written by a Catholic priest, Father John Bennett of Holywell, a friend of Gwyn's**
>
> *... [the hangman] asked the prisoner forgiveness ... whereupon the martyr taking him by the hand kissed it saying, I do forgive thee with all my heart ... Finally, as the executioner offered to put the rope about his neck, he smiled, advising him to leave the occupation, for it was but simple ... So the executioner came down and the Sheriff commanded the jailer to tell him to turn the ladder ... In the end, as he [Gwyn] was saying the prayer the executioner turned the ladder, and so he hanged.*

ACTIVITIES ?

1. How serious was the threat posed by Catholic recusants in Wales to Elizabeth's Religious Settlement?
2. Study Source W. What evidence is there in the source to suggest that the authorities were not in hurry to arrest the Catholics hiding in the cave?

Practice questions

1. What can be learnt from Sources W and X about support for the Catholic faith in Wales? *(For guidance, see pages 107–108.)*
2. To what extent does Source Y accurately explain the importance of the Catholic threat to Elizabeth in Wales? *(For guidance, see pages 109–110.)*

Conclusion: Why were the Catholics such a serious threat to Elizabeth?

While Elizabeth's Religious Settlement was accepted by the majority of her subjects, devout Catholics did not welcome it. They refused to attend Church of England services and were fined as a result. They particularly objected to the Settlement's compromise over the issue of real presence, believing that the blood and wine given during Mass was the actual body and blood of Jesus. Not wishing to give up this belief they celebrated Catholic Mass in secret, being administered to by the seminary priests who began to enter England after 1574 from their training colleges in northern France. They were quickly joined by Jesuit priests who, following the Pope's excommunication of Elizabeth in 1570, played a role in the Catholic plots to overthrow Elizabeth.

During the 1570s and 1580s these plots did pose a significant threat to Elizabeth as they all aimed to replace her as monarch with Mary, Queen of Scots, followed by the restoration of the Catholic faith as the main religion of the land. As long as she lived, Mary posed a threat to Elizabeth and her near twenty-year captivity caused her to become the centre of all the Catholic plots. While Elizabeth's Privy Councillors could find no direct evidence to link Mary to both the Ridolfi and Throckmorton plots, that was not the case with the Babington Plot. Having intercepted letters proving Mary's treasonable intent to overthrow the queen of England, Elizabeth was compelled by her councillors to sign her cousin's death warrant. The fear had always been that the Catholics might have been supported with foreign help and it was lucky for Elizabeth that this never materialised. Mary's death, however, did not end the Catholic threat which reappeared the following year in the form of the Spanish Armada.

While some English Catholics had proved to be disloyal to Elizabeth and had supported the plots, it must be remembered that they were relatively few in number and the vast majority of Catholics remained loyal. A propaganda campaign engineered by Cecil and Walsingham made the threat from plotters, Jesuits and seminary priests appear larger than it actually was.

Summary question

Now that you have completed this chapter, use the knowledge you have acquired to answer the following a question.

'The Northern Rebellion was the most serious of the Catholic Plots against Elizabeth.' How far do you agree with this statement?

In your answer you might like to consider the following factors:

1   the seriousness of the Northern Rebellion
2   the Ridolfi Plot
3   the Throckmorton Plot
4   the Babington Plot
5   and any other relevant factors you can think of.

6 The Spanish Armada

Reasons for the Spanish Armada

> **Source A:** Extract from the orders issued by the Duke of Medina Sidonia to his men prior to the Armada setting sail in May 1588
>
> *You must all know, from the highest to the lowest, that the principal reason which has moved His Majesty to undertake this enterprise is his desire to serve God, and to convert to His church many peoples and souls who are now oppressed by the heretical enemies of our holy Catholic faith, and are subjected to errors.*

The execution of Mary, Queen of Scots, in February 1587 was the last straw for King Philip II of Spain, particularly as it now ended his hopes of placing a Catholic ruler on the throne of England. As early as 1586 he had begun to draw up plans to launch an invasion of England to overthrow Elizabeth and restore Roman Catholicism as the country's official religion. Mary's execution now combined with other factors to make Philip even more determined to push ahead with launching an armada.

The ambitions of King Philip II of Spain

In 1554 Philip married Mary Tudor who, like him, was a devout Catholic. In October 1555, following the abdication of his father, the Emperor Charles V, Philip became King of Spain, the Netherlands and all Spanish dominions in Italy and America. He was now ruler of the most powerful and wealthiest empire in the world, while his native Spain possessed a large navy and one of the strongest armies in Europe. Determined to protect the Catholic faith, Philip now used his new power to instruct the Spanish Inquisition to attack the growth of Protestantism across northern Europe.

In July 1556, following the death of Edward VI, Philip became co-ruler of Wales and England with his wife Mary Tudor. He supported Mary's quest to re-establish Catholicism as the official religion and to punish Protestants severely. The couple had no children and Mary's death in November 1558 ended Philip's rights to the English throne. Not wishing to sever his ties with England, he attempted to arrange a marriage with the new queen, Elizabeth. His proposal however, was rejected by Elizabeth, and in 1559 Philip married Isabella, daughter of King Henry II of France. Elizabeth's Religious Settlement of that year, which created a new Protestant Church, alarmed Philip and he began to watch developments in England with some concern, wishing to find an opportunity for the country to revert to the Catholic faith. His eventual solution was to plan for an armada.

▲ **Source B:** A portrait of King Philip II of Spain (1555–98). It was painted in 1571 by the Spanish artist, Alonso Sanchez Coello

Philip possessed a firm belief that God was on his side and he viewed his plans as a 'holy crusade' to purge England of its heretic queen and its Protestant faith. His ultimate aim was to see the restoration of Roman Catholicism as the principal faith across Wales and England. It was a view reinforced by the commander of the armada, the Duke of Medina Sidonia (see Source A).

ACTIVITIES

1 How significant was the execution of Mary, Queen of Scots, in Philip's decision to invade England to restore the Catholic faith?

2 What reasons were given in Source A for Philip's decision to launch an Armada?

The war in the Netherlands

At the start of Elizabeth's reign relations between England and Spain were relatively friendly. The Netherlands was very important to Spain economically, and the most convenient trade routes involved ships sailing through the English Channel. Philip did not wish to end this valuable economic link by souring relations with England. Philip was therefore initially reluctant to see Mary, Queen of Scots, become ruler as he believed she would be more likely to side with France, that power being Spain's most deadly enemy.

However, a revolt by Dutch Protestants in the Netherlands did a great deal to undermine relations between England and Spain. In August 1566, Protestants in Ghent, Antwerp and other Dutch cities rose in rebellion against the Catholic rule of Spain and began rioting and smashing the Catholic icons and religious images that decorated their churches. In 1567 Philip responded by sending an army of 10,000 troops to the Netherlands under the command of the Duke of Alba. He was determined to crush the Dutch rebels (see Source C) and put down the rebellion ruthlessly, arresting over 18,000 Dutch Protestants and ordering over a thousand to be burnt to death.

> **Source C:** In 1566, in a letter to the pope, Philip expressed his determination to crush the Dutch rebellion in the Netherlands
>
> *Before suffering the slightest damage to religion and the service of God, I would rather lose all my states, and a hundred lives if I had them, because I do not propose to be the ruler of heretics.*

> **Practice question**
>
> What can be learnt from Sources C and D about Philip's attitude towards the Dutch Protestants? *(For guidance, see pages 107–108.)*

▲ Source D: A contemporary painting, *The Massacre of the Innocents*, by the Dutch artist Pieter Bruegel, *c*.1567. It shows the harsh policy adopted by Alba's forces in suppressing the Protestant rebellion

Elizabeth's reaction to events in the Netherlands

Elizabeth watched developments across the Channel with alarm and was concerned over the prospect of having such a large Spanish force being stationed so close to the English coastline. She received conflicting advice from her Privy Councillors, one faction led by Cecil wanting to avoid war with Spain at all costs, while another faction led by the Earl of Leicester and Francis Walsingham favouring direct military action in order to protect and support the Protestants. Elizabeth, however, was hesitant and chose to provide unofficial support to the Dutch rebels by supplying them with money and weapons, allowing rebel ships to stay in English ports, and allowing pirate activity to disrupt the transport ships supplying Alba's army.

In 1575 rebellion erupted again in the Netherlands and by 1579 the country had split in two. The southern provinces formed the Union of Arras and made peace with Spain. The northern provinces, led by William the Silent (otherwise known as William of Orange) formed the Union of Utrecht and rejected Spanish rule. Philip appointed a new commander, Alexander Farnese, the Duke of Parma, who began to recover land previously lost to the rebels. Facing the prospect of a Dutch defeat Elizabeth began to fund resistance against Parma and, following the assassination of William the Silent in 1584, which deprived the revolt of its key leader, the queen finally bowed to pressure from the Leicester faction and signed the Treaty of Nonsuch with the Dutch rebels in 1585.

By this Treaty Elizabeth agreed to become protector of the Dutch Protestants and to send a force of 5,000 troops and 1,000 cavalry under the Earl of Leicester's command, to help maintain the rebellion. It proved to be indecisive and Leicester fell out with the rebel leaders, returning home in 1587. England and Spain were now in a state of undeclared war. At the same time Elizabeth sent out a fleet under Francis Drake to raid Spanish shipping in the Caribbean.

ACTIVITIES ?

1 Use Source E and your own knowledge to explain why rebellion broke out in the Netherlands.

2 Explain why Elizabeth decided to help the Protestant rebels in the Netherlands.

▲ Source E: A contemporary painting showing the problems facing the Netherlands in the 1580s. The cow which represents the Netherlands is being milked of its resources by the Spanish commander, Parma, and it has to carry the burden of a foreign ruler, Philip II of Spain. Queen Elizabeth is offering nourishment to the cow, the food symbolising the aid she gave in the form of troops and money

The actions of English privateers in the Spanish Main

As relations with Spain deteriorated another area of conflict emerged in the Spanish Main, the provinces ruled by Spain in central and southern America. During the 1570s and 1580s Elizabeth encouraged English privateers or 'sea dogs' to attack Spanish treasure ships bringing gold and silver from the Spanish Main to Spain and also to attack Spanish settlements in South America. In 1572 Francis Drake attacked the Spanish stronghold of Nombre de Dios in the Caribbean and was able to ambush ships bringing silver back to Spain.

In 1577 Elizabeth sent Drake on a voyage which was to take 3 years, during which he became the first Englishman to sail round the world. In his ship the *Golden Hind* he sailed round South America into the Pacific from where he launched surprise attacks on Spanish treasure ships, capturing vast amounts of treasure (see Source F). One estimate claims he brought back gold, silver and jewels worth over £140,000 (roughly £200 million today). Philip II was furious with Drake and demanded his execution. Elizabeth was delighted and in 1581 boarded the *Golden Hind*, took out a sword and knighted him.

When war broke out with Spain in 1585 Drake was sent to the West Indies to attack Spanish settlements and disrupt trade routes. He captured several towns and returned to England with over £30,000 in treasure and 250 Spanish cannon. By the 1580s the continued damaging raids on Spanish bullion ships by Drake and other English privateers were starting to have a serious impact on Spain's economy.

Sir Francis Drake (c.1540–96)

- Gained experience of sailing through participating in the slave trade voyages of John Hawkins.
- First took command of a ship at the age of 22.
- Led pirate attacks on Spanish treasure ships during the 1570s.
- The Spanish came to fear him, referring to him as 'El Draque' (the dragon).
- Sailed around the world in the *Golden Hind* between 1577–80.
- Knighted by Elizabeth in 1581.
- Attacked the Spanish fleet in Cadiz harbour in 1587, delaying the Armada by a year.
- Made vice-admiral of the fleet to fight the Armada.
- In 1595 Elizabeth sent him on an expedition to the West Indies and central America.
- He died of yellow fever in January 1596, aged 53, and was buried at sea off the coast of Mexico.

ACTIVITY ?

How significant were the actions of English privateers in causing the outbreak of war between England and Spain?

▲ Source F: A contemporary drawing showing the *Golden Hind* in action in the Spanish Main attacking the Spanish ship, the *Cacafuego*

▲ Sir Francis Drake, 1540–96

Philip's preparation of the Armada

Britain being an island the only way Philip could attack Elizabeth's kingdom was launching an invasion by sea. He possessed a powerful army in the Netherlands but the problem he faced was how to transfer that army across the English Channel. His solution was an armada.

Philip's plan

First conceived in 1586, Philip's plan was to construct an armada of armed ships which were to be used to:

- sail north from Lisbon along the coasts of Spain and France into the English Channel, destroying the English fleet in the Channel
- advance through the English Channel and anchor the Spanish fleet off Calais
- a force of 17,000 experienced Spanish soldiers from the Netherlands would gather at Dunkirk ready to invade England; they were to be led by the Duke of Parma, considered to be one of the best generals in Europe
- the Armada would then guard Parma's soldiers as they crossed the Channel in huge flat-bottomed barges
- Parma's army would land at Margate in Kent, proceed up the Thames to London, capture the city and overthrow the Protestant heretic, Elizabeth, from the throne and turn England Catholic again
- as soon as the Spanish army landed on the south coast English Catholics would rise up in rebellion against the Protestant queen and government.

Drake's attack on Cadiz

With the amassing of the Armada in Cadiz harbour nearing completion in the spring of 1587, Philip II was horrified to receive news that on 20 April Drake had sailed a group of English warships into the harbour at Cadiz and attacked the Spanish fleet. Drake claimed to have destroyed 37 ships, the report sent to Philip said 24. This was a major setback for the Armada. Of equal significance was the fact that Drake burnt important timber supplies, particularly seasoned wood waiting to be used to construct storage barrels. Consequently, when the Armada set sail the following year many of the barrels leaked or split because they had been made of unseasoned wood. Drake's attack was said to have 'singed the king of Spain's beard' and it delayed the Armada for a year. This allowed Britain more time to prepare her defences against a possible Spanish invasion.

Changes to the plan

Philip's plan had serious flaws. There were no harbours in the Netherlands deep enough for the big Spanish ships to dock, which made the picking up of Parma's army difficult. There was also the serious problem of how to transport Parma's army across the Channel. It would need a large number of barges which would have to be built on the spot and if the weather was rough the barges might sink.

In addition to Drake's attack on Cadiz several other events also seriously hindered the sailing of the Armada.

- Philip ignored the advice from his ministers and military commanders to delay the launch (see Source G).
- In February 1588 the admiral in charge of the Armada died and Philip chose the Duke of Medina Sidonia to take over. The duke felt he was not qualified for the job as he hated sailing and was easily seasick (see Source H). Philip overruled his requests to be replaced.
- Shortly after the Armada set sail from Lisbon in April 1588 it ran into a dreadful storm and was blown off course. It was forced to seek refuge at La Coruña to enable repairs to take place and to take in supplies.

> **Source G:** Extract from a letter written by the Duke of Parma in the Netherlands to Philip II in 1588, advising delay as he had insufficient forces
>
> *Even if the Armada supplies us with 6000 Spaniards as promised, I shall still have too few troops. In a very short time my army will be so reduced as to be unable to cope with the great number of the enemy.*

> **Source H:** Extract from a letter written by the Duke of Medina Sidonia to Philip II in February 1588
>
> *I wish I possessed the talents and strength necessary to it. But Sir, I have not the health for the sea. I soon become seasick. It would not be right for a person like myself, possessing no experience of seafaring or war, to take charge of it.*

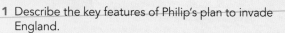

ACTIVITIES

1 Describe the key features of Philip's plan to invade England.
2 What evidence is provided in Sources G and H to suggest that Philip's plans for his Armada might experience problems?

Practice question

Why was the attack on Cadiz a significant event in weakening Philip's plans for the invasion of England? *(For guidance, see page 111.)*

The threat posed by the Armada

The Armada posed a serious threat to Elizabeth and England. Confident of success and in an attempt to intimidate the English, the Spanish government issued details of the Armada's size and composition just prior to its departure:

- 130 galleons and supply ships (64 battleships which included 22 huge galleons)
- 30,000 men (8,000 experienced sailors, 19,000 well-trained troops, 3,000 servants, including 180 friars and priests)
- 1,900 cannon and small guns; 123,790 cannon balls; together with powder, bullets, pikes, armour and swords
- extensive supplies of food and drink including biscuits, bacon, fish, cheese, rice, beans, wine, vinegar and water.
- 17,000 well-trained soldiers led by the Duke of Parma would be waiting to join it in the Netherlands.

England prepares for the invasion

Such a large task force posed a serious risk and England was forced to make hasty provision. A line of warning beacons were set up along the coast which would be lit when the Armada was sighted in the Channel and church bells would be rung to warn people.

English land defences were weak and as it was not known where the Armada might land it was difficult to place land forces appropriately. Most English soldiers were untrained and poorly equipped, which was in sharp contrast to Parma's army which was considered to be one of the best in Europe. If it landed on English soil it would be difficult to defeat. Elizabeth had, however, managed to raise a force of about 20,000 men which was organised into three armies, one based in the north of England, one based in Kent and one at Tilbury in Essex to guard the south coast.

While the army was relatively weak in comparison with its Spanish counter-part, the English navy would prove to be the country's main line of defence. It was commanded by Lord Charles Howard, the Duke of Effingham (see Source I), who appointed as his vice-admirals two experienced sea captains, Francis Drake and John Hawkins. Their 54 battleships had the advantage of being light, fast moving in comparison with the large and clumsy Spanish galleons and were fitted with long-range cannons. In addition, over 140 merchant ships had been converted into battleships, making up a total task force of about 200 ships.

▲ Source I: Lord Charles Howard, Duke of Effingham, commander of the English navy

---

ACTIVITIES ?

1 Working in pairs make a copy and complete the following table about the threat posed by the Armada.
   a) One of you should complete the list of strengths.
   b) The other should complete the list of weaknesses.

Strengths of the Armada	Weaknesses of the Armada

2 'The Armada posed a serious threat to Elizabeth.' How far do you agree with this statement?

The course of the Armada

The threat posed by the Armada hung over England throughout the summer and autumn of 1588.

The Armada set sail from Lisbon on 28 May. Hit by storms it was forced to put into harbour at Corunna on 19 June to undertake repairs and take on fresh supplies of food and water. On 21 July it left Corunna and sailed north towards the English Channel. On 29 July the Armada was sighted off Lizard Point in Cornwall and warning beacons were lit along the south coast to carry the news across the country.

Events in the Channel

Covering 11 km of sea, the Armada sailed through the English Channel in a crescent formation, making it difficult for the English to attack (see Source I). The slow unarmed store ships were placed in the centre, protected by the heavily armed galleons on the outer edges and the horns; if there was an attack from behind the horns would close in to protect the larger supply ships in the centre.

The English fleet led by Lord Howard, Drake and Hawkins sailed out of Plymouth, pursued the Armada for a week, engaging in regular fights but they were unable to break the crescent formation. By the time the Armada anchored off Calais it had lost just two ships.

ACTIVITY ?

Explain why the English found it difficult to attack the Armada as it sailed through the English Channel.

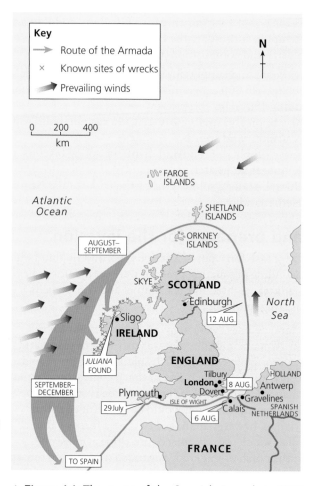

▲ Figure 6.1: The route of the Spanish Armada in 1588

▲ **Source J:** A drawing of the Spanish Armada in the English Channel. The Spanish fleet, in crescent formation, is on the right. The English ships are on the left. In the foreground some English ships are attacking a Spanish ship

Calais and the attack by fireships

On 6 August the Armada anchored off Calais. The Duke of Medina Sidonia was now faced with a delay; he received news that the Duke of Parma's forces would not be arriving for another week as they were delayed by attacks from Dutch forces. Lord Howard decided to take advantage of this opportunity to attack. On 7 August eight unmanned ships were filled with tar, gunpowder and loaded cannons. They were set alight and allowed to drift downwind towards the enemy ships anchored in Calais harbour. Seeing these 'hellburners' or fireships sailing towards them the Spanish ships in panic cut their anchor ropes to escape destruction. They headed out to sea in all directions, thereby breaking their protective crescent formation.

Source K: An account describing English tactics including the use of fireships, written by Petruccio Ubaldini, an Italian living in England in 1588

The English with their excellent ships did not fight as expected but kept at a distance and fired at the hulls and sails of their enemy. The English set eight ships on fire amongst the Spanish fleet. Their enemy were woken up and had to cut their cables to get away from their anchors.

Source L: An extract from the Duke of Medina Sidonia's report to Philip II, dated 7 August 1588

At midnight two fires were seen among the English fleet and these gradually increased to eight. They were eight vessels with sails set, which were drifting with the current directly towards our flagship and the rest of the Armada, all of them burning with great fury. When I saw them approaching, fearing that they might contain fire machines or mines, I ordered the flagship to let go the cables, the rest of the Armada receiving similar orders, with an indication that when the fires had passed they were to return to the same positions again. The current was so strong that most of the ships of the Armada were carried towards Dunkirk.

ACTIVITY ?

How useful is Source L to an historian studying the English attack on the Armada at Calais?

Practice question

What can be learnt from Sources K and M about the attack on the Armada in Calais? (For guidance, see pages 107–108.)

▲ Source M: Fireships attacking the Armada in Calais

The Battle of Gravelines, 8 August

On 8 August English warships attacked the scattered Armada at the Battle of Gravelines near Dunkirk. After 8 hours of fighting in rough seas the English ships began to run out of ammunition and by 4 p.m. they had fired their last shots and were forced to pull back. At least three Spanish ships had been lost, but no English ships. About 1,000 Spaniards had been killed and over 800 wounded, in contrast to the 50 English sailors who had been killed. The Spanish plan to join with Parma's army had been defeated and the English had gained some breathing space. The Battle of Gravelines was therefore a significant turning point. However, the Armada's presence in northern waters still posed a threat to England.

> **Source N:** An account of action in the Battle of Gravelines fought on 8 August 1588, given by a Spanish captain
>
> *The enemy opened heavy cannon fire on our flagship at seven o'clock in the morning, which carried on for nine hours. So tremendous was the fire that over 200 balls struck the sails and hull of the flagship on the starboard side, killing and wounding many men, disabling and dismounting guns and destroying much rigging. The holes made in the hull … caused such a great leak that two divers had as much as they could do to stop them with tar and lead plates, working all day. The galleon San Felipe of Portugal was surrounded by seventeen of the enemy's ships, which directed heavy fire on both sides and on her stern. The enemy approached so close that muskets and pistols on the galleon were brought into action, killing many enemy men on the enemy ships. The enemy did not dare, however, to come to close quarters, but kept up a hot cannon fire from a distance, smashing the rudder, breaking the foremast and killing over two hundred men in the galleon.*

Practice question

What can be learnt from Sources N and O about the battle of Gravelines in August 1588? *(For guidance, see pages 107–108.)*

▲ Source O: A scene showing the Battle of Gravelines, drawn by Philippe-Jacques de Loutherbourg in 1796

Elizabeth's rallying speech at Tilbury

Despite victory at Gravelines England still faced a possible invasion of Spanish forces at any time. On 9 August Elizabeth visited her troops at Tilbury and delivered a rousing speech (see Source P).

> **Source P:** Part of Elizabeth's speech to her troops at Tilbury, 9 August 1588
>
> *I ... am resolved in the midst and heat of battle to live and die amongst you all ... I know I have the body of a weak and feeble woman, but I have the heart and stomach of a King, and a King of England too, and think foul scorn that Parma, or Spain, or any prince of Europe should dare to invade the borders of my realm.*

Pursuing the Armada north

On 9 August the wind changed direction and the Armada sailed into the North Sea; it would not be able to return to Spain through the English Channel and would now have to proceed round the coast of Scotland and Ireland. The English fleet continued to pursue the Armada until it sailed past the Scottish border on 12 August. The English fleet then turned back; it was short of ammunition and food, and many sailors were sick.

Returning to Spain around Scotland and Ireland

The Spanish lacked accurate maps to chart a safe passage around the coasts of Scotland and Ireland. The Spanish lost more of their fleet through shipwreck caused by severe storms as it sailed round Scotland and Ireland than it did through actual fighting; two ships were wrecked off the coast of Scotland and 25 off the coast of Ireland. Thousands drowned and any Spanish sailors that made it to dry land were beaten up and killed. Only about 67 ships finally returned to Spain, limping back to Santander during September and October, full of wounded, starving and sick men (see Table 6.1).

	England	Spain
Ships	0	51 (5 sunk or captured by the English)
Men	c.100 English sailors killed in battle, but thousands died of disease	20,000

▲ Table 6.1: Losses sustained by England and Spain

ACTIVITIES

1 Study Source P. What was the purpose behind Elizabeth's speech at Tilbury in August 1588?
2 Explain why a large part of the Armada failed to return to Spain.

▲ **Source Q:** A seventeenth-century English playing card showing Spanish ships wrecked on the shores of Scotland

Reasons for the failure of the Armada

A combination of factors help to explain why the Armada failed to achieve its objectives.

English strengths

The English ships were smaller, faster and more manoeuvrable than the larger, more bulky Spanish galleons. They had heavier firepower, being fitted with superior long-range cannons allowing them to fire from a safe distance.

Spanish weaknesses

The Spanish cannons were largely ineffective; the shot was made of poor-quality iron and many cannon exploded when fired. The Spanish commander, the Duke of Medina Sidonia, was not as experienced at commanding a fleet as his English counterparts, Drake and Hawkins. The failure of the Duke of Parma to turn up on time proved to be a costly delay as it allowed the English an opportunity to attack the moored Spanish fleet at Calais.

Tactics

The English found it difficult to attack and break the tightly packed crescent formation as the Spanish fleet sailed up the English Channel, but once broken following the Calais attack, the Spanish ships were out-gunned and easier targets for the more experienced English ships. The turning point was the use of 'fireships' to break up and disperse the Armada, which then made it impossible for Medina Sidonia to maintain control over his fleet.

The weather

▲ Source R: This medal was issued on the orders of Elizabeth in 1588 to commemorate victory against the Armada. The inscription reads 'God blew with His wind, and they were scattered.'

The weather was an important factor, particularly after the Battle of Gravelines, as it blew the scattered Spanish fleet northwards. The Spanish did not have maps to chart their route around Scotland and Ireland and many perished on the rocks, especially off the coast of Ireland. Also significant was the fact that the Spanish ships did not have enough food or water for this long voyage. Sickness due to contaminated food and water meant that the sailors became too ill to sail their ships properly and morale was low, particularly after Gravelines (see Source T).

> **Source S: A comment made by Philip II as he talked to survivors of the Armada in 1588**
> *I sent my ships to fight against men, not against the wind and waves of God.*

> **Source T: An extract from a report on the Armada's defeat, written in September 1588, by Francisco de Bobadilla, the general in charge of the Armada's soldiers**
> *We found that many of the enemy's ships held great advantages over us in combat, both in the design, and in their guns, gunners and crews who could do with us as they wished. But in spite of this the Duke of Medina Sidonia managed to bring his fleet to anchor in Calais just several leagues from Dunkirk. If on the day that we arrived there, Parma had come out with his troops we should have carried out the invasion.*

ACTIVITIES

1 Identify THREE key weaknesses in the Spanish forces which help to explain why the Armada failed to achieve its objectives.

2 'The English ships were smaller, faster and had superior fire-power.' How significant were these factors in explaining why the English were able to defeat the Armada?

3 How useful is Source T to an historian studying the Duke of Medina Sidonia's leadership of the Armada?

Practice questions

1 Why was the weather a significant factor in explaining the reasons for the defeat of the Armada? *(For guidance, see page 111.)*

2 What can be learnt from Sources R and S about the reasons why the Armada failed? *(For guidance, see pages 107–108.)*

The results of the Armada

News of the Armada's defeat resulted in great celebrations across Wales and England. Church bells rang out and people gave thanks for their deliverance from a possible Spanish invasion. Philip's soldiers had been prevented from crossing the Channel and landing on English soil. The country remained Protestant and it continued to be ruled by Queen Elizabeth. English Catholics had not risen up in support of Spain in 1588 and there were no further Catholic plots or rebellions for the rest of Elizabeth's reign.

However, it is important not to over-emphasise the significance of the defeat of the Armada as its effects were limited:

- The war against Spain continued and dragged on for a further decade.
- There was still a successful Spanish army in the Netherlands under the command of a very able leader, the Duke of Parma.
- There was still a risk of a Spanish invasion and within a short time Philip had constructed a new armada of over 100 ships; on two occasions it was sent to invade England but in both instances it was driven back by storms.
- The English continued to support the Dutch Protestants in their rebellion against Catholic Spain.
- English sailors continued to attack Spanish treasure ships and ports across the Spanish Main.
- There was increased anti-Catholic feeling within England (see Source U) but it did not result in any major arrests.

> **Source U:** In his book, *Annales* (1615), the chronicler William Camden spoke about the backlash against English Catholics after 1588
>
> *In this difficult time, some beat it many times into the Queen's head, that the Spaniards were not to be as much feared as the Catholics in England. For safety, they advised the heads of the chief Catholics should be chopped off on a false charge. The Queen thought this cruel advice and did no more than imprison some.*

◄ **Source V:** The 'Armada Portrait' of Queen Elizabeth I, painted in 1588 by George Gower. The scene in the top right shows the battle raging in a stormy sea, the top left shows the victorious English fleet sailing in a calm sunny sea. The queen, dressed in royal majesty, has her right hand resting on a globe, her fingers pointing at the Spanish empire in America

ACTIVITIES ?

1 Study Source V.
   a) Explain how the artist has portrayed English supremacy over the Spanish.
   b) What do you think was the main purpose of this portrait?
2 Did the defeat of the Armada finally end the Spanish threat to Elizabeth and England?

Practice question

To what extent does Source U accurately reflect the seriousness of the Spanish threat to England in 1588? (For guidance, see pages 109–110.)

Conclusion: How much of a threat was the Spanish Armada?

In 1588 the major powers of Europe – Spain, France, Austria and their empires – were strongly Roman Catholic. As a Protestant power England was somewhat isolated and when it attempted to help fellow Protestants in the Netherlands rebel against its Catholic ruler Spain, the decision was made by Philip II to invade England, overthrow Elizabeth and re-establish the Catholic faith.

The Armada conceived to accomplish this invasion posed a serious threat. Its size made it difficult to attack in the English Channel and had it been successful in picking up Parma's army and transporting it across to English soil the consequences could have been severe for Elizabeth. England did not possess a strong army and the defence of the country rested largely upon a much smaller naval force to that of Spain.

However, several factors played into Elizabeth's hands. The Armada was led by an inexperienced naval commander, the Duke of Medina Sidonia, and the ships he commanded were large, slow to manoeuvre and outclassed by the smaller more agile English ships which possessed superior firing power. Drake's attack on the Armada at Cadiz had longer-term consequences in terms of interrupting the supply of provisions, resulting in the later spread of disease among the Spanish crews. This helped to diminish the threat.

Key turning points helped to further reduce the Spanish threat, notably the use of fireships at Calais, the battle of Gravelines and the deterioration in the weather, which forced the Armada north around Scotland. After Gravelines the real threat from the Armada had passed and Philip's army waiting in the Netherlands had no means of crossing the Channel. As a result, the invasion was called off.

Summary question

Now that you have completed this chapter, use the knowledge you have acquired to answer the following question.

'The Spanish Armada posed a serious threat to Elizabeth.' How far do you agree with this statement?

In your answer you might like to consider the following factors:

1 the size of Spanish naval and land forces
2 the difficulty the English had in attacking the crescent formation
3 the weakness of English land forces
4 the ability of English naval commanders
5 and any other relevant factors you can think of.

7 The Puritan threat

Key question: Why did the Puritans become an increasing threat during Elizabeth's reign?

Puritanism

As well as opposition from some Catholics, the Religious Settlement of 1559 also met with criticism and opposition from some extreme Protestants known as Puritans. They increased in number during Elizabeth's reign, becoming more radical in their views as the reign progressed.

Who were the Puritans?

Puritans were given their name because they wanted to rid the church of all Catholic associations and because they wanted to follow a simpler or 'purer' form of worship. They were sometimes referred to as the 'hotter sort of Protestants'. Puritan ideas had begun to spread during Edward VI's reign (1547–53). When Mary Tudor took to the throne after Edward's death and restored the Catholic faith as the religion, many Puritans were forced to flee abroad in order to escape persecution. Many went to the Protestant cities of Europe such as Geneva, Zurich, Frankfurt and Strasbourg, where some of them became radicalised, accepting the extreme Protestant beliefs and practices of the Swiss pastor and theologian, John Calvin.

Following Elizabeth's accession many Puritans returned to England, bringing with them their Calvinist ideals and they soon became critical of the Religious Settlement of 1559 (see page 97), believing that it did not go far enough as it still contained elements of Catholicism within it. They wanted the new church to be more Protestant, a church purged of all Catholic practices and ritual and one in which the focus was upon preaching and the study of the scriptures.

The role of bishops

Puritans were particularly opposed to the role of bishops within the church, arguing that it was the invention of the pope to maintain his power over the church and claiming that there was no mention of bishops in the Bible. Many of the bishops of the new Elizabethan Church together with the queen regarded Puritan ideas with suspicion and came to see them as a direct threat to the power of the

Crown and the unity of the country. Puritan ideals were seen by many as a direct challenge to Elizabeth's authority as supreme governor of the Church of England. However, a small number of bishops who were sympathetic to Puritan beliefs accepted positions within the new church hoping that they could work to bring about reform from within the church. They included:

- John Jewel, Bishop of Salisbury
- Edwin Sandys, Bishop of Worcester
- Edmund Grindal, Bishop of London
- Richard Cox, Bishop of Ely.

John Calvin (1509–64)

Born in France, the son of a lawyer:

- He was seen as Martin Luther's successor in the development of the Protestant faith.
- He studied theology in the University of Paris.
- Between 1528–33 he experienced a 'sudden conversion' to Protestantism.
- He moved to Geneva in 1536 which then became the centre of his religious work.
- His rule in Geneva was very strict.
- He believed in plain and simple religious services and placed great importance upon the sermon and the teaching of the scriptures.
- He opposed the use of bishops in the organisation of the church, advocating the use of elders and deacons instead.
- English Protestants who took refuge in Geneva during Mary Tudor's reign came under Calvin's influence and returned to England after 1558 with these beliefs.

Puritan beliefs and practices

Puritans believed that people should lead their lives according to the scriptures and were against practices which were not referenced in the Bible.

Puritans particularly opposed:

- bowing when the name of Jesus was said
- kneeling in order to receive communion
- the giving of a ring during a marriage ceremony
- the marking of the sign of the cross during baptism
- the celebration of saints' days
- the playing of organ music during church services
- the display of ornaments, colourful altar cloths, paintings and stained glass windows in churches (see Figure 7.1).

Puritans believed strongly that Sunday was the Lord's day and it should be devoted entirely to religious study. After attending church service with a lengthy sermon on a Sunday morning, the rest of the day was to be spent studying the scriptures and reading devotional books (see Source A). Their clothing was modest and made of plain materials, usually consisting of black and white outfits (see Source B).

Everyday life was to reflect a moral code, living a simple life based upon the scriptures. Things to be avoided included:

- playing of games or participating in any form of entertainment on a Sunday
- all forms of gambling
- visits to the theatre
- frequenting the alehouse
- drunkenness
- swearing
- dancing on the village green.

All the above were considered to be sinful as they were seen to be the works of the devil.

Different types of Puritans

Puritans were made up of a variety of different groups and during Elizabeth's reign three main strands emerged.

- Moderate Puritans reluctantly accepted the Religious Settlement of 1559 but continued to call for further reforms to purify the church.
- Presbyterians wanted further reform of the church and called for simpler services, the abolition of bishops and for each church to be run by a committee of Presbyters (elders or teachers) elected by the people who attended the church services. Presbyterianism was well established in Scotland.
- Separatists formed the most radical group. They wanted to break away from the national church and for each church to be independent and to run its own affairs on a parish-by-parish basis through local committees chosen from the congregation. They were sometimes known as 'Brownists' (see page 103).

> ## ACTIVITIES ?
>
> 1 What changes did the Puritans wish to make to the Religious Settlement of 1559?
> 2 Using Figure 7.1 and your own knowledge explain the differences between a Protestant and a Puritan place of worship.

> ## Practice question
>
> What can be learnt from Sources A and B about the lifestyle of Puritans? *(For guidance, see pages 107–108.)*

> **Source A:** A reference to the Puritan practice of studying the scriptures made by a contemporary, William Western in his book *The Autobiography of an Elizabethan* (c.1580)
>
> *From the very beginning a great number of Puritans lived here … Each of them had his own Bible, turning the pages and discussing the passages among themselves … they would start arguing about the meaning of passages from the scriptures – men, women, boys, girls, rustics [simple country folk], labourers and idiots – and more often than not, it was said, it ended in violence.*

▲ Source B: A contemporary woodcut showing a Puritan family at home. Their clothes are plain black and white garments

▲ Figure 7.1: The inside of a Protestant church (left) and a Puritan chapel (right) during Elizabethan times

Puritan challenges to the Religious Settlement

After Elizabeth introduced the Religious Settlement in 1559 many Puritans continued to push for further reform of the church. Their aim was to remove those elements of the Elizabethan Church which they considered to be too Catholic. Elizabeth was not prepared to make any further changes (see Figure 7.2).

The Vestments Controversy, 1566

In 1566 Matthew Parker, the Archbishop of Canterbury, issued a 'Book of Advertisements' which laid down rules for the conducting of services and the wearing of vestments, identifying the specific clothes to be worn by priests during church services. Many Puritan priests refused to follow these instructions and they argued that the vestments suggested by Parker were very similar to the clothing previously worn by Catholic priests.

As a result some priests were punished:

- Thomas Sampson, the Dean of Christ Church, Oxford, was dismissed from his position because he refused to wear vestments
- in London, 37 Puritan priests were dismissed from their jobs because they also refused to wear vestments.

Such protests were seen as a challenge to the queen's authority as supreme governor of the church. In response, Elizabeth insisted that the correct dress be worn and that all priests conformed. In this instance, the Puritans failed to get the reforms they wanted.

Proposals by Thomas Cartwright, 1570

In the spring of 1570, Thomas Cartwright, a professor of divinity at Cambridge University, gave a series of lectures in which he called for the introduction of a Presbyterian system of church government. He suggested:

- the abolition of the post of archbishop
- the abolition of all bishops
- that each church should be ruled locally by its own minister and elders from the community
- that ministers should be elected by their own church congregations.

The Presbyterian system he wanted to see introduced would have weakened the power of the queen to act as supreme governor and as a result Cartwright's proposals were bitterly rejected by both Elizabeth and her Privy Council. His views cost him his job and he was forced to leave England for Geneva.

Figure 7.2: Elizabeth's views ▶ about the Puritans

French marriage pamphlet of John Stubbs, 1579

In 1579, John Stubbs, a Puritan and political commentator, wrote a pamphlet which criticised the queen for engaging in marriage talks with the Duke of Anjou, a French Roman Catholic who was the brother of the king of France. Elizabeth was not pleased by the publication. Stubbs was arrested, put on trial and charged with 'seditious writing'. He was sentenced to have his right hand cut off (see Source C) and he was then imprisoned for 18 months.

The Marprelate Tracts, 1588–89

During 1588–89 a series of anonymous pamphlets were published called the Marprelate Tracts. They bitterly attacked the church and its bishops and their content offended many people. While the authors were never identified their publication lost the Puritans support and respect as the text of the pamphlets contained violent, sarcastic and often offensive language, completely opposite to Puritan attitudes on how people should behave.

To counter this criticism some Protestants wrote pamphlets against Puritan views. In 1593 Richard Hooker published his *Laws of Ecclesiastical Policy* as a defence of the Anglican Church and in that same year Richard Bancroft launched a

bitter attack on Puritanism through his pamphlet entitled *Survey of the Pretended Holy Discipline Dangerous Positions and Proceedings*.

ACTIVITIES ?

1 Make a copy and complete the following table about Puritan challenges to Elizabeth's position as supreme governor.

Puritan challenge	Threat it posed to Elizabeth's authority as supreme governor	Elizabeth's response
Vestments controversy		
Thomas Cartwright		
John Stubbs		
Marprelate Tracts		

2 Write a paragraph to accompany Source C, detailing the reasons why John Stubbs had his right hand chopped off.

PUNISHMENT OF STUBBS AND PAGE.

◄ Source C: A print of 1579 showing John Stubbs, a Puritan, have his right hand chopped off as a punishment for criticising Elizabeth's marriage talks

Puritan opposition in parliament and the Privy Council

Elizabeth found it difficult to ignore the Puritans as they were represented at every level of government. Within the Privy Council some of Elizabeth's most powerful councillors were Puritans, most notably the Earl of Leicester and Sir Francis Walsingham. These moderate Puritans hoped to use their influence to persuade the queen to continue with religious reform.

Within parliament there were many Puritan MPs who used their positions to introduce bills which proposed reform in favour of their religious beliefs. At the local level many JPs were Puritans, as well as many church ministers and tutors in universities. Many of these individuals supported calls for religious reform.

Individuals who attempted reform within parliament

Walter Strickland, 1571

In April 1571, Walter Strickland, the Puritan MP for Yorkshire, proposed a bill in parliament calling for the introduction of a new Book of Common Prayer and for the banning of vestments, the use of a ring in marriage and kneeling while receiving communion. Strickland was prevented from attending the House of Commons by the Privy Council and Elizabeth closed parliament down before his ideas could be discussed. The bill was not heard of again and to enforce conformity the Thirty-nine Articles (see page 60) were formally approved by parliament, requiring all clergy to accept these rules to keep their jobs.

John Field and Thomas Wilcox, 1572

In 1572, two London clergymen, John Field and Thomas Wilcox, published books with the titles *Admonitions to the Parliament* and *A View of Popish Abuses yet remaining in the English Church* (see Source D) in which they argued that the Presbyterian church structure was the one laid down in the Bible. They said that the Bible contained reference to the terms ministers, elders and deacons but not bishops. They were also critical of the Book of Common Prayer. It was a bitter attack on the Elizabethan Church and as a result both men were arrested and imprisoned for a year, having been accused of breaking the Act of Uniformity which had required them to swear under oath that they would follow the official procedure for services. Puritan printing presses were ordered to be destroyed and bishops were instructed to enforce uniformity.

> **Source D:** In 1572 John Field published a book, *A View of Popish Abuses yet remaining in the English Church* which was critical of the Elizabethan Church
>
> *[The Book of Common Prayer] is an unperfect book, culled and picked out of that popish [Roman Catholic] dunghill, the Mess book, full of all abominations [wrong practice]. ... In this book we are enjoined to receive the Communion kneeling, which has in it a show of popish idolatry [worship of idols] ... The public baptism ... is also full of childish and superstitious toys ... marking the child on the forehead with a cross.*

Peter Wentworth, 1576

In 1576, Peter Wentworth, the Puritan MP for Barnstable, complained in the House of Commons that MPs were not being allowed to discuss what they wanted in parliament (see Source E). Elizabeth responded by having him imprisoned in the Tower of London for a month and she closed parliament down. She also issued instructions that parliament was not to debate religious matters without her permission.

> **Source E:** Extract from a speech delivered by Peter Wentworth in the House of Commons on 8 February 1576
>
> *I have never seen in any Parliament but the last the liberty of free speech in so many ways infringed, with so many abuses offered to this honourable House. The Queen said that we should not deal in any matters of religion, except what we receive from the bishops. Surely this was a doleful message, for it meant, 'Sirs, ye shall not deal in God's causes, no, ye shall in no way advance His glory.' It is a dangerous thing in a prince unkindly to abuse his or her nobility and people, and it is a dangerous thing in a prince to oppose or bend herself against her nobility and people, yea against faithful and loving nobility and people.*

Peter Turner, 1584

In 1584, Peter Turner, the Puritan MP for Bridport, proposed a bill to change the government of the church to copy Calvin's system at Geneva. The bill failed to get much support and was forcefully attacked during a speech delivered in the Commons by Sir Christopher Hatton, one of Elizabeth's loyal Privy Councillors. Hatton was a moderate Protestant who hated Puritans and their beliefs.

Anthony Cope, 1586–87

Anthony Cope, the Puritan MP for Banbury, was sympathetic to Presbyterian ideas. In 1586 he introduced a bill in parliament that called for the abolition of all bishops and the replacement of the Book of Common Prayer with the Geneva Prayer Book of John Calvin. Peter Wentworth supported his right to speak, arguing that MPs should have the right to discuss religious matters in parliament. The bill was bitterly attacked by Hatton in the House of Commons. Cope and Wentworth, together with four of their supporters, were confined in the Tower of London for several months during 1587 and parliament was closed down.

These setbacks led many Puritans to believe that they could achieve little through parliament and so they began to seek out other means of calling for reform, such as the reinforcement of Puritan ideals through prayer meetings.

ACTIVITIES

1 What criticisms of the Elizabethan Church are made by John Field in Source D?
2 Study Source E. Why did Peter Wentworth believe it was important for MPs to have the freedom of speech in parliament?

Practice question

Explain the connections between any THREE of the following:
- Walter Strickland
- Peter Wentworth
- Anthony Cope
- Sir Christopher Hatton.

(For guidance, see page 112.)

Measures taken to deal with the Puritan challenge

Having successfully blocked demands for reform within parliament, Elizabeth applied equal force to stop the spread of extreme Puritanism at the local level. She was particularly concerned over the growth from the 1570s onwards of two developments within the Puritan movement – prophesyings and separatists.

Archbishop Grindal and the 'prophesyings'

During the 1570s the government became alarmed by the spread of meetings held by Puritans called prophesyings during which prayers and sermons were said. Intended as a means of improving the standards of the clergy, they came to be seen by the queen and the Privy Council as potentially dangerous as it was thought they served to encourage unrest and rebellion. In 1576 the queen ordered Edmund Grindal, her new Archbishop of Canterbury, to ban such meetings.

Grindal, however, was sympathetic to Puritan ideas and he concluded that prophesyings were not dangerous (see Source F). He therefore refused to follow the queen's instructions. Elizabeth reacted by confining him to his house at Lambeth Palace, suspending him from his duties and preventing him from functioning as leader of the church.

As Grindal would not act, Elizabeth issued her own instructions to her bishops in which she banned prophesyings (see Source G).

> **Source F:** Extract from a letter written by Archbishop Grindal to Queen Elizabeth in 1576
>
> *I and others of your Bishops have found by experience that these profits come from these exercises [prophesyings]:*
> 1. *The ministers of the Church are more skilful and ready in the Scriptures, and apter to teach their flocks*
> 2. *It withdraweth their flocks from idleness, wandering, gaming etc.*
> 3. *Some suspected of doctrinal error are brought to open confession of the truth*
> 4. *Ignorant ministers are driven to study, if not for conscience then for shame and fear of discipline*
> 5. *The opinion of laymen about the idleness of the clergy is removed*
> 6. *Nothing beateth down Popery [Roman Catholicism] more than that ministers grow to such a good knowledge by means of these exercises.*

Edmund Grindal (1519–83)

- *c.*1519 born the son of a tenant farmer at St Bees in Cumbria
- 1530s, educated at St Bees Priory, followed by Cambridge University
- *c.*1549 appointed chaplain to Edward VI
- 1553, forced into exile during Mary's reign, spending time in Strasbourg and Frankfurt
- 1558 appointed Bishop of London
- 1570 appointed Archbishop of York
- 1576 appointed Archbishop of Canterbury
- 1577 refused to carry out Elizabeth's order to suppress prophesyings and was suspended
- 1577–83 confined to Lambeth Palace
- 1583 died.

> **Source G:** Elizabeth's instructions to her bishops banning prophesyings, 1577
>
> *In sundry [various] parts of the our realm there are no small number of persons which, contrary to our laws established for the public divine service of Almighty God … do put into execution … unlawful assemblies of our people out of their ordinary parishes … which manner of invasions [meetings] they in some places call prophesying and in some other places exercises.*
> *… We will charge you that the same forthwith cease. But if any shall attempt, or continue, or renew the same, we will you to commit them unto prison as maintainers of disorders.*

▲ Portrait of Edmund Grindal, *c.*1580

John Whitgift's attack on Presbyterianism

When Grindal died in 1583 Elizabeth replaced him as archbishop by John Whitgift, a devout Anglican and member of the Privy Council. He had little sympathy with Puritan beliefs. To purge the church of all Presbyterian elements he issued his *Three Articles* in 1583 (see Source H). These laid down regulations to demand uniformity from the clergy by forcing them to swear:

- the acceptance of bishops
- the acceptance of all that was contained in the Book of Common Prayer
- the acceptance of the Thirty-nine Articles.

Between 300–400 ministers refused to swear acceptance of these terms and they were removed from office. For the rest of his time in office Whitgift continued to impose strict controls over his clergy to end all prophesyings and to suppress any other developments of Presbyterian practices.

Source H: Article Two from Whitgift's *Three Articles* of 1583

That the Book of Common Prayer, and of ordering bishops, priests and deacons containeth nothing in it contrary to the word of God. And that the same may be lawfully used; and that he himself will use the form of the said book prescribed, in public prayer and administration of the sacraments and none other.

John Whitgift (1530–1604)

- 1530 born the son of a wealthy merchant
- he was educated at St Anthony's School, London, followed by Cambridge University
- 1563 appointed Chaplain to Queen Elizabeth
- 1571 appointed Professor of Divinity at Cambridge
- 1571 appointed Dean of Lincoln
- 1577 appointed Bishop of Worcester
- 1583 appointed Archbishop of Canterbury and he was given the task of ensuring conformity to the Religious Settlement
- 1583 issued his *Three Articles* to enforce religious uniformity
- 1586 given a position on the Privy Council, becoming the only cleric to sit on the Council
- 1603 crowned James Stuart as King James VI
- 1604 died.

ACTIVITIES

1 What were prophesyings?
2 Study Source F. What reasons are put forward by Archbishop Grindal in defence of prophesying meetings?
3 Describe the measures taken by Archbishop Whitgift to rid the church of Presbyterian elements.

Practice question

To what extent does Source G accurately reflect the seriousness of the Puritan threat? *(For guidance, see pages 109–110.)*

▲ Portrait of John Whitgift

The development of the separatist movement in the 1580s

While Whitgift's efforts to enforce uniformity were largely successful, it forced strict Puritans underground. With the destruction of printing presses and the imprisonment of some Puritan extremists, a small number of Puritans who had been given the name 'separatists', decided to leave the established church and set up their own church. One of the main leaders of this breakaway movement was Robert Browne, and his followers were sometimes referred to as Brownists.

In 1580 Browne established a separatist congregation in Norwich. He believed that the Church of England still contained elements of the Catholic faith and demonstrated a lack of moral discipline. He wanted true Christians to break away and leave the church to set up separate, voluntary gatherings which would impose proper discipline. He was imprisoned for his beliefs for a short time and upon release emigrated to settle in Holland in 1582.

After Browne's departure new leaders emerged to take his place such as Henry Barrow and John Greenwood. Browne's ideas were a worry for Whitgift and in June 1583 two Brownists, John Copping and Elias Thacker, were ordered to be hanged for distributing Brownist pamphlets.

The Act against Seditious Sectaries, 1593

The Marprelate Tracts of 1588–89 (see page 98) were part of the separatist movement, being anonymously published pamphlets which bitterly attacked the organisation of the church and its bishops. Such pamphlets demonstrated that the separatists were not prepared to compromise and provided Elizabeth's ministers with ammunition to launch an attack on Puritanism.

Government propaganda linked Puritanism to separatism, and separatism to treason. The response by Elizabeth's government was the passing of the Act against Seditious Sectaries in 1593 which gave the authorities power to execute those suspected of being separatists. It imposed the severe penalties of imprisonment, banishment and even death on those who held unauthorised meetings or who refused to go to Anglican Church services. As a result of this Act the separatist leaders Henry Barrow and John Greenwood, along with the Welsh Puritan John Penry, were arrested and executed in May 1593. The arrests and executions marked the end of the separatist movement.

> **Source I:** Extract from the Act against Seditious Sectaries, 1593
>
> *If any person or persons above the age of sixteen years shall obstinately refuse to repair to some church ... to hear divine service, established by her Majesty's laws ... by printing, writing or express words or speeches advisedly and purposely practise or go about to move or persuade any of her Majesty's subjects ... to deny ... her Majesty's power and authority in causes ecclesiastical [to do with the church] ... or to that end or purpose advisedly and maliciously move or persuade any other person ... to abstain from coming to church to hear divine service ... that then every such person so offending ... shall be committed to prison there to remain until they shall conform. ... And if any such offender shall refuse to make such abjuration [swear an oath] as is aforesaid ... the person so offending shall be adjudged a felon [which carried the death penalty].*

> **Interpretation 1:** A view of the threat posed by separatists made by the historian John Warren in his book *Elizabeth I: Meeting the Challenge, England 1541–1603*, published in 2008
>
> *Separatists were not a threat in practice. They were too few in number, too addicted to bickering with each other and totally devoid of elite support. In addition, the Queen could and did employ savage penalties against them.*

ACTIVITIES ?

1 What were the aims of the separatist movement?

2 Explain how Elizabeth's government dealt with the separatist movement.

Practice question

Study Interpretation 1. How far do you agree with the interpretation about the threat posed by the separatist movement? *(For guidance, see pages 113–114.)*

The Puritan challenge in Wales

There were very few signs of Puritan activity in Wales before the last decades of Elizabeth's reign. The movement tended to be introduced into Wales from England along trade routes and it was in ports like Swansea and the towns of the Welsh borders where Puritanism picked up most support. In Wrexham in the north-east, the Puritans were beginning to make themselves felt and during the 1580s sabbath breakers and maypole-dancers in this region were attacked by Puritans for their lifestyle. Individuals like Walter Stephens, Vicar of Bishop's Castle, and Stanley Gower, Vicar of Brampton Bryan, were known Puritans, active on the Welsh borders. In these areas the authorities did not see Puritanism as a serious threat and little action was taken against them.

In other areas of Wales, Puritanism made little inroads. The conservative nature of the Welsh people and their isolation geographically made the spread of Puritan ideas difficult, especially as the main language of Puritanism was English. The one Welsh person who did have an impact upon the Puritan movement was John Penry but even he operated outside of Wales.

John Penry, a Welsh Puritan martyr

John Penry was born in 1563 at Cefn Brith, near Llangamarch in Breconshire. While a student at Cambridge and later Oxford University he became heavily influenced by the ideas of the Puritans. He grew to dislike Elizabeth's Religious Settlement and he began to write pamphlets in which he called for a reform of the church. He desired a church not run by bishops but by a democratic assembly of presbyters or elders and he believed that true salvation could only come through an understanding of the scriptures explained through preaching.

In 1587, Penry published a pamphlet called *An Exhortation to the governors and people of Wales* which attacked the state of religion in Wales. He complained about poor church services and unsuitable clergy who could not speak Welsh. He said that services should be in Welsh and that the Bible should be translated into Welsh. He attacked the bishops, calling them 'soul murderers'. Upon the orders of Archbishop Whitgift he was arrested and put in prison for a month.

Upon release Penry became involved with a secret printing press which during 1588–89 published a number of pamphlets attacking the lifestyle and work of bishops of the Church of England. These were the Marprelate Tracts. The authorities began a search for the secret press and Penry was forced to flee to Scotland to avoid capture. Whilst in Scotland he wrote *A Briefe Discovery* which defended the Church of Scotland.

In 1592, he returned and settled in London where he joined a community of Separatists or extreme Puritans. Such associations caused him to be arrested in 1593. He was put on trial accused of having: 'feloniously devised and written certain words with intent to excite rebellion and insurrection in England.'

He was found guilty and while awaiting his punishment he appealed to Sir William Cecil for clemency but his appeal was ignored (see Source J). He was executed in London on 29 May 1593. He was just 30 years old and he became the first Puritan martyr in the history of Wales.

ACTIVITY

Explain why John Penry was a problem for Elizabeth I.

> **Source J:** An extract from a letter written by John Penry to Sir William Cecil, a week before his execution on 29 May 1593
>
> *I am a poor young man born and bred in the mountains of Wales. I am the first since the last springing up of the Gospel in this latter age that publicly laboured to have the blessed seed thereof sown in these barren mountains ... I leave the success of these my labours unto such of my Countrymen, as the Lord is to raise up after me for the accomplishing of that work, which in the calling of my country unto the knowledge of Christs blessed Gospel, I began.*

Conclusion: Why did the Puritans become an increasing threat during Elizabeth's reign?

The Puritans became an increasing threat during Elizabeth's reign due to the development of the Puritan movement itself and also because of the queen's refusal to allow any further reform of the Religious Settlement of 1559. To begin with the differences between moderate Puritans and Protestants were small and posed no real threat to the Settlement. There was the hope by many Puritans that, over time, Elizabeth would allow changes to be made to eliminate the last traces of the Catholic faith.

The Presbyterian branch of the Puritan movement posed more of a threat as it pushed to have the structure of the church amended to model the Calvinist system which took away control from archbishops and bishops. Such change, however, was unacceptable to Elizabeth who demanded complete uniformity to the Settlement. She increasingly came to see the Presbyterians as a threat and took action to suppress all calls for reform from both within and outside parliament.

Elizabeth's refusal to consider making even minor concessions did drive some Puritans to more extreme actions such as printing radical pamphlets and religious works calling for changes to the structure of the leadership of the church. The setting up of prophesying meetings to purify the church from within was seen as a major threat as such meetings were seen to have the potential to lead to treasonable plotting. The actions of Archbishop Whitgift to suppress such meetings in many ways led to the development of a more radical branch in the form of the separatist movement.

The separatist movement posed the greatest threat to the Settlement as its suggestions for a church structure without controls would take away Elizabeth's power as supreme governor. It took government legislation to remove this threat. However, while Elizabeth may have crushed the radical wing she had not destroyed the Puritan movement itself.

Summary question

Now that you have completed this chapter, use the knowledge you have acquired to answer the following question.

'The spread of prophesying meetings was the most serious threat posed by the Puritan movement.' How far do you agree with this statement?

In your answer you might like to consider the following factors:

1 the reforms demanded by Puritan MPs
2 the writings of Puritan authors
3 the Presbyterian movement
4 the separatist movement
5 and any other relevant factors you can think of.

WJEC Examination Guidance

This section will give you step-by-step guidance on how best to approach and answer the types of questions that you will face in the exam. Below is a model exam paper with a set of exam-style questions (without the sources).

Unit one: studies in depth

In Question 1 you have to analyse and pick out key details from two sources linked to the theme of the question

In Question 2 you have to analyse and evaluate the accuracy of a source, using your knowledge to identify strengths and weaknesses

In Question 3 you have to demonstrate knowledge and understanding to help construct a reasoned judgement upon the significance of an identified issue

In Question 4 you have to demonstrate knowledge and understanding in order to explain relevant connections between three chosen features

In Question 5 you need to demonstrate knowledge and understanding of a key issue, analysing and evaluating how and why interpretations of an issue differ, before reaching a judgement about the accuracy of the interpretation based upon its authorship

Wales and the wider perspective
1A The Elizabethan Age, 1558–1603
Time allowed: 1 hour

1   What can be learnt from Sources A and B about the Privy Council in Elizabethan times?
    [4 marks]

2   To what extent does Source C accurately explain the importance of the Catholic threat?

    [In your answer you should refer to the strengths and limitations of the source and use your own knowledge and understanding of the historical context.]
    [6 marks]

3   Why was vagrancy seen as a significant threat to law and order during the reign of Elizabeth?
    [12 marks]

4   Explain the connections between any THREE of the following:

    - Philip II
    - Duke of Medina Sidonia
    - The Netherlands
    - Calais
      [12 marks]

5   'The theatre burst into life during Elizabeth's reign. Shakespeare wrote at least 37 plays during her reign, many of them being the most famous plays ever written. The popularity of such plays helped to make Elizabeth's reign the "Golden Age" of English drama.'

    (Andy Harmsworth writing in a GCSE history textbook, *Elizabethan England*, published in 1999.)

    How far do you agree with this interpretation about the popularity of the theatre in Elizabethan times?
    [16 marks]

    [In your answer you should refer to how and why interpretations of this issue differ. Use your own knowledge and understanding of the wider historical debate over this issue to reach a well-supported judgement.]

    Marks for spelling, punctuation and the accurate use of grammar and specialist language are allocated to this question.
    [3 marks]

Total marks for the paper: 53

Examination guidance

Examination guidance for Question 1

This section provides guidance on how to answer the question on what you can learn from two sources. Look at the following question.

> What can be learnt from Sources A and B about the English attack on the Armada at Calais?

> **Source A:** An account describing English tactics including the use of fireships, written by Petruccioi Ubaldini, an Italian living in England in 1588
>
> *The English with their excellent ships did not fight as expected but kept at a distance and fired at the hulls and sails of their enemy. The English set eight ships on fire amongst the Spanish fleet. Their enemy were woken up and had to cut their cables to get away from their anchors.*

▲ Source B: A late-sixteenth-century painting by a Dutch artist, showing the fireships attacking the Armada in Calais harbour

How to answer

- Compose an opening sentence to say that both sources provide useful information upon the topic.
- Pick out several key facts/points for Source A, linking them to the question.
- Pick out several key facts/points from Source B, linking them to the question.
- Make sure your answer displays a balanced use of both sources. An imbalanced answer which concentrates too much on one source will not score you top marks.

Example answer

Step 1: Opening statement which links to the question

> The two sources provide useful information about the English attack on the Armada as it was anchored off Calais.

Step 2: Identify two or more facts from Source A

> Source A comments that the English had kept their distance whilst the Armada has sailed through the English channel, firing their cannon at the Spanish fleet from a distance and avoiding direct fighting. When the Armada anchored off Calais the English sent in fireships which caused the Spanish to cut their anchor cables in an attempt to escape.

Step 3: Identify two or more facts from Source B

> Source B shows the attack of the fireships in more detail. The artist has painted the fireships fully ablaze and drifting towards the Armada. The Spanish ships are anchored close together for protection but this now caused them a serious problem. The painting shows the English ships sailing towards the Armada immediately behind the fireships, ready to attack the Spanish ships as they attempt to break free.

Now try answering the following question:

What can be learnt from Sources C and D about the execution of Mary, Queen of Scots, in February 1587?

Source C: A contemporary account of Mary's execution sent to Lord Burghley in February 1587

Groping for the block, she laid down her head, putting her chin over the block with both her hands, which, holding there still, would have been cut off had they not been seen. Then she, lying very still upon the block, one of the executioners holding her slightly with one of his hands, she endured two strokes of the other executioner with an axe, she making a very small noise or none at all, and not stirring any part of her from where she lay. And so the executioner cut off her head, save for one little gristle.

▲ **Source D:** An anonymous painting of the execution of Mary, Queen of Scots, in February 1587, drawn by an eyewitness

Examination guidance for Question 2

This section provides guidance on how to answer the question on the accuracy of a source.
Look at the following question.

> To what extent does this source accurately reflect the threat the new theatres posed to maintaining law and order during Elizabethan times?
>
> [In your answer you should refer to the strengths and limitations of the source and use your own knowledge and understanding of the historical context.]

> **Source E:** A letter sent to the Privy Council written by the Lord Mayor of London in 1597 in which he complained about the problems caused by the rise in the number of theatres in the city
>
> *Theatres are places of vagrants, masterless men, thieves, horse-stealers, whoremongers, cheats, swindlers, traitors and other idle and dangerous persons to meet together to the great displeasure of Almighty God and the hurt and annoyance of the Majesty's people. We cannot prevent this for the theatres are outside the area of our control.*
>
> *They maintain idleness in such persons as have no work, and draw apprentices and servants from their work, and all sorts of people from attending sermons and other religious services, causing great damage to the trade and religion of the realm.*
>
> *In times of sickness many who have sores amuse themselves by hearing a play, whereby other are infected.*

How to answer

- Identify the key points/issues raised in the source – this can be done by underlining or highlighting the most important points.
- Use your knowledge of this topic area to place the source into its historical context – you need to test the accuracy of what the source says against your knowledge of this topic area.
- Consider the attribution of the source to identify strengths and limitations:
  - who wrote it?
  - when did they write it?
  - why was it written?
  - what was its purpose?
- How does this impact upon the reliability and accuracy of the information?
- Make a reasoned judgement upon the accuracy of the source, making clear links to the question.

Example answer

Step 1: Identifies and discusses the key points raised in the source

> The source shows how the new theatres were seen as a considerable threat to the maintenance of law and order during the 1590s. The Lord Mayor identifies a number of specific problems. He says that the theatre attracts people from the poorest classes, especially those not respectful of law and order. He quotes examples of vagrants, thieves, swindlers and cheats, all of whom he believes can be the cause of lawlessness, especially when they mix with the large crowds which the theatre attracts. The Lord Mayor also makes the point that the theatre acts like a magnet, drawing people away from their work and from Sunday worship. Such large crowds, he believes, can be the cause of the spread of disease and illnesses.

Step 2: Use of own knowledge to provide historical context to test the accuracy of the source

> The source highlights the chief concerns of the Lord Mayor, some of which are justified and can be confirmed by an examination of the historical context. The gathering of large crowds did attract a lawless element, who intended to use the event to engage in crimes such as pickpocketing, the stealing of horses and swindling the audience out of their money. It also confirms the contemporary belief that the coming together of such large crowds of people drawn from a wide area of the city of London helped to spread disease.

Step 3: Reaches a substantiated judgement upon the accuracy of the statement posed in the question

> However, the Lord Mayor is writing from a particular standpoint and as the man responsible for maintaining law and order within the city of London he is bound to be concerned about the potential problems the gathering of such large crowds at the new theatres could have on civil unrest. As the theatres were built outside the city walls he had no control over them. He is obviously going to be biased in his view, painting a negative picture and possibly exaggerating the degree to which lawlessness was a problem. His mission is to win the support of the Privy Council to have such theatres closed down and he therefore may have exaggerated the threat posed. The Lord Mayor wanted to avoid such large gatherings and to stop the mixing of the classes. While some contemporaries do comment upon the increase in crime at such venues, the Lord Mayor seems to be exaggerating the depth of the problem.

Now try to answer the following question.

To what extent does the source accurately reflect the seriousness of the threat posed to Elizabeth by Mary, Queen of Scots, after 1572? [*In your answer you should refer to the strengths and limitations of the source and use your own knowledge and understanding of the historical context.*]

Source F: Extract from Parliament's charges against Mary, Queen of Scots, made in May 1572

She has wickedly challenged the Crown of England.

She has sought to withdraw the Duke of Norfolk from his natural obedience, against the Queen's express prohibition.

She has stirred the Earls of Northumberland and Westmoreland to rebel.

She has practised [tried] to procure [get] new rebellion to be raised within this realm.

We, your true and obedient subjects, do most humbly beseech your Majesty to punish and correct all the treasons and wicked attempts of the said Mary.

Examination guidance to Question 3

This section provides guidance on how to answer a question on significance. Look at the following question.

> Why was the Puritan movement seen as a significant threat to the Religious Settlement of 1559?

How to answer

- ■ Use you knowledge to place the key issue in context.
- ■ Explain what was happening at that time.
- ■ Include specific factual detail to help construct an argument.
- ■ Make regular links to the key issue, providing some judgement.
- ■ Conclude with a reasoned and well-supported judgement.

Example answer

The threat posed by the Puritans increased as Elizabeth's reign progressed. This was largely due to how the Puritan movement itself developed. Initially many Puritans hoped that the Religious Settlement of 1559 would be the start of a reform package that would ultimately wipe out the last traces of the Catholic faith from the new Elizabethan Church. Elizabeth, however, saw the Settlement as permanent and refused to allow any further changes. This caused some Puritan MPs to attempt reform through Parliament but their efforts were largely unsuccessful.

Step 1: Begin by placing the key issue into context, providing some background detail

While the main body of Puritans did not pose a threat to the Religious Settlement, the emergence of more radical branches within the Puritan movement did come to pose a more significant threat. Lack of progress with calls for reform helped the Presbyterian movement to develop, the key part of their belief being the abandonment of a church structure based upon archbishops and bishops. While this represented little real threat, more serious was the emergence in the 1570s of Prophesying meetings which alarmed the government. To deal with this threat Archbishop Whitgift introduced measures to enforce conformity amongst the clergy.

A more worrying challenge to the Religious Settlement came from developments within Puritanism during the 1580s which saw the emergence of the separatist movement. First established in Norwich in 1580 by Robert Browne, the movement wanted its members to break away and leave the Church to set up separate, voluntary gatherings, which would impose strict discipline.

Step 2: Continue to develop the context, provide specific detail and make links to the key issue, attempting some judgement

The beliefs of the separatists posed a significant threat to Elizabeth as they undermined her position as supreme governor. The movement was supported through the publication of the Marprelate Tracts which bitterly attacked the organisation of the Church and its bishops. Elizabeth saw this as a serious challenge to the Religious Settlement and the government response was the passing of the Act Against Seditious Sectaries in 1593. This, together with the arrest of some of its leaders, killed off the separatist movement. Of all the branches of the Puritan faith this was by far the most radical, and the one which posed the greatest threat to the established order. However, the main branch of the Puritan Movement, while it continued to push for religious reform, posed little real threat and its members remained loyal and faithful to the Religious Settlement of 1559.

Step 3: Conclude with a reasoned and well-supported judgement upon the key issue

Now try the following question.

Why was poverty seen as a significant threat to law and order during the reign of Elizabeth I?

Examination guidance for Question 4

This section provides guidance on how to answer the question on connections between three features. Look at the following question.

> Explain the connections between any THREE of the following:
> - Translation of the Scriptures into Welsh
> - Richard Davies
> - William Salesbury
> - William Morgan.

How to answer

- Select three factors which you think show clear connections.
- Use your knowledge to explain the three factors, making links between them.
- Aim to cover a number of points to illustrate how the factors are connected.
- Conclude with a final sentence demonstrating relevant connections.

Example answer

Issues chosen: translation of the Scriptures into Welsh, William Salesbury and William Morgan

Step 1: Select three factors and introduce them, pointing out a connection.

> One of the most important religious and cultural events in Welsh history during Elizabeth's reign was the translation of the Scriptures into Welsh. This was achieved through the passing of an Act of Parliament in 1563 which laid down that the Bible and Prayer Book were to be translated into Welsh by St David's Day 1567. Copies were to be placed alongside English versions in every church in Wales. The undertaking of the translation involved a small team of Protestant clerics and scholars, the most important being William Salesbury and William Morgan.

Step 2: Use your knowledge to explain and develop the connections further.

> Through the help and encouragement of Bishop Richard Davies, the Welsh scholar William Salesbury began work on translating the New Testament and Prayer Book in Welsh shortly after 1563 and by the deadline date of 1567 he had completed the task. As there were no printing presses in Wales the printing was performed in London. The publication marked an important date in the religious history of Wales but it had its drawback. Salesbury's translation proved difficult to read and therefore its impact was limited.

Step 3: Aim to cover a number of points to demonstrate how one factor relates to the other factors.

> Salesbury could not be persuaded to continue with the work of translating the Old Testament into Welsh and that task was performed by William Morgan, the vicar of Llanrhaeadr-ym-Mochnant. Unlike Salesbury, Morgan adopted a more readable style of written Welsh in his translation. It took him many years to complete the translation and during the printing process he moved up to London so that he could correct the printer's proofs. When the translation of the Old Testament was finally published in 1587 it met with immediate success. Morgan then went on to produce revised versions of Salesbury's translation of the New Testament and Prayer Book.

Step 4: Conclude with a final few sentences demonstrating clear connections between them.

> By the time of Morgan's death in 1604 the translation of the Scriptures into Welsh had been completed and copies of the Old and New Testaments together with the Prayer Book were to be found in every Church in Wales. The process had taken over twenty-five years to complete and was chiefly the work of two men, William Salesbury and William Morgan. However, without the Act of 1563 it is doubtful the translation of the Scriptures would have taken place.

Now you try the following question:

Explain the connections between THREE of the following:
- Portraits of Elizabeth
- Royal progresses
- Royal patronage
- The Queen's character.

Examination guidance for Question 5

This section provides guidance on how to answer the interpretation question. Look at thier following question.

> How far do you agree with this interpretation of the Catholic threat to Elizabeth? [*In your answer you should refer to how and why interpretations of this issue differ. Use your own knowledge and understanding of the wider historical debate over this issue to reach a well-supported judgement.*]
>
> *Marks for spelling, punctuation and the accurate use of grammar and specialist terms are allocated to this question.*

> **Interpretation:** Susan Doran, a university lecturer and specialist in Tudor history, writing in her book, *Elizabeth I and Religion*, published in 1994
>
> *In reality the danger from English Catholics was exaggerated. The vast majority of them were loyal to their Queen and country and simply hoped for better times when the Catholic Mary Stuart [Mary Queen of Scots] would succeed to the throne. In many instances the constant exposure to Protestantism caused many Catholics to turn away from their faith and only the most committed Catholics became recusants and refused to accept the Religious Settlement.*

How to answer

- Outline the interpretation given in the extract.
- Provide context:
  - ☐ discuss the content of the extract linking it to your knowledge of the events
  - ☐ what evidence can you include to support the main message of the extract?
- Consider the author:
  - ☐ how does what you are told about the author impact upon the reliability and accuracy of the information in the extract?
  - ☐ why was the extract produced?
  - ☐ who was the intended audience?
  - ☐ does this impact upon the interpretation?
- Identify other interpretations:
  - ☐ suggest that other historians may have differing viewpoints
  - ☐ outline some of the arguments of other interpretations, explaining how they differ
  - ☐ explain why these interpretations differ
- Conclusion:
  - ☐ provide a substantiated judgement which addresses how and why interpretations on this issue differ.

Example answer

The interpretation clearly states that the threat posed by English Catholics both to the country and to Elizabeth's position as queen was exaggerated. The author, Susan Doran, makes the point that the majority of the population were loyal to their queen and country and did not engage in activities that could be classed as treasonable. Most people accepted the Religious Settlement of 1559 and saw it as a workable compromise, a middle way with elements of the Catholic faith still being allowed to continue, such as the wearing of vestments and the marking of the sign of the cross during baptism. Few people were fined for recusancy and the vast majority accepted the Elizabethan Church without protest.

Step 1: Outline the interpretation given in the source

It is true that Elizabeth faced a number of Catholic plots designed to overthrow her and replace her with a Catholic monarch, Mary, Queen of Scots, which would be followed by the re-instatement of the Catholic faith as the official religion. However, in reality these plots were supported by only a small number of individuals and they were easily dealt with by Walsingham. In many respects the Catholic threat was exaggerated, especially by the likes of Walsingham who wanted evidence to enable him to act against the Catholics.

Step 2: Provide context – use your knowledge to expand and develop the content of the source

Step 3: Authorship – develop the attribution to make a judgement upon the reliability and accuracy of the interpretation based upon what you know about the author

The author of the interpretation, Susan Doran, is a professional historian who lectures in history at a university. She is an expert in Tudor history and would have detailed knowledge of this period based upon many years of academic research. She is writing with the benefit of hindsight, and would have reached a judgement based on extensive evidence.

Step 4: Other interpretations – suggest other interpretations, commenting upon how and why they differ from the given interpretation

However, there are other interpretations of this issue. Extreme Protestants known as Puritans believed that the Religious Settlement had not gone far enough to eradicate Catholic practices and therefore saw any Catholic challenges as a serious threat. Their view has been taken up by historians with a Protestant leaning, some of whom have accepted the government propaganda saying that the threat posed by several Catholic plots such as the Ridolfi and Babington Plots posed a real and serious threat to Elizabeth and the country. They also emphasised the seriousness of the Northern Rebellion. Catholic historians may also offer an interpretation which differs from that put forward by Susan Doran. They may argue that a large percentage of the population was Catholic at heart and only accepted the 1559 Settlement because they feared the consequences of not doing so. They were hoping Elizabeth's reign would be short.

Step 5: Conclusion – provide a reasoned judgement upon the validity of the interpretation given, weighed up against other interpretations

The view of Susan Doran is that of a specialist historian who has written a very detailed study called *Elizabeth I and Religion* about one aspect of the queen's reign. However, the quotation is rather short and its content is generalised, lacking full context. Such a view would be challenged by historians writing from a different perspective, such as the viewpoint of extreme Protestants which might concentrate more upon particular issues such as the threat posed by Mary, Queen of Scots or a particular plot and not explore the attitudes of the population as a whole. Alternatively Catholic historians might argue that they posed no threat and that Walsingham and his secret service deliberately exaggerated the influence of Mary, Queen of Scots, in order to take action against them. Susan Doran's interpretation should therefore be viewed as part the wider historical debate which includes a range of differing viewpoints.

Now you try the following question.

How far do you agree with this interpretation of William Cecil's position in Elizabeth's government? [*In your answer you should refer to how and why interpretations of this issue differ. Use your own knowledge and understanding of the wider historical debate over this issue to reach a well-supported judgement.*]

Interpretation: Stephen Alford, a university lecturer and Tudor specialist, writing in his biography of Cecil called: *Burghley William Cecil at the Court of Elizabeth I*, published in 2008

He [William Cecil] was everywhere and everything in Elizabethan government. He controlled the machinery of power. He ran the royal secretariat and chaired meetings of the Privy Council. He advised the queen daily and read every piece of paper that was sent to her. With ready access to Elizabeth in her private rooms and a mastery of the government machine, he saw and heard all that went on in court.

Depression, War
and Recovery,
1930–1951

1 The coming of the Depression

Key question: What were the main causes of the Depression?

On 29 October 1929, Wall Street, the US stock exchange, collapsed. Hundreds of thousands of people lost their life savings. Banks collapsed because loans were not repaid. Businesses went bust as people stopped buying goods and the Great Depression began, causing very high unemployment. The USA could no longer afford to lend money to European countries and recalled some of its earlier loans. Consequently, economic depression soon hit the United Kingdom and the rest of Europe because of their over-dependence on the USA.

It is easy to blame the economic depression that Britain experienced in the early 1930s on the impact of the Wall Street Crash in 1929. It played an important role in the timing of the depression in Britain, however, other underlying factors also contributed to the Depression.

In the 1920s, Britain was full of contrasts. While southern England and the Midlands saw growing prosperity, for many areas of Britain it was a time of despair and disillusionment. The population living in the countryside was declining as farming became more mechanised, and as prices for farm goods fell so too did rural incomes. In parts of Britain that had older industrial communities – the north and north-east of England and South Wales – life for many consisted of poor living conditions, illness, disease and a lower life expectancy.

It is against this background that the consequences of the Wall Street Crash need to be seen in order to fully understand why Britain experienced a Depression in the early 1930s. When the Crash happened, it added further economic problems to a country that was already economically unstable.

Reasons for the decline of traditional industry in Britain

Britain was the first industrial nation. Its textile, coal, and iron and steel industries benefited enormously from the lack of competition from other countries, and profited from being able to sell all over the world. However, as the nineteenth century progressed, other countries not only copied Britain's industrial development, but started to move ahead as they developed new methods of production and competed with Britain for markets. By the 1920s, Britain had major economic rivals in the USA, Japan and, despite the effects of the First World War, even Germany. This meant that Britain was experiencing economic problems before the Wall Street Crash happened.

Competition from abroad

Much of British industry in the early twentieth century had developed around the coalfields of the North because they depended upon steam power, which the coalfields powered. These old industries mostly produced raw materials or heavy goods, such as ships, textiles (cotton and wool), coal, iron and steel.

The main problem affecting the old industries at this time was that they depended on exports. The coal, iron and steel, shipbuilding and textiles industries were only profitable if they could sell to worldwide markets. From the early 1920s, British industry faced more and more competition from abroad. Often the foreign competitors were much bigger than their British counterparts, so they could produce goods at a price that the small British companies, such as Palmers shipyard in Jarrow, could not compete with.

New markets

Finding new markets to buy British goods was proving difficult, and the situation was made worse by the policies of successive British governments. They followed a policy of free trade in the 1920s, which allowed foreign goods to come into Britain freely. Conversely, British companies that exported goods often had to pay import duties to foreign governments.

The worst hit industry of all was shipbuilding. If no one was buying or selling anything, then no new ships were needed to transport goods around the world. In 1930, British shipbuilders built 1,400,000 tonnes of shipping. In 1933 the figure had fallen to 133,000 tonnes. Unemployment spread from shipbuilding to steelmaking and coalmining.

Obsolete methods

During the 1920s in the USA, new methods of production were seen in many of its industries. Mass-production was pioneered in the production of the motor car and this was copied in many other consumer type industries emerging in the USA. This was not the case in many of Britain's major industries. They were slow to move to new, quicker and more efficient methods of production, and at the same time national resources were not switched quickly enough to new emerging industries such as chemicals, rayon and automobiles.

The impact of the three factors explained above on Britain's major industries by the 1920s can be seen in Table 1.1. The impact of the Wall Street Crash only added to the decline of industry (see page 118).

Coal	Iron and steel
Coal could be produced much more cheaply abroad. In the mid-1920s coal could be produced in the USA for 65p a tonne compared to £1.56 a tonne in Britain. British coal was more expensive because it was more difficult to mine. Mines had not invested in up-to-date machinery and the industry was run by coalmine owners who, in most cases, did not want to invest in modernisation. This was particularly true in relation to the mining industry in South Wales. Once the home of the raw materials of Britain's Industrial Revolution, by the 1920s and early 1930s the industry was in a poor way. It had lost European markets because Germany was making some of its reparations payments (cost of the First World War) to countries in coal. The French favoured buying coal from the USA rather than Britain, and this meant that demand for coal from the Welsh coalfields had dropped significantly. Also, investment in the coal industry was stagnant, meaning that modern mining methods had not been introduced like in competitor countries. This resulted in unemployment in Swansea and Merthyr Tydfil reaching 25 per cent, and as high as 80 per cent in Dowlais.	The iron and steel industry suffered for several reasons. There was far less demand for ships and armaments in the years after the First World War. Competitors such as the USA and Japan regularly undercut British prices and their steel-making plants were generally larger, more efficient and modernised than those in Britain. The steel industry in South Wales was particularly ill-equipped to cope with the pressures of changing markets and new competitors. It faced stern competition from both the USA and Germany, whose steel-making plants were more technologically advanced and more efficient. In 1929, steel making ceased completely at Ebbw Vale, and in 1930 a major part of the steel works at Dowlais closed leaving 3,000 steel workers unemployed.
Textiles	**Shipbuilding**
Shipbuilding declined more rapidly than other industries. There was a fall in world trade in the years after the First World War. This meant less need for ships. International disarmament meant a fall in demand for warships. Moreover, foreign countries such as Japan and the USA could produce ships much more cheaply than Britain.	The market for textiles, such as wool and cotton, declined as man-made fibres, invented in the 1920s, soon became popular. When man-made fibres were mixed with cotton and wool they produced clothes that were more hardwearing and easier to wash. British textile industries also faced increasing competition from Japan and the USA during the 1920s. Both of these countries had developed their own industries during the First World War. So-called 'safe' home markets became vulnerable to foreign competition, particularly Lancashire which could not compete with cheaper cotton produced in India.

▲ Table 1.1: The impact of competition, new markets and obsolete methods on British industry

The impact of the Wall Street Crash and its effects on industry in Britain

It was famously said at the time of the Wall Street Crash that 'when America sneezes the whole world catches a cold', implying that whatever happened in the American economy would be replicated elsewhere (see Source A). Many countries around the world did indeed 'catch a cold', and Britain was no exception.

The following economic impacts were seen in Britain:

- Business confidence fell dramatically and international trade declined.
- Between 1929 and 1931 exports from Britain fell by a half.
- Britain's balance of trade (the relationship between exports and imports) was badly affected and by 1931, it had a trade deficit of £114 million, compared to a trade surplus of £104 million in 1928.
- The slump in exports affected those industries also supplying the home domestic market.
- There was a rapid growth in unemployment and by the middle of 1930, it had reached 2 million unemployed, and continued to rise to over 3 million by 1932.

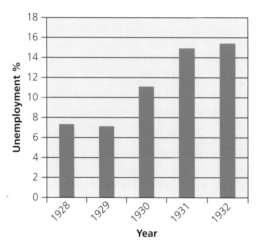

◀ Figure 1.1 Unemployment in Britain 1928–32

Source A: A cartoon about ▶ the USA's economy and its impact on the world

ACTIVITY ?

What can you learn from Figure 1.1 about unemployment in the years 1928 to 1932?

Source B: From *The Road to Wigan Pier* written by George Orwell, published in 1937. Orwell was a left-wing novelist and political writer

When you see the unemployment figures quoted at two millions, it is fatally easy to take this as meaning that two million people are out of work and the rest of the population are comparatively comfortable. I admit that till recently I was in the habit of doing so myself. I used to calculate that if you put the registered unemployed at around two millions and threw in the destitute and those who for one reason and another were not registered, you might take the number of unfed people in England as being, at the very most, five millions. This is an enormous under-estimate. I think it is nearer six millions.

Source C: From *Brynmawr: A study of a distressed area* written by Hilda Jennings and based on the results of a social survey. Published in 1934

While some of the effects of unemployment are general, individual men and their families of course react in different ways, and out of some six hundred families normally dependent upon unemployment benefit probably few have precisely the same attitude to life and circumstances. One man will approach the Exchange with impatience and bitterness at his dependence and impotency to help himself; one in a mood of growing apathy; one in a growing feeling of the need for change in the economic and social system.

Practice question

What can be learnt from Sources B and C about the impact of the Depression on Britain? *(For guidance, see pages 190–191.)*

ACTIVITY

In groups, use the information and the sources on pages 118–119 to decide what the most important cause of Britain experiencing the Great Depression in the early 1930s was:

- competition from abroad
- obsolete industrial methods
- the Wall Street Crash.

Present your ideas and judgement to the rest of class.

Conclusion: What were the main causes of the Depression?

The Depression was not caused by only one cause and one event. It was multi-causal and triggered by events both in Britain and abroad. The consequences of being one of the first industrial nations included great benefit but also brought with it competition from other countries. By the 1920s, Britain was being overtaken economically and industrially by those countries. Britain's industries were no longer leading the world and found competition difficult. The First World War had been costly and added an extra burden to Britain's economic problems. These issues then combined with an event in the USA – the Wall Street Crash – that had economic repercussions around the world, and as a consequence Britain suffered a major economic depression in the 1930s.

2 Life during the Depression

The impact of the Depression created a certain impression of Britain in the 1930s, not only at the time, but also in the decades that followed. That impression focused on the negative rather than the positive. The 1930s were labelled as 'the black years', 'the devil's decade' and 'the hungry thirties'. It was also characterised as a decade of mass unemployment, dole queues and hunger marches. However, the negative impact of the Depression was not evenly spread. During the 1930s, many people enjoyed longer holidays, shorter working hours and higher real wages. They owned motor cars, listened to the radio and went to the cinema. They went to dancehalls, cafés and cocktail bars. Understanding this contrast is important when reaching judgements about what life was like during the Depression, and how people coped with the challenges that the Depression years presented to them.

The dole and the means test

In 1920, the government introduced the Unemployment Insurance Act 1920. This created a system of payments for unemployed workers. The aim was to give workers who became unemployed some financial support while they found new employment. It provided 39 weeks of benefits to those who were registered as unemployed. The system became more commonly known as 'the dole' (meaning 'one's allotted portion') and those who received it were often referred to as being 'on the dole'. When the Depression hit Britain some traditional economists believed that the cost of providing this benefit was too great, and as unemployment grew, the cost would be even greater. They also believed that the benefit would prevent the economy recovering properly as workers would not return to work when they had become used to the 'dole'. So, they suggested that the 'dole' should be cut by at least 10 per cent. The issue of cut or not then split the minsters in the Labour government, and the Prime Minister, Ramsey MacDonald, resigned. He then joined the Conservatives and Liberals in a coalition government. This government became known as the National Government.

The introduction of the means test

In 1931, the National Government introduced one of the most hated measures of the period, the means test. This was designed to control and reduce the amount of dole that was paid. The policy showed little or no understanding of the plight of the families of the long-term unemployed and those increasingly affected by the Depression. For those families, especially in the depressed areas, life was very hard. There was a dramatic fall in living standards. Moreover, long-term unemployment often had negative psychological effects on the unemployed.

The means test meant that after six months on unemployment benefit, people went on to uncovenanted benefit. This continued to be known as the 'dole'. However, before they could receive the dole, people had to have their houses inspected to check all their possessions and their savings – that is, go through a means test. The tests were carried out by inspectors from the local Public Assistance Committees (PACs), which had been set up in 1930. Families could be forced to sell possessions, such as furniture, if they wanted to receive the dole. If a family had any other sources of income, such as a part-time job, or the pension of an elderly relative, deductions were made from the weekly payments. The amount paid was based on the income of the whole family with the maximum payment varying from area to area. The average maximum for a family of two adults and three children was fixed at £1.46 per week, but many were paid less because of earnings from other members of the family. In 1936, the maximum sum was raised to £1.80 per week but it was still well below the average wage of £3.

Reactions to the means test

The means test was very unpopular for several reasons:
- Many claimed that it was more about the government trying to save money than helping the unemployed.
- People hated having an inspector go through all of their belongings and then force them to sell some of them.
- People did not like having to make relatives go to live somewhere else if they wanted to receive the full amount each week.
- It was humiliating for families to have to reveal their earnings, savings and the value of possessions.

- If the officials thought that there was enough money in the house, they would stop the dole.
- Some local authorities applied the means test very harshly, while others, such as those in County Durham, refused to carry it out.
- The means test was a great strain on family life, especially if, say, an older child (who was working) was forced to pay more towards family funds.

There were many protests against the means test, the most important of which were hunger marches. These were columns of unemployed men who marched across the country trying to bring attention to their plight. The marches began in the autumn of 1931. By the end of 1931 there had been protest marches against the means test in more than 30 towns. However, not all these marches were peaceful. In 1932, there were clashes with the police in Rochdale and Belfast where two demonstrators were killed. The National Unemployed Workers' Movement (NUWM) was set up to try to put pressure on the government. It organised a march on London in October 1932, with marchers attempting to present a petition to Parliament but they were stopped by the police.

Source A: From *The Road to Wigan Pier*, written by George Orwell in 1937

The means test breaks up families. An old age pensioner would usually live with one of his children. Under the means test, he counts as a 'lodger' and his children's dole will be cut.

Source B: An unemployed man describes the effects of the means test on his life in 1933

My wife obtained a job as a house-to-house saleswoman, and was able to earn a few shillings to supplement our dole income. This strained our relationship. It was a burden on her and constant bickerings over money matters, usually culminating in threats to leave from both of us. The final blow came when the means test was put into operation. Eventually, after the most heart-breaking period of my life, both my wife and son, who had just begun to earn a few shillings, told me to get out, as I was living on them and taking the food they needed.

ACTIVITIES ?

1 In groups, decide on the most important reason for why the means test was so hated. Present your ideas to the rest of the class.

2 Study Sources A and B. How far do these sources agree about the effects of the means test? Explain your answer, referring to the sources.

3 Work in pairs. Imagine you had to advertise the protest march against the means test shown in Source C. Produce a poster criticising the means test and encouraging people to take part in the march.

Practice questions

1 To what extent does Source B accurately explain the effects of the means test? (*For guidance, see pages 192–193.*)

2 Why was the introduction of the means test and the dole significant during the 1930s? (*For guidance, see page 194.*)

◄ Source C: A photograph of thousands of demonstrators arriving in London's Hyde Park from all parts of Britain in a protest against the means test, organised by the National Unemployed Workers' Movement, 1932

Hunger marches

By the time of the Depression in Britain, 'hunger marches' had become a traditional way for working people to express their concerns about their living and working conditions to those who governed them. The first hunger march took place in 1905. This type of protest drew the wider public attention to the sufferings of people who lived in areas that politicians seemed to ignore. However, regardless of whether the Prime Minister was Conservative, Labour or National Government they invariably refused to meet with the leaders of the hunger marches. This has led some commentators and historians to question whether or not this form of protest achieved anything.

The Jarrow March

In 1936, the most famous hunger march originated in Jarrow, in the north-east of England, and went to London. It became known as the Jarrow Crusade. It captured the imagination of many people at the time and has continued to capture the imagination of people since.

Causes of the hunger march

Jarrow was the worst affected town during the Depression. Most people in the town were either employed by or dependent on one firm, Palmers shipyard, for their livelihood. The shipyard began to decline after the First World War. By the early 1930s, orders had dried up completely. Unemployment rose from 3,245 in 1929 to 7,178 in 1933.

Palmers also suffered from another problem. By the 1930s the yard was too small for the type of ships that were being built. The *Queen Elizabeth* and *Queen Mary*, which were launched in the 1930s, were over 80,000 tonnes. Palmers could not match that. The end came in 1934, when a group of shipyard owners set up a company called National Shipbuilders' Securities. They decided to buy up smaller yards and then scrap them. Palmers was one of the first to go. It was announced that no ships would be built there for 40 years. The closure of the yard had a terrible effect on Jarrow with unemployment reaching 80 per cent.

Normal life almost ceased to exist as families tried to find any way they could to survive. The death rates and infant mortality rates in Jarrow were monitored by the Jarrow Public Health Committee and published. The figures for Jarrow were very high, showing that malnutrition and poor health were widespread in the town (see Table 2.1). Families were totally dependent upon support from the local community or the government. Some people responded by suggesting that more drastic action needed to be taken in order to make people fully aware of what was happening in Jarrow (see Source E).

Source D: David Riley, the organiser of the Jarrow March, speaking in 1936

I think we should get down to London with a couple of bombs in our pockets. These people do not realise that there are people living in Jarrow today in conditions in which a respectable farmer would not keep pigs. We must do something outrageous which will make the country sit up.

Death rates per 1,000 of population			
	1919	1931	1936
Jarrow	20	15	15
National average	13	10	9
Infant mortality – deaths (0–1 year) per 1,000 of population			
	1919	1931	1936
Jarrow	151	159	114
National average	58	62	57

▲ Table 2.1: Death rates and infant mortality rates 1919–36

The people of Jarrow sent a number of deputations to the Board of Trade in London. They got nowhere. In 1936, the last deputation met the President of the Board of Trade, a cabinet minister who told them to go back to Jarrow and work out their own salvation. In 1936, Jarrow made one last effort. A march was organised by the people of the town from Jarrow to London. The object was to attract attention to the plight of the town by taking a petition all the way to parliament.

However, the government was very suspicious of hunger marchers similar to the one from Jarrow. This was because one of the leaders of previous hunger marches, Will Hannington, was a communist, which alarmed the authorities, and the marches had often led to clashes with the police. Stanley Baldwin, the Prime Minister, was especially unsympathetic towards hunger marches. Moreover, the Trades Union Congress (TUC) and the Labour Party did not support these marches, believing they only brought bad publicity for the Labour movement and the plight of the unemployed. Additionally, the Jarrow Crusade was one of the few hunger marches of the 1930s not run by the National Unemployed Workers' Movement (NUWM). The NUWM opposed the march for two reasons:

■ The Jarrow marchers refused to co-operate with a much larger march organised by the NUWM in which several groups were to converge on London at the same time.
■ The NUWM objected to the non-political nature of the Jarrow March. The Jarrow marchers did not favour any of the political parties with both Labour and Conservative party officials helping with its organisation.

▲ Source F: A life-sized statue entitled *The Spirit of Jarrow,* created in 2001 to commemorate the 65th anniversary of the Jarrow Crusade

Source E: From an account written by the mayor of Jarrow in 1936

A campaign was started by the Labour Party to send a petition. Then it was decided to march with the petition. I opposed the decision. There were hunger marches going on all over and I didn't want to embarrass and put down the men. I eventually had to agree, and I marched to Darlington with some of the men. I managed to get time off from Spiller's in Newcastle. Communists wanted to join us on the march, but we wouldn't let them.

What happened during the Jarrow March?

The Jarrow March was carefully planned and prepared and the final route decided. Two hundred men marched from Jarrow to London, led by the mayor, the MP Ellen Wilkinson and town councillors. They marched in step in their best clothes so that they would have the greatest possible impact on the people that they passed. The men were turned out as smartly as possible and were clean-shaven. It took the marchers eight months. They covered over 450 kilometres in 22 stages (see Figure 2.1).

As the marchers made their way south, they were completely surprised by the reception that they received. Everywhere they went they received great support and sympathy. They were put up in church halls and given free meals and their shoes were repaired free of charge. The Bishop of Ripon spoke out in their support and newspapers published accounts of their progress. But when they arrived in London, there was little support or sympathy from members of the government.

> **Source G: Ritchie Calder, a journalist who covered the march**
>
> *In one family here were four volunteers from whom only one could go. And the brothers gave the trousers and jacket and the father gave the boots and the uncle gave the raincoat ... the family marched with one man.*

> **Source H: From a memo by the Special Branch of the Metropolitan Police, 1936**
>
> *The promoters of the match from Jarrow to London have now made definite arrangements for 200 marchers to take the road on the 5 October. The plans are being carried out by Miss Ellen Wilkinson MP, a former communist.*

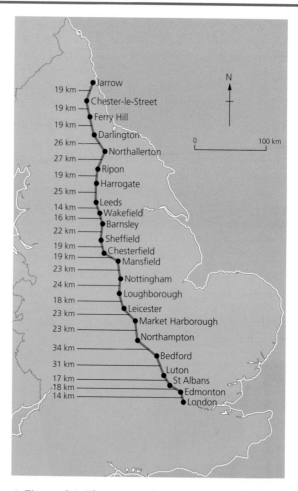

▲ Figure 2.1: The route taken by the marchers on the Jarrow Crusade

> ## Practice question
>
> What can be learnt from Sources G and H about the preparations for the Jarrow March? *(For guidance, see pages 190–191.)*

▲ Source I: Jarrow marchers with Ellen Wilkinson at the front

▲ Source J: Jarrow marchers stopping for a meal near Bedford

What did the Jarrow March achieve?

There is much debate over the achievements of the Jarrow March. On the one hand, it has been seen as providing much needed publicity for the plight of the unemployed in general, and Jarrow in particular. On the other hand, some have argued that little was actually achieved. The achievements and limitations are summarised in Figure 2.2.

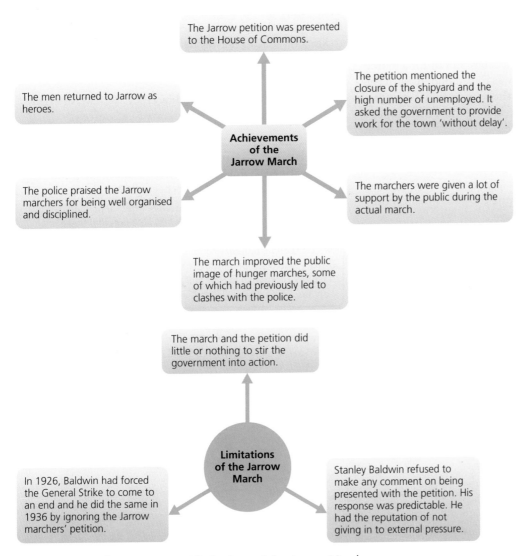

▲ Figure 2.2: Achievements and limitations of the Jarrow March

> **Interpretation 1: From the memories of the Jarrow March by Kathleen Haigh, who was interviewed for Radio Newcastle in October, 2008**
>
> *My uncle, Jimmy McCauley, was the second last of the marchers to die. He said he wore out many pairs of shoes on the match and that all of the marchers looked forward to being fed by the people in whichever town they arrived! In retrospect, he believed that the march was in vain because nothing happened afterwards to bring jobs to the town. The legacy which does remain is that Jarrow has found its place in history thanks to their brave efforts.*

Practice question

Read Interpretation 1. How far do you agree with this interpretation of the outcome of the Jarrow hunger march? *(For guidance, see pages 196–197.)*

Hunger marches from the Rhondda valley

As well as protests from the north-east of England there was also protests from South Wales, particularly from the Rhondda, an area of 16 mining communities built around the River Rhondda (see Figure 2.3). Even before the Depression started, this area suffered economic problems.

On Sunday 18 September 1927, at the Red Sunday in Rhondda valley demonstration, a call went out for a march to be organised. Its destination was to be London, with the purpose of raising awareness of the economic difficulties faced in the Rhondda area. However, it gained little support and the march did not take place.

As the Depression deepened, unemployment and its consequences hit South Wales and the Rhondda valley particularly hard. People returned to the idea of protest and hunger marches as a way of making the government more aware of the issues.

On 14 October 1932, a nationwide hunger march began with the aim of converging on London. A total of 2,500 marchers set off from different points around Britain. From South Wales 375 marchers set off from the Rhondda area. The intention was to present a petition to parliament demanding the abolition of the means test and Anomalies Act, the ending of cuts to social services, and the ending of the 10 per cent reduction in unemployment benefits. These marches concerned the government so much that they deployed spies, informers and the Metropolitan Police to keep a watchful eye on their movements. Force was also used to confiscate the petitions so that the marchers could not deliver them to parliament.

In 1935, the MP for the Rhondda valley, W.H. Mainwaring, wrote a letter to the Home Secretary (see Source J).

> **Source K:** From a letter written in 1935 by W.H. Mainwaring MP. Published in *Wales between the Wars* edited by G.E. Jones and T. Herberts (1988)
>
> *The Minister, perhaps, can make some attempt to imagine the depth of feeling in the Rhondda when I tell him that there is a total population of less than 140,000 and a week ago yesterday, 100,000 people demonstrated there. There was nobody in that district who was not demonstrating except those who were in hospital. I only wish to God that the same thing would happen in London.*

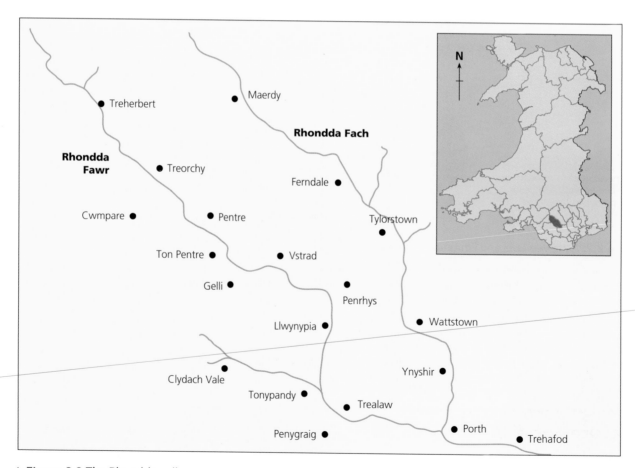

▲ Figure 2.3 The Rhondda valley

However, rather surprisingly, an unsympathetic pamphlet appeared in the *New Statesman and Nation* magazine in 1935 (see Source L). The tone of the pamphlet showed little sympathy for the plight of the unemployed in South Wales and the economic hardships they were suffering.

> **Source L:** From the pamphlet 'What's Wrong with Wales' which appeared in the *New Statesman and Nation* magazine in 1935
>
> *So many remedies have been tried in vain. South Wales has become a bore. It is like a crying babe in the hands of an ignorant mother. It is smacked by one Government Department and kissed by another. Why won't it go to sleep like Dorsetshire?*

Even the new monarch, King Edward VIII, reportedly said while on a tour of Wales in 1936 'something must be done', regarding the conditions that he witnessed when talking to unemployed miners and their families. Some residents of Pontypool had a letter they had written to the King published in the *Western Mail*, a newspaper with a predominantly South Wales readership (see Source M).

> **Source M:** From a letter published in the *Western Mail* in 1936
>
> *Today you will be visiting the towns and villages of our valleys, and a valley blighted by the dead hand of poverty. We regret that your tour has been planned in such a way that the terrible effects of this poverty will not be seen.*

Finally, in October 1936, a hunger march was organised from South Wales. It numbered 504 marchers and had the backing of the Labour Party, which had not been the case with other such marches. Yet again the government kept a close eye on the march by using spies and informants, but did not use the Metropolitan Police Force this time. It has been suggested that the backing given to this march by the Labour Party gave the march an air of credibility, and the government did not want the police involved. The march achieved little.

ACTIVITY ?

In pairs, use the information and sources on pages 126–127 and prepare two arguments about the South Wales and Rhondda hunger marches: one that focuses on the achievements and one on the failures. Compare your arguments with other pairs in the class.

Practice activity

Read Interpretation 2. How far do you agree with this interpretation of the impact that hunger marches had in the 1930s? (For guidance, see pages 196–197.)

Interpretation 2: From *English History 1914–45* written by A.J.P. Taylor and published in 1965

Select bands of unemployed from the depressed areas marched on London where they demonstrated to little purpose. Their progress through the country, however, was a propaganda stroke of great effect. The hunger marchers displayed the failure of capitalism. Middle-class people felt the call of conscience. They set up soup kitchens for the marchers and accommodated them in local schools.

◄ **Source N:** The Rhondda valley hunger marchers holding a Jarrow Crusade banner

'Making ends meet' and 'self-help'

In the areas of Britain where the old industries (see Chapter 1, pages 116–117) had grown, such as the north-east of England, South Wales and Central Scotland, the Depression led to very high levels of unemployment, sometimes over 50 per cent, and it lasted for a long time. This long-term unemployment often led to a fall in the standard of living and health of the families of those out of work.

Poverty and diet

Seebohm Rowntree, a social researcher and son of the chocolate manufacturer Joseph Rowntree, carried out a survey of York at the beginning of the twentieth century and found that 30 per cent of people in York lived below the poverty line. In 1936, Rowntree completed a second survey and found this percentage had remained the same. Moreover, his findings revealed that 72 per cent of unemployed workers lived below the poverty line. More evidence of hardship is shown in a survey of Stockton-on-Tees in the early 1930s. This compared the average weekly income of a family in which the wage earner was out of work with that of a family in which the wage earner was in work. The average weekly income of an unemployed family was £1.46. For an employed family the average income was £2.57.

Item	Weekly spending
Rent	43p
Coal	17.5p
Gas	12.5p
Union and insurance subscription	16p
Savings club	5p
Meat	10p
Milk	12.5p
Bread	23.5p
Margarine	10p
Jam	4p
Clog-irons (Shaped metal nailed under a shoe's heel to make the sole last longer)	2.5p
Total	£1.56.5

▲ Table 2.2: The weekly spending of the family of an unemployed textile worker in Lancashire in 1931. Their weekly dole payment was £1.59

As a consequence of this, families of the unemployed had less to spend and had to make whatever savings they could. They lived by 'making ends meet', a term originally used when checking income against expenditure, but in this context it meant that families could only spend what money they now had. One way was to buy cheaper food, but cheaper food could lead to malnutrition. The same survey in Stockton-on-Tees showed that a poor family was likely to spend only 3 shillings (15p) a head on food per week, while a richer family would spend at least 6 shillings (30p).

In 1936, John Boyd Orr published the results of a survey into the diet and health of the British people. He concluded that 4.5 million people had a diet that was completely inadequate in all respects. A further 5 million people suffered from some form of deficiency. Overall he believed that one tenth of the population was seriously undernourished. This percentage included one fifth of all children. Families of the unemployed ate a lot of bread, margarine, potato, sugar and tea but little meat, fresh fruit, vegetables and milk. The diets of wives and mothers were most inadequate as they sacrificed their own needs for those of their husbands and children.

Interpretation 3: From a television interview with Frank Cousins, a trade union leader, in 1966

I happened to be in a transport café on the Great North Road, when a young couple came in with a child in a nearly broken-down pram. They were walking from South Shields (near Newcastle) to London because the man understood he could get a job. They sat down and fed the baby with water. They lifted the baby's dress up. She was wearing a newspaper nappy. They took it off and sort of wiped the baby's bottom with the nappy they'd taken off and then picked up another newspaper and put than on for another nappy. I immediately thought someone ought to do something about this situation.

Practice question

Why was 'making ends meet' significant during the 1930s? *(For guidance, see page 194.)*

ACTIVITY ?

Try to convert the weekly pending figures into today's money. The website http://gwydir.demon.co.uk/jo/units/money.htm can help.

Women

'Making ends meet' probably had the biggest impact on the women in unemployed families. Women in work were generally the first to be laid off, especially in the cotton industry. In contrast, the number of women in domestic service went up in the 1930s, as women looked for any chance of finding work so that they could 'make ends meet'. In addition, National Insurance usually only covered the worker, which would normally be the man. That meant that women and children were often not covered for medical treatment. They would have to pay for visits to the doctor and for any medicine. Furthermore, many women sacrificed themselves to feed their children or pay for their medical treatment rather than their own. Government statistics showed that from 1931 to 1935 the death rate for women aged 15 to 35 was more than twice as high in some areas of high unemployment as it was in other areas.

Children

A major consequence of 'making ends meet' was a poor diet which particularly led to the higher infant mortality rate and poorer health of children in depressed areas. For example, in the south-east of England, in 1935, the infant death rate was 42 per 1,000 live births. In Northumberland and Durham it was 76. As well as the difference in the death rate in different regions, there was also a difference between rich and poor. For example, in the 1930s, for every three children from richer families who died young, there were eight children from poorer families. Local medical officers of health frequently reported on the poor health of districts in the depressed areas. In 1933, an investigation in Newcastle revealed that one in three schoolchildren were physically unfit because of poor health. Comparisons with children from richer families showed that the poor were ten times more likely to catch bronchitis, eight times more likely to catch pneumonia and five times more likely to suffer from rickets.

Self-help

Another way of dealing with the consequences of the Depression was 'self-help'. There were many ways in which unemployed people helped themselves, others and their communities. 'Self-help' could be informal, communal or familial.

- Women operated credit mechanisms for pawning goods, paying rent, buying food and clothing, borrowing money.
- Neighbours rallied around during times of crisis, for example child birth, intrusion by rent collectors or the police.
- Communities would come down harshly on those broke its unwritten conventions.

Other organisations also attempted to 'help' the unemployed to 'help' themselves. In many parts of the country, clubs for the unemployed were set up, often initiated by the Church and Mayors' funds (money put aside by the mayor of a local authority to use to support unemployed people). The clubs were often located in a church hall and became a frequently used meeting point. In 1930, a national conference was held by the British Association of Residential Settlements and the YMCA to promote the idea of effective use of the 'leisure' time the unemployed had until they could return to work. In 1932, the British Institute of Adult Education called a conference that led to the establishment of the Central Advisory Council for Unemployed Workers. This Council subsequently received funds from the newly appointed Commissioners for Special Areas (see page 134) which then led to an increase in educational programmes for the unemployed. Also, the British Library organised a National Book Appeal for the unemployed.

> ### Practice question
>
> Why was 'making ends meet' and 'self-help' significant during the Depression? *(For guidance, see page 194.)*

▲ Source O: Men reading newspapers in an unemployment club, 1936

Emigration from Wales

During the Industrial Revolution, Wales had attracted thousands of immigrants who found work in the coal, iron and steel industries. However, this was not to last. In the years that followed the First World War, immigration numbers started to fall and by the time the Depression hit, the reverse was happening; people were emigrating from Wales in massive numbers and with significant effects. Between 1921 and 1938, approximately 440,000 people left Wales to find work and a better life elsewhere. The valleys of Glamorgan and Monmouthshire in South Wales saw migration on a massive scale, with approximately 85 per cent of the people who were leaving Wales coming from those areas. In Pembroke Dock one quarter of the population (3,500) had left by1933. The population of the Rhondda valley fell by approximately 18 per cent in the 1930s. Merthyr Tydfil also saw a large drop in its population.

Some of these migrants looked to other countries for a new start. Others did not want to leave Britain but decided to look for work in other, more potentially prosperous areas around the world. Welsh communities were established in the USA, Canada, Australia, New Zealand and South America. The work opportunities these places offered, even though some of these places had been affected by world-wide depression, seemed more attractive that what was left in Wales.

In Britain, the government, through the Ministry of Labour, set up a scheme to help unemployed Welsh workers and their families. The new light engineering and car manufacturing areas of the Midlands saw an influx of Welsh people who were encouraged to settle in towns such as Coventry. Similarly, towns such as Oxford and Slough also saw an increase in Welsh settlers. The Morris Motor company in Cowley (Oxfordshire) became one of the biggest employers of Welsh migrants.

One side effect of this migration was a significant impact on Welsh language and culture (see Interpretation 4).

Practice question

Explain the connections between any THREE of the following:
- the Depression
- hunger marches
- 'making ends meet'
- self-help.

(For guidance, see page 195.)

ACTIVITIES ?

1 Why do people emigrate during times of economic hardship?

2 What can you learn from Source P about the work done by emigrating Welsh workers?

▲ **Source P:** Morris Cowley cars on the assembly line at the Cowley works, Oxford, 1930

The importance of radio and cinema

Both radio and cinema offered people the opportunity to escape their daily lives whether or not they had been badly affected by the Depression.

Radio

Radio provided a distraction from the harsh reality of Depression life as well as making the world seem smaller. By 1939, there were 9 million registered radios in houses across Britain. The cost of a radio licence was 15s (35p). The electrical department store Currys sold radios, with two or three valves, for £1 to £3. The store even had a hire purchase agreement of between one and two shillings per week for those who could not afford to buy a radio outright. By 1939, nearly 75 per cent of British families owned a radio. The BBC broadcast schools programmes, plays, popular music and comedy. Regular reports from around the British Empire imparted news and information. Sport was also featured on the radio. In 1936, on Boxing Day, the first ever radio broadcast was made of a Swansea Town FC football game played against Aston Villa.

▲ Source Q: Women workers at Perivale Philco radio factory, Middlesex, 20 April 1936

Cinema

Despite the Depression, cinema-going remained as popular in the 1930s as it was during the 1920s. In 1927, for the first time films had sound, and people heard Al Jolson talking in the feature film 'The Jazz Singer'. Consequently, cinema became even more popular. In 1934, Wales had over 320 cinemas, with over 20 in Cardiff alone. People could go and watch stars such as Clark Gable, Greta Garbo and Errol Flynn in the latest Hollywood blockbuster. Special Saturday matinees were offered to children for a penny entry. Young people met at the cinema and it became a place for couples to date.

In 1935, the first Welsh language 'talkie' was screened. Films such as 'How green was my valley' portrayed a romantic view of life in a typical mining community in South Wales, which was very different from the reality. By 1936, there were 1,000 million cinema admissions per year in the United Kingdom. In 1937, in Liverpool, it was estimated that 40 per cent of the city's population went to the cinema at least once a week. In the town of York it was estimated that almost half of the town's population went to its seven cinemas. Cinemas themselves became more luxurious in their décor, and for many people became 'dream palaces'. Even the names of cinemas, for example, The Empire, The Majestic, The Paramount, and The Royal, conjured an image that, for many, was very different to their daily experience.

▲ Source R: Boys standing outside the Ideal Cinema, Lambeth, c.1930. The silent film showing is *Don Q, Son of Zorro*

Practice question

Why were radio and cinema so significant during the 1930s in Britain? (For guidance, see page 194.)

ACTIVITY ?

What can you learn from Source R about the role of cinema in the 1930s?

Television

Television broadcasting, though still in its infancy in the 1930s, was beginning to get in on the act, however, even in the more prosperous south and south-east of Britain few people owned a television. Nevertheless, for the lucky few, watching live sporting events was possible from the comfort of their own home (see Source R).

Other forms of entertainment were impacted by the Depression and provided opportunity for people to escape their everyday experience.

Rugby

By the 1930s, rugby had become one the most popular games, particularly in Wales. Most villages had teams, particularly mining villages. Miners mixed with people from the so-called higher professions, for example, doctors, teachers and the clergy, in these amateur rugby teams. However, once the Depression hit many talented players went to the north of England where they could play in professional Rugby League teams and earn a living wage.

Association football

By the 1920s, association football was played extensively throughout Wales and England. Regarded by many as a working-class sport, it was labelled the 'people's game'. Thousands of supporters travelled the country to watch and support their teams. Many of these supporters travelled by train. When the Depression hit supporters travelling waned and this did not fully recover until 1937. However, during the 1930s many football clubs set record attendance figures. A game between Manchester City and Chelsea saw a crowd of over 80,000 in attendance, while Halifax Town FC regularly had attendances of over 30,000.

Boxing

Boxing was a sport that attracted working-class supporters as well as supporters from the wealthier classes who were prepared to bet large amounts of money on the outcome of a fight. In the 1930s, the best boxers were American and the heavyweight section was dominated by Joe Louis. In 1937, Tommy Farr, a former miner from the Rhondda, fought Louis and was paid £10,000 (the equivalent of approximately £500,000 today) for the fight. Despite taking Louis to the maximum fifteen round distance, Farr lost on points.

> **Practice question**
>
> Why was 'popular entertainment' important during the 1930s? *(For guidance, see page 194.)*

Source S: BBC TV's first broadcast of a football match – Arsenal versus Arsenal Reserves in September 1937

Growing light industry in parts of Britain

Not all areas of Britain were affected by the Depression in the same way. For many people the 1930s was a time of increasing prosperity. Those employed in newer industries, such as motor vehicles and electrical goods, especially in south-east England and the Midlands, often had a relatively good standard of living. Mass-production methods (first seen in the USA in the 1920s) were applied to the motor car industry. By 1938, the number of cars sold in Britain had risen to approximately 2 million. Mass-production lines needed workers to do aspects of the car assembly as the process moved from start to finish.

This type of work proved very attractive to workers who had lost their jobs during the Depression; however, far too many people had lost their jobs for the new industries to take them all. The new technology of the production line also required an efficient source of power – electricity. Electricity was clean, cheap and efficient and it began to replace coal as a main fuel supply. Electricity not only powered new industries, but by 1938, the number of consumers supplied with electricity to their homes had reached 9 million. The government tried to encourage these new industries with grants and by allowing land to be turned into industrial estates. Apart from the aircraft and chemical industries, the factories of these new light industries were smaller and employed fewer people. By 1939, the sale of consumer goods still only accounted for 15 per cent of the nation's total exports.

ACTIVITY ?

What can you learn from Source T about the use of electricity in the 1930s?

THE
HOUSE
YOU
WANT

▲ Source T: From a 1930s booklet on electricity at home

The Special Areas Acts

Practice question

What can be learnt from Sources U and V about the impact of the Special Areas Acts? *(For guidance, see pages 190–191.)*

ACTIVITIES ?

1 How reliable is Source U as evidence of the Special Areas Act being a success?

2 Study Source V. What was the purpose of this photograph? Use details from the photograph and your knowledge to explain your answer.

The worst hit areas of unemployment were north-east and north-west England, Clydeside, South Wales and Northern Ireland. These became known as the 'special areas'. In 1934, the government passed the special areas Act, which offered grants of £2 million to companies that would move to the special areas. Also, 44,000 workers were encouraged to move to other towns, and 30,000 unemployed men were put on retraining courses enabling them to learn new skills. In 1936, a further Special Areas Act was passed. This offered factories and businesses remission of rents, rates and payment of taxes of up to 100 per cent.

New industrial estates were created, the first of which was the Team Valley Trading Estate in Gateshead in 1938 (see Source U). However, unemployment numbers came down very slowly in those areas. By 1938, about £8,400,000 had been spent but only 121 new firms had been set up, creating 14,900 jobs. Small industrial estates could not replace the coalmining or shipbuilding industries. In addition, many companies in the newer industries were reluctant to move to the special areas. The general view about the Special Areas Act was that while they were well intentioned, in reality they did not achieve a great deal. Those in Parliament who opposed the government claimed that all the government was doing was a 'hollow gesture' towards those suffering the hardest aspects of the Depression. Although by 1938 unemployment in these special area had gone down, some have suggested that it was not the Acts that achieved this, but the migration of workers from these areas to more prosperous areas such as the Midlands and the south-east of England.

Source U: From the 'Third Report of the Commissioners for the Special Areas,' 1936

There is evidence that the work done and the measures initiated are proving helpful to the Special Areas and that their benefits will in many cases be increasingly felt. Nevertheless, it has to be admitted that there has been no appreciable reduction of the number of those unemployed ... My recommendation is that by means of state-provided inducements a determined attempt should be to attract industrialists to the Special Areas.

Source V: A photograph taken by the Special Areas Board of the Team Valley Trading Estate in Gateshead, 1938

The Treforest Industrial Estate

The Treforest Industrial Estate in South Wales was established in June 1936. It was a non-profit company whose aim was to provide some alternative forms of employment to the coal and steel industries, which had been hit hardest by the Depression. In 1937, three small factories were completed on the Estate, employing 69 people. The government invested in the Estate from 1939 to 1945. As a consequence the number of people working on the industrial Estate grew to 16,000.

▲ Source W: The site before the development of the Trading Estate showing the rural nature of the landscape, and then during development

ACTIVITIES ?

1 Why did the government create 'Special Areas' in the 1930s?

2 Compare the two photographs in Source V. Identify similarities and differences shown in them.

3 How successful where 'Special Areas' in dealing with the economic problems of the 1930s?

Contrast of old industrial regions with areas of greater employment

The Depression had a massive impact on Britain, both negative and positive, but those impacts were not evenly spread across the regions of Britain. Some observers at the time, and since, have suggested that during the Depression there were 'two Britains: the old and the new'. It was dependent on where you lived as to which one you experienced. It is very evident that areas like the north-east of England and South Wales had a very different experience of the Depression than the Midlands and the south-east. New investment, new housing, new roads and rail links significantly changed some areas of the country, while other areas languished in poverty.

> **Interpretation 5:** From *Rebirth of a Nation: Wales 1880–1980* written by historian Kenneth O. Morgan and published in 1981
>
> *Some historians of late have tended to paint a more cheerful picture of the thirties than once used to be prevalent. No doubt amongst the owner-occupiers of London, the home counties, and the east Midlands, with their cars, their housing estates, their thriving new light industries based on consumer durables, hire purchase and the newer technologies, the thirties were not such a bad time in which to live. But in South Wales, this verdict cannot possibly be accepted. The thirties there were a time a whole society was crucified by mass-unemployment and near-starvation.*

Practice questions

1 Read Interpretation 5. How far do you agree with this interpretation of the impact of the Depression on people in Britain? *(For guidance, see pages 196–197.)*
2 Explain connections between any THREE of the following:
   ● growing new light industry
   ● Special Areas Acts
   ● Treforest Industrial Estate
   ● old, heavy industrial regions.
   (For guidance, see page 195.)

ACTIVITIES

1 Use the information and sources from Chapter 2 to create a list of the negative and positive effects of what life was like during the Depression in the 1930s.
2 Compare your list with other students in your class.

Conclusion: How were people able to cope with the challenges of the Depression years?

The economic depression of the 1930s, has gone down in the history of Britain as one of the worst economic depressions ever experienced. As you have seen from the information and sources in this chapter it was a very difficult time for many people to experience, and they coped in a variety of ways, some successful others not. However, it was also a time of positive change and innovation that changed the lives of many people. Human beings are very resilient and it takes a lot to stop them, and make them completely give up. The economic depression of the 1930s tested that resilience, maybe at times, and for some people, to its limits, but it did not stop people completely from wanting to get on with their lives. The challenge that was to come at the end of the 1930s, another world war, was possibly an even greater challenge, and the experience of the economic depression in some way prepared them for what was to come.

3 The coming of war

When the First World War occurred, from 1914 to 1918, many people used the phrase 'the war that will end war'. People could not imagine going through that kind of horrific experience again. Many believed that the newly created peacekeeping organisation, the League of Nations, would ensure this. Some believed the terms set out in the 1919 Treaty of Versailles, the main peace agreement that formally ended the war, were harsh enough to deter countries from acting aggressively again. Germany, in particular, suffered economically as it was blamed for starting the war and made to pay reparations (the cost of the war) to other countries. However, by 1934, Adolf Hitler had become the Führer of Germany and leader of the Nationalist Socialist German Workers (Nazi) Party. His main aim was to restore Germany as a major European, if not a global, power. As Hitler's ambition and aggression grew, some people believed that everything that could be done to avoid war or prepare for war must be done, regardless of the consequences. Others believed that a second world war was inevitable.

The threat from Germany

As early as 1924, Hitler had made his aims clear in his book *Mein Kampf* ('My Struggle'), and repeated these at speeches and rallies in the 1920s and 1930s, when he had gained more power. These aims included:

- To unite all German-speaking people under his rule.
- To gain *Lebensraum* (living space) for the German people.
- To restore Germany as a Great Power (a country with economic, political and military power).

In order to achieve these aims, Hitler would have to tear up the Treaty of Versailles. Many of its terms treated Germany harshly. Germany was effectively disarmed:

- Its army could only number 100,000.
- Conscription was no longer allowed.
- It could not have tanks.
- It could not have an air force.
- Its navy was reduced significantly in size, and could not have submarines.

Additionally, land was taken from Germany and given to European countries such as France, Poland and the newly created Czechoslovakia, which meant that millions of Germans were now living in these countries. A significant area of Germany, the Rhineland, was demilitarised, leaving Germany unable to protect its border with France. Germany's overseas empire was taken from it and much was given to Britain and France. They controlled them as 'mandates'. Britain controlled Palestine and France controlled Syria.

▲ **Source A:** A cartoon by David Low, 'Just in case there's any mistake', published in the *Evening Standard* newspaper, 3 July 1939

ACTIVITY ?

What is the cartoonist in Source A suggesting about Britain's preparedness for going to war with Germany in 1939?

As you work through this chapter, look at your response to the activity, and decide if you would change your response and if the cartoonist was right.

Foreign policy under Hitler

Hitler became leader of the Nazi Party during the 1920s, making promises to the German people that he would restore German pride (after the humiliation of the First World War) and make Germany a world power. In 1933, he was appointed as the Chancellor of Germany (the equivalent of being the British Prime Minister), and on the death of President Hindenburg, in August 1934, he named himself the Führer. This meant he was in total charge of Germany.

By the time Hitler became the Führer of Germany in 1934, a number of events had occurred that not only started the process of tearing up the Treaty of Versailles, but also gave Hitler further opportunities to fulfil his aims. For example, in 1932, Germany's reparation payments had been completely cancelled. Countries such as Britain and France were of the opinion that charging Germany for the cost of the First World War was wrong and reparations were no longer necessary. In 1933, Germany withdrew from a disarmament conference and left the League of Nations, as Hitler did not want to be bound by the rules and regulations of being a member country.

Some of Hitler's early actions, however, convinced some countries that his aims and intentions were peaceful:

- In 1934, Germany signed a Non-Aggression Pact with Poland that was supposed to last for ten years. It seemed to confirm that Hitler accepted the border between Germany and Poland set by the Treaty of Versailles and that he would not try and take back the 'Polish Corridor'. This gave the impression to other countries, including Britain, that Hitler was a man of peace, not war.
- In 1934, the failure of the Austrian Nazi Party to gain *Anschluss* (the union of Germany and Austria), which had been forbidden in the Treaty of Versailles, appeared to be a setback for Hitler, but he backed down when Mussolini moved his army to the Austrian border.
- In 1935, Germany signed the Anglo-German Naval Agreement. The agreement limited Germany's navy to 35 per cent of the size of the British navy. While this agreement satisfied Britain because it meant that Britain's navy would always be larger, it concerned both France and Italy. They felt that Britain had given Hitler the opportunity to expand his navy well beyond the limits imposed by the Treaty of Versailles.
- In 1935, an area of Germany called the Saar voted to return to German control. Under the Treaty of Versailles it had been controlled by the League of Nations for 15 years. The vote was known as the Saar Plebiscite and 90 per cent of the Saar population voted to re-join Germany, 8 per cent to remain under League of Nations control, and 2 per cent to join France. Hitler and the Nazi Party used this event to great effect as it gave them the perfect propaganda opportunity. Many outside Germany considered the return of the Saar region to Germany illegal.

▲ Source B: Refugees who fled Nazi vengeance following the plebiscite at the border with France

By 1935, Hitler had started a re-armament programme in earnest. At first it had been done secretly. In 1933, Hitler ordered his army generals to plan to triple the size of the army to 300,000 soldiers. He also ordered the Air Ministry to build 1,000 military aircraft. In 1935, Hitler went public with what had already been done and what was to be done further. The army would be increased to 550,000 by the introduction of conscription and the number of military aircraft would quickly increase to 2,500.

▲ Source C: The set of four stamps above was issued by the Third Reich on January 16, 1935, a few days after the Saar Plebiscite, to celebrate the return of the Saar to Germany. The stamps show the Saar (a child) returning to the arms of Mother Germany

Practice question

What was the significance of the Saar Plebiscite for Hitler and the Nazi Party in the 1930s? *(For guidance, see page 194.)*

ACTIVITY

In groups, use the events that took place between 1933 and 1935 (see pages 137–139), and decide how much of a threat Hitler was to European peace. Present your judgement to the rest of the class.

The re-militarisation of the Rhineland

On 7 March 1936, an event took place which further divided opinion about the threat of Hitler and his intentions: the re-militarisation of the Rhineland. The Rhineland was German land that it had been demilitarised as a consequence of the Treaty of Versailles. The events of the re-militarisation are shown in Figure 3.1 below.

The re-militarisation of the Rhineland was against the Treaty of Versailles (1919) and the Treaty of Locarno (1925).
In 1935, the Franco–Soviet Pact made Hitler feel 'encircled' and vulnerable as, without re-militarisation, Germany could not protect its border with France.
Hitler was advised by generals to send only a small number of troops to the Rhineland. 22,000 troops and a handful of aircraft were involved in the re-militarisation.
When French troops were reported to be on the French border, Hitler was advised by his generals to withdraw his troops, as the French troops did not cross the border, Hitler did not take their advice.
Hitler offered France and Britain a 25-year non-aggression pact, claiming that 'Germany had no territorial demands to make in Europe'.
Britain and France condemned the re-militarisation, as it broke the terms of the Treaty of Versailles, but neither took action to reverse it, nor saw it as an act of war.

▲ Figure 3.1 The re-militarisation of the Rhineland

◀ Source D: The Goose-Step. A British cartoon about the re-militarisation of the Rhineland in 1936

THE GOOSE-STEP

"GOOSEY GOOSEY GANDER,
WHITHER DOST THOU WANDER?"
"ONLY THROUGH THE RHINELAND—
PRAY EXCUSE MY BLUNDER!"

ACTIVITY

1 Look at the information above and find evidence to complete a copy of the table below.

The re-militarisation of the Rhineland was an aggressive act	The re-militarisation of the Rhineland was a non-aggressive act

2 What is the message in Source D about the re-wtarisation of the Rhineland by Germany in March 1936?

The events of 1938

Anschluss, 1938

Despite what had happened in 1934 regarding *Anschluss* with Austria (see page 138), the Nazi Party remained committed to the union of Germany and Austria (which had been forbidden since the Treaty of Versailles in 1919). On 12 March, battalions of the German army entered Austria. Opponents of this action were either eliminated or put in concentration camps. Approximately 80,000 were put in camps. During the coming weeks Hitler gained control of the Austrian government and the *Anschluss* was proclaimed. In April 1938, a plebiscite was held in which 99.75 per cent of the population agreed to the *Anschluss* (which, in reality, had already happened). Austria was now part of the Third Reich and Greater Germany. Britain and France protested about what had happened but did not stop it.

The Czechoslovakia Crisis

Hitler now turned his attention to Czechoslovakia. As a consequence of the Treaty of St Germain (one of the peace treaties which ended the First World War) more than 3 million German-speaking people had been living the Sudetenland area of western Czechoslovakia. This area had borders with both Germany and Austria. Hitler now encouraged the leader of the Sudetenland Nazi Party, Henlein, to call for independence for the Sudetenland. This area was rich in raw materials and was heavily fortified; an area, therefore, that Czechoslovakia could ill-afford to lose. The British Prime Minster, Neville Chamberlain, decided that he could help settle this situation. Chamberlain met Hitler, at Berchtesgaden, on 15 September 1938. He learned that Hitler wanted the Sudetenland to become part of Germany as it contained German-speaking people. Chamberlain, with the support of France, forced Edvard Beneš, the leader of Czechoslovakia, to agree to the demand. Chamberlain hoped this would ensure that war would not happen. When Hitler heard the deal had been accepted he demanded more. Chamberlain returned to Britain convinced that war would break out as Hitler was now demanding too much.

However, Hitler called a conference of four powers, Germany, Britain, Italy and France, to formally agree a deal. Czechoslovakia was not invited. On 30 September, the four powers signed the Munich Agreement. The terms were that:

- The Sudetenland would become part of Germany.
- Britain and France would guarantee the independence of the rest of Czechoslovakia.
- If the Czechs decided to fight against this, they would be on their own.
- Hitler and Chamberlain would sign a declaration that Britain and Germany would never go to war.

Beneš was forced to accept the Munich Agreement, and Chamberlain returned to London with the signed declaration (see Source F). While he hoped that his actions had prevented war then and in the future, others, like Winston Churchill, a prominent politician, were not so sure.

ACTIVITIES

1 Why would Hitler hold an *Anschluss* plebiscite after the *Anschluss* had already taken place?
2 In groups, use the events that took place between 1936 and 1938 (pages 139–140) and decide how much of a threat Hitler was to European peace. Present your judgement to the rest of the class.

Britain's policy of appeasement

Throughout the 1930s it seemed that Britain had a particular way of dealing with problems that emerged in Europe: appeasement, or giving into demands to keep the peace. It is believed by some that if you apply 'appeasement' to a difficult situation it will not only solve the problem, but ensure it will not happen again. However, others believe that when applying 'appeasement' to a problem you are basically giving in. While appeasement may solve the immediate problem, it may not prevent the problem from happening again, and in fact may encourage it to happen again on a bigger scale. While there is evidence that Britain applied the policy of appeasement towards Germany from 1933, the policy is most closely associated with the actions of Neville Chamberlain, the British Prime Minister from 1937–40.

In adopting appeasement, Britain was gambling that Hitler was reasonable in his ambitions for Germany. If Hitler could have his way on some issues and other countries were seen to be listening to Germany's grievances, then this may satisfy Hitler and restore Germany's economical and political power.

▲ Neville Chamberlain

POLITICAL CAREER OF NEVILLE CHAMBERLAIN

1924	Appointed Minister for Health
1931	Appointed Chancellor of the Exchequer
1937	Elected Prime Minister
1939	Declares war on Germany
1940	Resigns as Prime Minister (succeeded by Winston Churchill)

The arguments for and against appeasement

The arguments for and against appeasement are summarised in Table 3.1 below.

Arguments for appeasement	Arguments against appeasement
• It made Germany feel that it was being listened to regarding its grievances in relation to the Treaty of Versailles (being disarmed, losing land, paying reparations, having millions of Germans living in other countries, not being able to unite with Austria). • It could avoid war by use of negotiation rather than action. • The horrors of the First World War were still in people's minds – anything that could avoid this happening again should be followed. • The Depression of the early 1930s meant that Britain's economy was still recovering, and going to war was costly. • Appeasement seemed a better option than relying on the League of Nations. • Communism, now established in the USSR under Joseph Stalin, was regarded by some as more threatening than Hitler. Keeping Hitler 'happy' would help make Germany a barrier between the USSR and countries such as Britain and France.	• It made Britain look weak, as it was Britain that always appeared to give in, and in turn this made Hitler more confident that he could keep demanding more and would always get what he wanted. • It suggested that Britain was prepared to betray other countries, or reverse decisions that had been previously agreed, to keep Hitler happy. • It seemed to undermine Britain's key role as a permanent member of the League of Nations. • Each act of appeasement (the Rhineland, Austria, Czechoslovakia) allowed Hitler to become stronger politically, economically and territorially – which could be seen as an encouragement of war.

▲ Table 3.1 The arguments for and against appeasement

ACTIVITY

In groups, use the information about the events of 1933–38 (pages 137–142), and the bullet points on this page to develop an argument, for or against appeasement being the best way to deal with Hitler.

The outbreak of war

Despite being labelled as the 'prophet of doom' during the 1930s, Churchill's warning in Source E (see below) proved to be right. By March 1939, the rest of Czechoslovakia had been carved up between Poland, Hungary and Germany. The Czech leader, Hácha, was forced by Hitler to hand over control, and German troops were sent in to restore order in the areas now under the control of the Third Reich. This seemed to confirm that appeasement had failed.

The policy of appeasement had made the USSR and Stalin suspicious of Britain and France. Fearing that the USSR could not rely on Britain and France, the USSR decided that a deal with Germany would be better that no deal with Britain and France. In August 1939, the Nazi–Soviet Pact was signed. It stated:

- Germany and the USSR would not interfere against the other power in the event of a war.
- Poland was to be divided between them with the USSR regaining land they had lost during the First World War, and Germany regaining western Poland, Danzig and the 'Polish Corridor'.

As Britain had a guarantee agreement with Poland to defend it, Hitler knew the agreement with the USSR could lead to war. However, he was prepared to gamble that, as at the Munich Conference, Britain would stand by and not stop him. On 1 September 1939, German troops entered Poland to claim the areas agreed in the Nazi–Soviet Pact. Britain issued an ultimatum: withdraw these troops or go to war. Hitler ignored this. On 3 September 1939, Britain declared war on Germany.

Practice questions

1 What can be learnt from Sources E and F about the policy of appeasement? *(For guidance, see pages 190–191.)*
2 Explain the connections between any THREE of the following:
- The introduction of conscription in Germany in 1935
- The re-militarisation of the Rhineland, 1936
- The Munich Crisis, 1938
- Britain's policy of appeasement in the 1930s.
(For guidance, see page 195.)

We, the German Führer and Chancellor and the British Prime Minister, have had a further meeting today and are agreed in recognising that the question of Anglo-German relations is of the first importance for the two countries and for Europe.

We regard the agreement signed last night and the Anglo-German Naval Agreement as symbolic of the desire of our two peoples never to go to war with one another again.

We are resolved that the method of consultation shall be the method adopted to deal with any other questions that may concern our two countries, and we are determined to continue our efforts to remove possible sources of difference and thus to contribute to assure the peace of Europe.

Neville Chamberlain

September 30. 1938.

▲ Source F: The Anglo-German Pact promising 'peace for our time', signed by Neville Chamberlain and Adolf Hitler, on 30 September, 1938

Preparation for war

Some preparations for war had begun by 1938 and continued in the early months of 1939. Britain was in a better position to fight a war by the autumn of 1939 than had been the case during the Munich crisis. By the time Britain had declared war on Germany, the following were in place:

- The government had created and started to enact a plan for a war that could possibly last for three years.
- The government had started a programme to build new warships for the navy.
- People had been encouraged to cut up and donate metal that could be melted down for the manufacture of war machinery and ammunition.
- People were encouraged to plant vegetables on any spare ground to supplement rations.
- The government spent money on educational information to inform people about the dangers of possible gas attacks, how to use their food rations, and stay healthy.
- In July 1939, the government set up the Ministry of Supply to oversee preparations for war.
- The government had met with trade unions and through negotiation had agreed wartime working regulations and wages.
- The government insisted that 'blackouts' (covers over windows to prevent light being seen from the outside) were to be used in all homes.
- The government insisted that all people carry gasmasks.

Despite Britain declaring war on Germany on 3 September 1939, no actual military action was seen until the late spring of 1940. During this time Hitler was busy taking over much of northern Europe. For Britain, this period of time is often referred to as the 'phoney war'. However, it did not stop further war preparations being put in place.

> **Interpretation 1:** *Welsh Journals* **Vol. 28 1984 'Preparations for Air Raid Precautions in Swansea, 1935–9'**
>
> *If 1938 had witnessed much ARP activity in Swansea, 1939 saw an escalation of it, since, from March of that year, the ARP Department began to put itself on a war footing. Indeed, in April, the Corporation was directed by the government to give ARP priority over all its other activities. In response to this, on 20 April, the Town Clerk, H.L. Lang-Coath, was appointed as ARP Controller for the County Borough in the event of war. This was a voluntary, unpaid post, which did not come into effect until war was declared, after which the Controller was to be responsible for the co-ordination of all ARP services whenever attacks occurred. His role should not be confused with that of the ARP Officer, who was a salaried, executive official, responsible for the day to day running of the ARP Department. In the same month an Emergency Committee was formed, while an air raid control room was established in the Green Room at the Guildhall, and from here the ARP resources would be directed in the event of attacks.*

ACTIVITY

In groups, using the information on this page and other research you have done, present a presentation about how people in Wales prepared for war.

Practice question

How far do you agree with Interpretation 1 about how people coped with the effect of the war? *(For guidance, see pages 196–197.)*

Wardens and shelters

The government was keen to recruit people to serve as air raid wardens and had started to do so during 1937 by creating the Air Raid Wardens' Service. By 1938, 200,000 people had joined the Service. During the Czechoslovakia crisis another 500,000 people had joined. By September 1939, 1.5 million people were now in the newly named Air Raid Precautions (ARP), which later became known as Civil Defence. One in six of the wardens were women. Their role was:

- To work from home, or a shop or office.
- To register all people in their sector.
- To enforce the 'blackout' (this led to some Wardens being considered as 'nosy').
- To sound sirens during an air attack.
- To help people to communal shelters, and check on people who had their own shelter.
- To carry out first aid, put out small fires and co-ordinate other emergency services once a bombing raid was over.

Most wardens were volunteers and therefore unpaid. In some areas some wardens were full-time and received a wage. They were not issued with a uniform but were given a steel helmet, a pair of Wellington boots and an armband as a means of making them identifiable.

LORD WARDEN OF THE EMPIRE

▲ **Source G:** A cartoon published in Punch magazine. Winston Churchill standing on a cannon dressed as an air raid warden at the beach at Dover during WW2 as RAF planes fly overhead

Practice question

Why were air raid wardens so significant during the Second World War? *(For guidance, see page 194.)*

Air raid shelters

The government supplied its citizens all over the country, and particularly in major cities, with air raid shelters. The first shelters, known as Anderson shelters, were delivered in February 1939. In total 400,000 Anderson air raid shelters were distributed. People were instructed to dig a hole in their garden to put the shelter in and cover it with earth. They were designed to protect people against falling brickwork if the houses were bombed. In areas where it was impossible to use Anderson shelters, large concrete shelters with curved roofs were constructed.

However, Anderson shelters were not popular because they meant sleeping outside. Some people used Morrison shelters, which were given out in 1941. These were steel cages, which fitted under a dining table with enough room for two adults and two small children.

Many people, however, had no shelters, particularly those living in city centres or in flats. Some people moved in with friends or relatives during raids and others moved to the ground floor. There, or sometimes in a cellar, they constructed a safe room. When the raids became serious in the second week of September 1940, people began to try to force their way into underground stations in London. At first the government did not allow the Underground stations to be used as shelters. It wanted to ensure that the trains could be used for transport. However, the early attacks were so severe and so damaging to morale that the decision was reversed. One of the first stations to be opened was Bethnal Green in the East End. The shelters were often packed. Children queued in the afternoon in order to stake a claim to a patch of platform for the family. A white line was drawn 2.5 metres from the edge of the platform. This was to let passengers reach the train. At 7.30 p.m. the line was moved to 1.2 metres from the edge. That was the last chance to find a bed space. Latecomers slept in the passages or on the stairs. Electricity to lines was switched off at 10.30 p.m. and adults would sleep in the fifth bay between the lines. People preferred the Underground stations as a shelter because they could socialise with other families and share a common threat. In addition, voluntary services began to provide hot drinks. Despite all of these precautions, it was still estimated that 60 per cent of Londoners stayed in their own homes throughout the Blitz.

Source I: An interview with a Londoner who remembers the Blitz

People would rush to get to the tubes, almost knock you down to get to the escalator. We lived like rats underground. People spread newspapers on the floor to show it was their territory. Sometimes you'd get people squaring up and fights.

ACTIVITY

Using the information and sources on pages 143–145, do you think enough was done by the government to provide people with shelter during air raids in the Second World War?

Practice question

What can be learnt from Sources I and J about the use of the London Underground during an air raid? *(For guidance, see pages 190–191.)*

▲ Source H: An Anderson shelter

▲ Source J: A photograph of children sleeping in an Underground station

Radar, barrage balloons and anti-aircraft guns

Radar

In the mid-1930s, the British had developed a sophisticated defence system against enemy bombing known as radar. Radar stations made it possible to track German planes and so concentrate the defence just where it was needed. The British had sector stations that acted as a nerve centre collecting the information from radar and sending the fighter planes to intercept the German planes.

▲ Source K: The inside of a radar station in 1940. Radar station operators were able to detect the position and direction of German aircraft using signals from radio waves that showed up on a screen

Barrage balloons

Barrage balloons had first been used during the First World War. They consisted of a large balloon filled with gas that was lighter than air and were attached to a steel cable. They were designed to 'float' in the air at altitudes that would deny low level air space to attacking enemy aircraft, thus, forcing the aircraft to fly at higher altitudes which could make bombing less accurate.

In 1936 the Committee of Imperial Defence decided to have 450 barrage balloons built to protect London in the event of a possible future attack. Their foresight proved to be very accurate. When war broke out in September 1939, not only would London need this type of defence, but other major industrial cities, naval ports and airfields would as well. By August 1940 2,368 barrage balloons flew over major strategic sites across the Britain. These were to prove invaluable during the Blitz.

▲ Source L: A photograph of a barrage balloon over London

Anti-aircraft guns

Anti-aircraft guns were capable of rapid high-rate fire and could fire at high angles. The Bofors 40-mm anti-aircraft gun had been developed by a Swedish manufacturer in the 1930s, and the British government had acquired a licence to build these guns and put them into service. They could fire 120 rounds per minute, and fire a round (a two pound shell) to a height of two miles above the ground.

▲ Source M: A photograph of an anti-aircraft gun and crew September 1940

ACTIVITY

How effective do you think anti-aircraft guns would be against an attacking air force?

Conscription and reserved occupations

The government introduced conscription into the armed services in April 1939. The Military Training Act made it compulsory for single men aged between 20 and 22 to join the armed forces. In September 1939, the National Services (Armed Forces) Act made it compulsory for men aged between 18 and 41 to join the armed forces. In both cases men could apply to be exempted (see below).

One of the many lessons learned from the First World War was that if people are conscripted without considering their work skills and how they might be better deployed at home, rather than at the warfront, fighting the war would prove difficult. In 1938, a 'Schedule of Reserved Occupations' was created by the government and published by the Ministry of Labour. It gave exemption from conscription to skilled workers in key areas of work.

The system was quite complicated, but over the course of the war it accounted for some 5 million men of conscription age staying at home and working. It included railway and dock workers, farmers and other related agricultural workers. Schoolteachers and doctors were also included. Workers in engineering industries were also exempted, as were those who worked as wardens in the ARP (see page 144). The government frequently reviewed the Schedule in response to the war effort. At the start of the war, coalmining was not a reserved occupation but was later added. Despite this there was such a shortage of miners that in December 1943, one out of every ten conscripted men was randomly chosen to work down the mines. These miners became known as 'Bevin boys', after Ernest Bevin, Minister for Labour and National Service, who had created the scheme. Also, as the war progressed, many women worked in reserved occupations. Many workers in reserved occupations received negative views from some people who thought they were hiding rather than taking part in the actual fighting.

▲ Source N: Propaganda poster from the Second World War. Builders! Speed is vital minutes saved – Lives saved

Conclusion: How effectively did Britain prepare for war?

Britain's preparations for war were carried out mostly during the later months of 1938 and the beginning of 1939. Some of those preparations were based on lessons that had been learnt during the First World War. It was expected that in a future war the country would be bombed from the air as well as attacked on ground, so many of the preparations reflected this thinking. It was also assumed that gas (which was used in the First World War) would be used again, but in greater quantities. The mobilisation of the armed forces and the organisation of the civilian population were seen as priorities for the government in the preparation for war, as was the protection of young and vulnerable people. When war did come some of the preparations had put Britain in a strong position to cope with the potential hardships, but that did not mean that people did not experience the horror that war brings.

4 Life during wartime

How people cope with the experience of war has fascinated people for centuries. We can learn about their experiences from a variety of sources. Some examples are: official documents from the government of the time, propaganda posters, photographs, cartoons and individual personal memoires. Historians use these types of sources to make their own interpretations and judgements about how they think people coped with the experience of war. It is too easy to say that 'everybody in society coped well with the experience of war', or 'the experience of war was terrible for all people.' As you move through this chapter you will have the opportunity to reflect on British people's experience of the Second World War through a variety of events, contexts and experiences. Then you will be able to make judgements about how people in Britain coped with the experience of war.

Source A: Wally's barber ▶ shop, St. Martin Street has defiant signs outside after losing its windows during the London blitz, November 1940

ACTIVITY ?

Discuss in pairs how Source A portrays how people coped with the experience of war. When you have worked through this chapter, come back and decide how accurate this photograph was in its portrayal.

The bombing of British cities

After Hitler gave up his attempt to invade Britain, he put into action a new strategy. From September 1940, Hitler decided to bomb Britain into submission. This became known as the Blitz. During the period of September 1940 to May 1941 the *Luftwaffe* (German air force) bombed Britain's major towns and cities. The British government brought in various measures to deal with being bombed from the air, including the blackout, air raid shelters and the Home Guard. Having survived this first Blitz, the British were then attacked by Hitler's revenge weapons, the V-1 and V-2 bombs, in 1944–45. Hitler's aims were:

- To force Britain to surrender.
- To break the morale of the British people.
- To destroy the homes and lives of the civilian population so that government would come to terms with him.
- To destroy industry, shipyards and railways that would support Britain's war effort.

Initially, London was the primary target for the German bombings, especially the East End with its docks and factories. Between 2 September and 2 November 1940, London was bombed every night. The House of Commons building was destroyed and Buckingham Palace damaged. King George VI and Queen Elizabeth (the late Queen Mother) were often on the scene soon after a severe raid to cheer and encourage people as they struggled to save those trapped under the debris. Over 15,000 people were killed and 250,000 made homeless. These raids continued

through 1941 with the worst on 10 May when thousands were left without electricity, gas and water.

The focus of the German bombing campaign spread to other highly populated areas and cities. Coventry suffered its worst attack on the night of 14 November 1940. Over 30,000 incendiary bombs were dropped on the aircraft factories there. Much of the city, including Coventry Cathedral, was destroyed. People were so terrified that they fled the city each night, sleeping with relatives or in farmers' barns or camping in open fields. Yet in spite of this savage raid, the factories in Coventry were back in full production within five days.

The north-west and Manchester in particular was attacked in December 1940. Liverpool was attacked regularly and on 3 May 1941 suffered the biggest single raid on a mainland city, involving over 600 bombers. The city lost some of its finest buildings, with fires burning out of control because water mains were hit. A freighter, the SS*Malakand*, carrying 1,000 tonnes of explosives received a direct hit. The docks around the ship and the nearby packed terraced homes were devastated.

> **Source B: A German radio report, 18 September 1940**
> *The legend of British self-control and coolness under fire is being destroyed. All reports from London agree in stating that the people are seized by fear – hair-raising fear. The 7 million Londoners have completely lost their self-control. They run aimlessly about the streets and are victims of bombs and bursting shells.*

Practice question

What can be learnt from Sources B and C about the impact of the Blitz on London? *(For guidance, see pages 190–191.)*

◀ Source C: A market stall open for business in London after a bombing raid

Swansea

As early as 1937, it was thought that in the event of a war Swansea would be a target for aerial bombardment. It had a port and docks and was vital in the import and export of coal. This capacity would be vital in wartime. The Swansea Council recognised this likelihood and planned and implemented strategies to ensure the town was prepared.

- In 1937, the Swansea Police and Fire Service had under gone anti-gas training in the event of the town being bombarded with gas shells.
- During 1938, the town had an ARP department (see page 144), volunteer wardens, a team of ambulance drivers and firemen, specially designated mortuaries and key first aid posts deployed around the town,
- Plans had also been made to dig trenches.
- The Council built 500 communal air raid shelters and requisitioned cellars and basements for 'shelter' use during an attack.
- In March 1939, 6,549 Anderson-style shelters (see page 145) were distributed to private homes across the town.
- It was hoped that there would be sufficient shelter for the town's population of 167,000.

It was good that the assumption made was that Swansea would at some point be a target for German aerial bombardment, and that this action had been taken. Swansea faced an aerial bombardment before London suffered the Blitz (57 consecutive nights of air-raids) and many other major British cities suffered extensive bombardment.

The bombardment of Swansea

On 27 June 1940, at 3.30 a.m. residents of the Danygraig area of Swansea were awakened by the sound of high explosives being dropped from aircraft that belonged to the German *Luftwaffe*. Fortunately, on this occasion few casualties were reported. However, emergency services had to deal with unexploded bombs that had been dropped on the Kilvey Hill area.

It was another eight months before the *Luftwaffe* returned, but this time it was for more than one night. The nights of 19, 20, 21 February 1941, have gone down in local and Welsh history as 'The Three Nights' Blitz'. The consequences were death, injury and significant destruction of buildings of all types and uses. Major parts of Brynhyfryd, Townhill and Manselton were destroyed. Over the three nights a total of 1,273 high explosive, and 56,000 incendiary bombs were dropped. They accounted for 230 deaths, 397 injured and the destruction of 7,000 homes. Other damage was:

- The seventeenth-century grammar school building in Mount Pleasant took a direct hit.
- Roads were blocked with masonry, and impassable due to craters.
- Sewers were fractured and exposed.

- Electric cables were down.
- Gas and water supplies were cut off.
- The once vibrant central market, with many food stalls, lay in tatters.

The Council set up communal feeding stations and water-tank lorries negotiated the damaged areas so that people could fill any containers they had with fresh water.

Reports of how the people of Swansea coped with those three nights vary. The government ensured that news was censored, and photographs of the damage were only allowed to be released in stages. When the BBC reported that the people of Swansea were still smiling, some people reacted angrily. *The Times* newspaper reported that 'The men looked tired and bereft of hope, and most of the women seemed to be on the verge of tears, their sadness and helplessness is very tangible'. It was also reported that during the three-day blitz, a Swansea woman had replied to a question about the whereabouts of her husband with 'He is in the army, the coward.'

Between 1940 and 1943 Swansea was bombarded from the air 44 times, which accounted for 340 deaths and thousands of injured. While the scale and intensity may not have been on the scale of the London 'Blitz', the experience was the same.

Thursday, 2 January 1941	Two small high explosive bombs dropped on an empty field in Ynystawe just before midnight. No damage.
Sunday, 5 January 1941	Twelve high explosive bombs and 200 incendiaries dropped on St Thomas, Swansea town centre, Sketty, Derwen Fawr and Glais just after midnight. Many small fires reported but all were easily extinguished. 20 casualties reported.
Monday, 13 January 1941	Two high explosive bombs dropped on King's Dock Road by a solitary plane just after 10.00 p.m. Five people slightly injured. Only slight structural damage.
Friday, 17 January 1941	Extensive damage as 178 high explosive bombs and 7,000 incendiaries landed on a snow-covered Swansea during its heaviest raid to date. St Thomas was easily the most affected region with other significant damage being recorded at Hafod and Bonymaen. Ninety-seven casualties and 55 deaths reported.
Wednesday, 19 February, Thursday 20 February, Friday 21 February 1941	The 'Three Nights' Blitz'. Over these three nights of intensive bombing, which lasted a total of 13 hours and 48 minutes, Swansea town centre was almost completely obliterated by the 896 high explosive bombs employed by the *Luftwaffe*. A total of 397 casualties and 230 deaths were reported.

▲ Source D: Timeline of the Swansea blitz

SWANSEA WILL REMEMBER

ONE OF THESE DAYS THEY WILL BE DROPPING PARACHUTE TROOPS.

▲ Source E: A cartoon published in *The Echo*, a Swansea newspaper, February 22, 1941

▲ Source F: A photograph of a Swansea family in 1941 after the 'Swansea Blitz'

Interpretation 1: David Roberts, an historian, writing in *Swansea's Burning*, published in 2011

As the flames subsided and the smoke cleared to reveal the true scale of the destruction, the words on everyone's lips were that things would never be the same again in Swansea. There was hardly an aspect of life in the town that wasn't, in some way, affected.

Practice question

Read Interpretation 1. How far do you agree with this interpretation of the impact of the bombing on Swansea in 1940 and 1941 during the Second World War? *(For guidance, see pages 196–197.)*

ACTIVITY

Use the information and sources on pages 149–151 and answer the following question. Do you think Swansea was fully prepared for the start of war?

151

Belfast

Belfast was devastated by four German bombing raids that took place during April and May 1941. Over 1,000 people were killed, 1,500 people were injured and 150,000 people were made homeless. While the factories and shipyards had been preparing for war by been a vital provider of naval ships, aircraft and munitions, preparing the civilian population had been relatively ignored. Approximately 4,000 women and children had been evacuated from the city, but that still left 80,000 in their homes.

▲ Source G: Rescue workers searching through rubble after an air raid on Belfast in 1941

Glasgow

Glasgow and the Clyde shipyards were hit hard in the spring of 1941. During 13 and 14 March the Germans bombed the shipbuilding area of Glasgow in what became known as the 'Clydebank Blitz'.

> **Interpretation 2:** From clydewaterfront.com. The website of a partnership between the Scottish Government, Scottish Enterprise and Glasgow city, whose purpose was to promote economic and social regeneration
>
> *Though the 260 planes were meant to target the shipyards and industrial locations in the Clydebank area on those two nights in March, it was inevitably the housing that suffered the most damage. The population had grown recently and as a result the housing was overcrowded. Over 16,000 houses were completely destroyed and 35,000 were made homeless. Hundreds of shops were ruined and five out of eleven schools. Hospitals and churches were affected, as well as power and water supplies, roads and railways. The casualties were around 1,083, which was quite low due to the strength of the shelters available. Over the next few days most of the remaining population was evacuated to the neighbouring areas of Renfrew, Lanark and Dumbarton. Remarkably, much of the industry survived and Clydebank continued to supply the country with much needed wartime manufacturing.*

ACTIVITY ?

Compare the bombing of Swansea, Belfast and Glasgow. What are the similarities and differences in:

■ Why the Germans bombed these cities
■ The effects of the bombing
■ The outcome of the bombing?

Evacuees and their host communities in Wales

The government expected that the Germans would attack Britain from the air, so it took precautions to protect its civilians from bombings. Children were to be protected by being moved from the likeliest targets, the cities, to the countryside where it was thought they would be safe.

Organisation

The evacuation began on 1 September 1939, the day that Hitler invaded Poland. In the first wave during 1939 and 1940, 1.5 million children, pregnant women, and women nursing babies were evacuated. Although many parents were reluctant to be separated from their children they accepted they would be safer in the countryside. Parents were told what the children needed to take with them and where they were to assemble for evacuation. Many city schools were closed and teachers went with the children to the countryside to carry on teaching them. At their destinations the evacuees gathered in village or school halls where they were chosen by the foster family they were to live with. Homesickness and the 'Phoney War' when little fighting took place and there were no enemy bombing raids, saw many children drift back to the cities by Christmas 1939. When German bombers began blitzing London in 1940, a second evacuation from the cities took place. There was a further wave of evacuations in 1944, when the Germans used their V-1 flying bombs and V-2 missiles to bomb Britain.

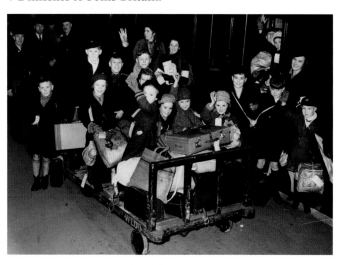

▲ **Source H:** A group of children wave and cheer as they are evacuated from London to Devon

---

ACTIVITY ?

Create your own version of the table below and use the boxes to complete it. Do you think evacuation was a success or not? Share your judgement with the class.

Successes of evacuation	Limitations of evacuation

- Evacuation saved many lives.
- There is evidence that some people tried to avoid taking evacuees.
- The organisation of the evacuation was criticised as children would arrive in village halls where they were 'chosen' by their host families.
- The organisation was sometimes poor, especially the way in which the evacuees were lined up in village halls and inspected by their host families.
- Evacuees were not used to rural life and there was a clash between city and country values. Evacuees often found themselves in much wealthier homes. Host families had to cope with different standards of behaviour.
- A number of evacuees were homesick. They missed their own families and evacuation children were sometimes split up from their brothers and sisters.
- Some children from poor inner-city areas saw the countryside for the first time.
- Many evacuees stayed with better-off people and were given a better standard of living including a healthier diet, fresh air and walks in the countryside.
- Evacuation showed better-off people in the countryside the social problems of families living in inner-city areas and increased the demand for change.
- Some evacuees experienced bullying by children who already lived in the countryside and resented these intruders from the cities who were causing overcrowding in schools.

Evacuation and Wales

As you have already learned, Swansea was unlikely to be a safe place to stay as it quickly became a strategic bombing target for the German *Luftwaffe*. After the first raid in June 1940, some families organised for themselves arrangements so that their children could be moved to the immediate countryside. However, within a 30-kilometre radius of Swansea town centre there was significant damage, and families had to look further afield for possible accommodation. After the Three Nights' Blitz (see page 150) some families even took to the road to escape on foot in order to find a safe haven. This type of evacuation was not planned by the authorities. It was chaotic and some people effectively became refugees. The Gower countryside, cold and remote in winter, proved to be an attractive alternative, given the circumstances. Some people tried to work out which parts of Swansea might be less susceptible to bombardment, and gamble that trying to seek accommodation their might be 'safer'. Sketty, on the west side of Swansea was one of those areas.

The accounts of evacuees in Interpretation 3 and 4 are from *Swansea's Frontline Kids 1939–45* by Jim Owen, published by Amberley 2014.

> **Interpretation 3: Peggy O'Neil Davies recalls her life as an evacuee**
>
> *I was nearly ten years of age when the Second World War was declared and really didn't think it would make a difference to me. It was the grownups that were talking about it. However, life changed dramatically for us children. My mother and father decided I should be evacuated. They didn't talk to me about it, I was just told I was going. My mother came with me to see me settled and to see where I was going to live. We went by train to the nearest town, then up the valley by bus. I had always lived in a town and here I was going through these mountains and green fields. The house I went to stay at had two children, a boy and a girl. Their mother did her best to make me feel welcome before my mother left me with these strangers. However, they were so good I really didn't feel homesick. At the beginning we were 'the evacuees', but soon we were accepted in the village and in school (in the next village) to which we had to walk every day.*

> **Interpretation 4: John Lewis was a lone evacuee. Here his wife, Maureen, talks about his experience**
>
> *John wore a label on his coat that clearly stated his name. He was taken by his mother to the local school. There he met other children labelled the same way. They were shepherded onto a bus. Small faces, tears running down their cheeks. The bus travelled some twenty miles to a school in Llangennech, Carmarthenshire. John was apprehensive and frightened. The children were handed over to people who had volunteered to 'take' and house a child. John spotted the most ugly woman he had ever seen. She must surely be a witch. He quickly hid under the teacher's desk. Then he heard a woman's voice bemoaning the fact that there were no children left, and she wanted a boy. He crawled out from under the desk he knew when he looked at her he would like Mrs Ebsworth. John still thinks fondly of this lady.*

ACTIVITY ?

Compare Interpretations 3, 4 and 5 about what it was like to be evacuated from Swansea during the war.

- What are the similarities and differences?
- What can you infer from their recollections about their experience?
- Why do you think it is John Lewis's wife that tells his story?
- How reliable, as pieces of historical evidence, do you think these recollections are?

> **Interpretation 5: Brenda Roberts (née Cox) was a lone evacuee. She was born in Swansea in 1931 and still lives there. In January 2017, she recalled her time as an evacuee**
>
> *I was evacuated in May 1940, aged 8. My sister Muriel, who was 15, came home from school with a note telling parents that children were to be evacuated from Swansea. She said she would not go. However, my parents said that I would be evacuated. Parents met at my school, and my father even took the day off work to come with us. I and the other children were being evacuated to Ystradgynlais, everyone was crying. When we got there, we were dropped off at the cinema where adults were waiting to take us in. I was put with a family that owned a wallpaper shop, and my best friend was put next door with an old lady. However, the old lady could not cope and my friend came to live with us. We lived above the wallpaper shop and the toilet was at the bottom of the garden. It was just a shed with a pit and a bucket. I didn't want to be there, and sometimes I got the bus to Swansea on my own to see my parents. My mother had to bribe me to get me to go back to Ystradgynlais. My sister came to visit me once while I was there. Every day we went to the local school, we evacuees had lessons in the morning, the local children had lessons in the afternoon. If I am honest I hated it, I was so young and I just wanted to be at home with my parents.*

The need for rationing

Although war had been on the horizon for several years, when it broke out in 1939, it was a shock to the British people. Most citizens could remember the horrors of the First World War and how it changed their everyday lives. They knew how the government had taken greater control of such things as industry, transport and, by the end of the war, food distribution. Unlike the First World War, in the Second World War the government introduced rationing almost immediately. A new ministry was set up to look after propaganda and censorship and it became almost impossible to escape the hand of the government. Most crucial of all was the introduction of rationing of food and clothing, something that affected everyone and became a source of irritation throughout the war and after.

In 1938, Britain imported 55 million tonnes of food, which was almost three-quarters of its total consumption. More than half of the meat consumed was imported and the majority of cheese, fruit, cereals and fats came from abroad. The government had been making plans since 1936 to combat food shortages in the event of war and gradually food rationing was brought in. The government's fears about attacks on British merchant ships proved right, and by Christmas of 1939 the Germans had sunk 96 ships. The situation worsened and in one month alone, March 1942, the Germans sank 275 British merchant ships. As the Battle of the Atlantic developed, food stocks dwindled and Britain had to take drastic steps to ensure that not only was there sufficient food for everyone but that everyone received a fair and equal amount.

◄ Source I: A photograph of the Tower of London moat, published in 1940 with the caption 'Even the Tower of London moat was turned into a vegetable garden'

Source J: From a leaflet produced by the Ministry of Food in 1941

Food is a weapon of war, don't waste it. You women at home are winning the war as much as your menfolk in the services. You have withstood the Blitz, economised and saved. Now here is one more way to help and it's up to you. We must eat more potatoes. The government has grown large crops especially because potatoes are a healthy food and because they save shipping space.

Practice question

What can be learnt from Sources I and J about the importance of food during the Second World War? *(For guidance, see pages 190–191.)*

Rationing

The first stage in the rationing process was National Registration Day, 29 September 1939, when every householder had to fill in a form giving details of the people who lived in their house. The government then collated this data and issued everyone with an identity card and ration book. These books contained coupons that had to be handed to or signed by a shopkeeper every time rationed goods were bought, so people could only buy the amount they were allowed.

Lord Woolton became the Minister of Food and he oversaw the introduction of the rationing programme which was combined with a nationwide propaganda campaign to ensure that people did not waste food and grew as much of their own food as was possible. The government knew that there was a danger of food prices rising quickly as certain foods became scarce, so by intervening with price controls and rationing, ordinary people were never in any danger of being unable to afford the necessities of life. In 1941, the government introduced a points system for rationed goods (which were given a specific points value) and each month a person could spend the allowance of 20 points on those goods that were available. Campaigns such as 'Dig for Victory' were also introduced (see Chapter 5, page 165).

Item	Rationing began
Petrol	March 1939
Bacon, butter and sugar	January 1940
Meat	March 1940
Tea and margarine	July 1940
Jam	March 1941
Cheese	May 1941
Clothing	June 1941
Eggs	June 1941
Coal	July 1941
Rice and dried fruit	January 1942
Soap	February 1942
Tinned tomatoes and peas	February 1942
Coal, gas and electricity	March 1942
Sweets and chocolate	July 1942

▲ Table 4.1: Britain's Second World War rationing timeline

Item	Allowance
Meat	350–430 grams
Milk	1.6 litres (3 pints)
Eggs	1 fresh (or 1 pack dried per month)
Cheese	85–112 grams
Bacon and ham	112 grams
Tea	56 grams
Sugar	224 grams
Butter	56 grams
Cooking fat	56 grams
Other rationed foods (subject to availability)	20 points

▲ Table 4.2: Adults weekly food ration in 1943

Practice question

Why was rationing significant during the Second World War? *(For guidance, see page 194.)*

The contribution of women to the war effort

At the beginning of the war in 1939 many women registered for voluntary work with organisations such as the Women's Voluntary Service (WVS), but others demanded part-time work in industry. The government's reaction was to ask women to stick to their existing jobs or stay at home. The work of women was not properly organised by the government until April 1941, by which time there were labour shortages as more men were conscripted into the armed forces. All women were forced to register for work. In October of the same year, a report was published by the Ministry of Labour which showed that 2 million more workers were needed in the armed forces and war industries. In December 1941, conscription for war work of women aged 19 to 30 was introduced. From then on, the number of women working steadily increased. By 1943, 17 million women aged between 14 and 64 were either in the forces or in essential war work. That included 90 per cent of single women and 80 per cent of married women with children over 14.

The women's armed forces

The women's armed services included the WRNS (Women's Royal Naval Services), the WAAF (Women's Auxiliary Air Force) and the ATS (Auxiliary Territorial Service). The WRNS was the most popular service followed by the WAAF. By 1944, there were 450,000 women in these services, with 212,000 in the ATS. The women did the routine office, driving and domestic duties which freed the men up for combat duty. Despite not being involved in combat, women nevertheless did hard and often dangerous jobs. They worked as mechanics, welders, pilots, carpenters and even gunners on anti-aircraft guns – although they were not allowed to fire the guns. Some 335 women were killed in the ATS and another 300 wounded. In the navy they overhauled and serviced torpedoes and depth charges and repaired ships. As well as carrying out administrative tasks in the army, they also drove convoys, acted as dispatch riders and worked in intelligence. Many of the code-breakers at Bletchley Park were women. Bletchley Park is an estate in Buckinghamshire that was used as the government code-breaking headquarters during the Second World War.

As with their male counterparts, many women entered the voluntary services as well as doing a full- or part-time job. By 1943, there were 180,000 volunteers in civil defence and a further 47,000 in the fire services. Some 130,000 women volunteered as messengers and dispatch riders for the Post Office. Many other women worked in medical centres, first-aid posts, mobile canteens and rest centres.

> **Source K: A statement issued by a government minister during a radio broadcast of May 1941**
>
> *Today we are calling all women. Every woman in the country is needed to pull her weight to the utmost – to consider carefully where her services would help most and then let nothing stand in the way of giving such services. Like her, many women have made their sacrifices already and are doing their utmost to win the war. But to those thousands who have not yet come forward I would say here and now that every one of us is needed.*

▲ Source L: A government poster of 1941

Practice question

What can be learnt from Sources K and L about the contribution of women to the war effort? *(For guidance, see pages 190–191.)*

Heavy industry and transport

Women worked in all kinds of industries. In aircraft factories they worked a sixteen-hour day, seven days a week, without bank holidays. Many worked in munitions. Others worked as engineers, mechanics and lorry, train and bus drivers. By 1943, women had proved how valuable they were in the war effort. They occupied 57 per cent of the jobs in factories, and, when they were in direct competition with men, often showed that they could do better. The Ministry of Information published details of women's achievements. A woman welder produced '30 feet [9 metres] more than a man on similar work'. A woman in a munitions factory produced 120 pieces of equipment a day, compared to 100 by her male colleagues. However, pay and conditions were often poor. Many of the women working in factories faced a twelve-hour day in places that were a long way from home. To avoid the risk of bombing, the new munitions factories were often built in remote areas, so travel to the factories was often difficult. Women's pay was lower than it was for men: women usually received about 75 per cent of a man's wage, even if they were doing the same job. In engineering, women earned 43 shillings (£2.15) a week when they started, compared to a man's pay of 65 shillings and sixpence (£3.28).

ACTIVITY ?

Use the information and sources on pages 158–159 and answer the following question. Do you think women were treated fairly in the workplace during the Second World War?

Practice question

Read Interpretation 6. How far do you agree with this interpretation of the impact and effect of women's contribution to the war effort in the Second World War? (For guidance, see pages 196–197.)

Source M: A young woman describes her working day in a factory in 1943

The room was about 40 yards long by 20 broad [37 metres by 18 metres]. There are three benches of small machines and a few large drilling machines on the floor. Altogether there are about 40 women and about a dozen men. My machine is a drilling one, and I am given a heap of small brass plates to drill holes in. It is quite dark when we come out – which strikes one with a curious shock of surprise, for one feels not so much tired, rather as if one has missed the day altogether.

Source N: From the personnel manager of a war factory, 1942

They had been told stories of nice clean factories with everything up to date and all modern amenities. I am genuinely sorry for these girls who highlight some of the facilities that should be provided for them. Our canteen is not so good. Lavatory accommodation will revolt these girls.

Interpretation 6: Steve Waugh and John Wright, writing in *GCSE Modern World History for Edexcel: War and the Transformation of British Society 1931–1951*, published 2010

Women played an important part in the Second World War, particularly in their contribution to the armed forces, and their work in heavy industry, farm work and transport. This, however, made little difference to the status of women in society in the years that followed the war.

▲ **Source O:** A government propaganda poster encouraging women to work

Conclusion: How did people in Britain cope with the experience of war?

The experience of war varied depending on where you lived in Britain, who you were and the part you played, or did not play, in the war. Some people found that the war opened up new opportunities and changed their lives for the better, while others found their lives changed in ways that were difficult to come to terms with and understand. For many people, the war separated them from their families, friends and work colleagues, and they had to get used to being told by the government how to act, think and live their lives. The perception of how British people coped with the experience of war is quite often referred to in the phrase 'the Blitz spirit', but while that contains some truth it also hides many of the experiences that post war generations have never had to experience.

5 Keeping up morale

Key question: How important was it to maintain people's morale during the war?

During wartime maintaining morale is just as important as maintaining an effective fighting force. When war broke out in September 1939, most citizens could remember the horrors of the First World War and how it changed their everyday lives. They knew how the government had taken greater control of industry, transport and, by the end of the war, food distribution. In the Second World War, government intervention was seen from the start, rather than towards the end. In fact, some intervention had begun even before the war started (see conscription, page 147). A new Ministry to look after information, propaganda and censorship was created. Rationing was set up immediately, strictly controlling the distribution of food and clothing. Campaigns were launched to actively involve citizens in the war effort. As the war progressed, everyone, in some way, was affected by these controls. Many people accepted this as a necessity during wartime, but some people came to resent it and saw it as a source of irritation. However, when the war ended, many people expected the government to continue to intervene and control aspects of their daily lives, as they had become used to it during the war.

As the threat of war approached in the summer of 1939, the British government introduced the Emergency Powers (Defence) Act 1939. This was passed on 24 August and it allowed the British government to take up emergency powers to:

- secure public safety
- defend the realm
- maintain supplies and services essential to the life of the country
- carry out the war effectively.

The Act gave the government the power to create regulations, without reference to Parliament, which covered almost every aspect of everyday life in the country. In order to carry these powers out, the Prime Minister, Neville Chamberlain, created five new Ministries:

- Home Security (attached to the Home Office)
- Information
- Shipping
- Economic warfare
- Food.

In addition, much British industry and transport was taken over by the government. You have already seen that the government began the evacuation of over 1 million children before the official outbreak of war (see page 153). Once fighting had started, it soon became clear that the government would use the Act extensively and, in doing so, radically change the relationship between the people and government.

ACTIVITY

Why was it so important for the government take control of people's lives when the Second World War started?

The role of radio and cinema during the war

Radio and cinema became widespread ways of communicating information and keeping up morale during the war.

Radio

On 1 September 1939, the BBC closed down its television transmissions and they did not re-commence until 1946. However, the BBC continued to broadcast radio programmes to a huge audience. There were almost 9 million licence holders, which meant that almost every family had access to a radio. The radio became an important way of involving the population and keeping them informed. The Ministry of Information had control of the BBC but it hardly ever interfered, and the BBC became well versed in self-censorship. The BBC newsreaders became very popular across the nation. At the outbreak of war it was decided that they should give their names at the start of each broadcast, so that listeners would get used to their voices, and be able to detect any enemy impersonations in the event of invasion.

BBC war reporters such as Richard Dimbleby and Frank Gillard sent back vivid accounts of British forces in action during the war and attracted huge audiences. Dimbleby once recorded a report from a British bombing raid over Berlin, for broadcast the following day. Radio programmes such as 'It's That Man Again' and 'Music while you work' became great favourites and maintained morale:

- 'It's That Man Again' was a comedy programme that poked fun not only at Hitler and the Germans but also at the British way of dealing with the war.
- 'Music while you work' was a programme introduced following a government suggestion that morale in industry would be improved if there were daily broadcasts of cheerful music piped into the factories. It proved to be most successful.

▲ Source A: A family listening to the radio

Cinema

Before the war the cinema was a cheap and therefore popular form of entertainment. In 1938, about 980 million cinema tickets were sold, and by 1945, this had reached more than 1,500 million. The Ministry of Information produced many short films about coping with the problems created by the war; there were documentaries such as *Fires were started* about firefighting in London. The British cinema industry also continued to make films during the war. The films were patriotic and dealt with the realities of war but had a biased approach, such as *In Which We Serve* and *Went the Day Well?* One of the most famous films of the war was *Henry V* starring Laurence Olivier. The film was made in 1943 and issued just before the D-Day invasion.

▲ Source B: A still from the film *Went the Day Well?* The film was made in 1942 and was about the capture of a British village by German paratroopers. The villagers and the Home Guard eventually defeat the Germans

ACTIVITIES

1 In groups, create your own three-minute radio broadcast feature designed to keep up the morale of the civilian population.
2 What does Source A show about the significance of radio during the war?

Propaganda posters and censorship

The government was aware that it had to ensure that people would support the war at all costs. It was hoped that by constant persuasion and suggestion people's attitudes would be positively influenced. The government tried to achieve these aims by means of propaganda. In addition, the government wanted to ensure that information would not be given away to the enemy, or given to the British people that might damage morale. This meant introducing censorship. There was censorship on overseas mail (see Source C) and the government examined all letters going abroad. If there was any sensitive material in the mail, it could be blacked out, cut out or returned to the sender. Soldiers' letters sent home were subject to censorship to ensure that military secrets were not inadvertently given away. Telephone calls were also subject to censorship (even King George and Winston Churchill faced this restriction).

Certain items of news were not broadcast or published because the Ministry of Information thought they would damage the morale of the people. On occasion photographs were not published because they were felt to be too distressing and would reduce enthusiasm for the war effort. Newspapers were carefully monitored, but there was only one case of closing down the press. This was in January 1941, when the Communist newspaper the Daily Worker was banned because it supported Stalin and continually attacked the British government and its leaders with rarely any condemnation of Hitler.

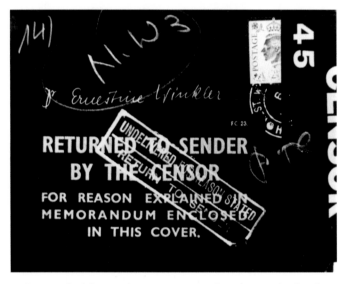

▲ Source C: A letter that was returned to the sender by the censor

▲ Source D: The censor's office, Liverpool, November 1939. Many of the workers could speak several languages

Practice question

What can be learnt from Sources C and D about censorship during the Second World War? *(For guidance, see pages 190–191.)*

ACTIVITY ?

How reliable are Sources C and D as evidence of censorship during the Second World War?

The work of the Ministry of Information

In order to make sure that propaganda and censorship were carried out effectively, the Ministry of Information was set up within hours of the outbreak of war. By the end of the war more than 3,000 people worked in the ministry. At first the Ministry of Information was not very successful and some of its poster campaigns failed to win much support. The aim of propaganda posters was to:

- encourage support for the war
- sell ideas
- convince people to act and think in a particular way
- appeal to people's sense of patriotism
- educate people about key issues during the war.

▲ Source E: One of the first posters of the Ministry of Information. It failed to win people over

ACTIVITY

Source E was not as successful as other propaganda posters. In pairs, using the bullet points about the aims of propaganda, why do you think this poster failed to win over civilians? Compare your ideas with the rest of the class.

Campaigns and appeals

The Ministry of Information sought to tell the British people what they should do for the war effort, and this sometimes meant telling them what they could not do. Source F describes a range of campaigns and instructions given to people. The Ministry published huge numbers of pamphlets, books, short information films and newsreels to ensure that the morale of the population did not diminish.

> **Source F:** From an interview with a member of the public by Mass Observation. (Mass Observation started in 1937 and looked at everyday life in Britain using untrained volunteer observers who kept diaries, answered questionnaires and interviewed members of the public)
>
> *In just one short walk I counted 48 official posters ... on hoardings, shelters, buildings, including ones to tell you to eat National Wholemeal Bread, not to waste food, to keep your children in the country, to know where the rest centre is, how to behave in an air raid shelter, to look out in the blackout, to look out for poison gas, to carry your gas mask always, to join the ATS, to fall in with the fire bomb fighters, to register for Civil Defence duties, to help build a plane, to recruit for the Air Training Corps, to save for Victory.*

The rationing policy

Rationing was introduced as a temporary measure, but it actually lasted until 1955, ten years after the war ended. The first stage in the rationing process was National Registration Day, 29 September 1939, when every householder had to fill in a form giving details of the people who lived in their house. The government then collated this data and issued everyone with an identity card and ration book. These books contained coupons that had to be handed to or signed by a shopkeeper every time rationed goods were bought, so people could only buy the amount they were allowed.

Lord Woolton became the Minister of Food and he oversaw the introduction of the rationing programme which was combined with a nationwide propaganda campaign to ensure that people did not waste food and grew as much of their own food as was possible. The government knew that there was a danger of food prices rising quickly as certain foods became scarce. By intervening with price controls and rationing, ordinary people were never in any danger of being unable to afford the necessities of life. In 1941, the government introduced a points system for rationed goods (which were given a specific points value) and each month a person could spend the allowance of 20 points on those goods that were available.

Despite the hardships caused by rationing, the people of Britain were healthier than before the war – they had a more balanced diet, even if it was rather boring. Fewer mothers died in pregnancy than before the war, and young children were fitter, because they were given milk and orange juice to improve their health. Some posters, such as Source G were targeted towards children's health.

Basic food such as eggs, sugar, butter, meat, tea and fruit, were all rationed and people were warned not to waste food. The government used nutritionists to ensure that its legally regulated ration entitlement gave a balanced diet to all. Children, and pregnant and nursing mothers, were given special attention through the Vitamin Welfare Scheme. Types of meals changed to reflect the shortage of ingredients, and soups, corned beef hash, carrot cake, and potato pie became typical meals. The Utility Scheme ensured that items such as shoes, clothes and carpets carried a utility mark (which indicated that they were necessary items needed during wartime) and were affordable. Soap and other toiletries were also rationed.

However, there was an illegal trade (black market) in rationed goods where people with money paid higher prices for extra rations. The government tried to stop such trade and Parliament passed laws that were quite severe. Courts could impose fines of up to £500 and imprison the guilty for up to two years. The Ministry of Food employed about 900 inspectors to try to root out the black market.

▲ Source G: A government poster, unknown date

> ### Practice question
>
> To what extent does Source F accurately explain how the government made use of propaganda during the Second World War? *(For guidance, see pages 192–193.)*

The 'Dig for Victory' campaign

The 'Dig for Victory' campaign was set up by the British Ministry of Agriculture. Men and women across Britain were encouraged to grow their own food to supplement what was available through rationing. People turned their lawns into vegetable gardens, and open spaces were turned into allotments (many of which still continue to this day). The lawns next to the Tower of London became a vegetable garden, see page 155. Many people in towns began to keep hens, rabbits and even pigs to supplement their ration allowances. In 1939, there were just over 800,000 allotments in Britain and this figure had almost doubled by 1943. The campaign included many posters and leaflets designed to educate people about the efficient use of food. In addition to posters and leaflets the 'Dig for Victory' campaign also had its own anthem.

> Dig! Dig! Dig! And your muscles will grow big
> Keep on pushing the spade
> Don't mind the worms
> Just ignore their squirms
> And when your back aches laugh with glee
> And keep on diggin'
> Till we give our foes a Wiggin'
> Dig! Dig! Dig! to Victory

The use of carrots was a particular focus, often introduced to British public, in posters and leaflets, by a character called 'Doctor Carrot'. The 'Doctor' encouraged people to make curried carrot, carrot jam and a drink called Carrolade (made from the juices of carrots and swede).

The potato received similar treatment through a character called 'Potato Pete' who had his own song that was regularly played on the radio:

> Here's the man who ploughs the fields.
> Here's the girl who lifts up the yield.
> Here's the man who deals with the clamp, so that millions of jaws can chew and champ.
> That's the story and here's the star,
> Potato Pete
> Eat up,
> Ta ta!

Practice question

Why was the 'Dig for Victory' campaign significant during the war? *(For guidance, see page 194.)*

Source H: A 'Dig for Victory' poster ▶

The Spitfire Fund

In 1940, this government-backed scheme led by Lord Beaverbrook, head of the Department for Aircraft Production, spread across Britain (see Source I). If an individual or business raised £5,000 they could have a Spitfire fighter aircraft named after them. Your name would be painted in yellow on the fuselage. While the £5,000 did not cover the full cost of building a Spitfire, which was between £8,000 and £12,000 (nearly half a million pounds today), it did cover the cost of building the frame. Money collected ranged from pennies to thousands of pounds. Local communities staged 'Spitfire' events so that people could contribute anything they could afford (see Source J). In Brighton, a special 'Spitfire' dog race raised £400.

The Nazim (sovereign) of Hyderabad, a princely state in India, which was part of the British Empire, donated so much money that 152 (Hyderabad) Spitfire Squadron was built and named in his honour. The MP for Macclesfield, Garfield Weston, personally donated £100,000. The Gold Coast (a region in Australia) raised £25,000 which paid for five Spitfires.

▲ Source I: Government posters about the Spitfire Fund

▲ Source J: A shopper at London's Lambeth Walk's market contributes to the Spitfire Fund in January 1940

Practice questions

1   What can be learnt from Source I and J about the importance of the Spitfire in the Second World War? *(For guidance, see pages 190–191.)*
2   Explain the connections between any THREE of the following:
    ● The role of radio
    ● Propaganda posters
    ● The Dig for Victory campaign
    ● The Spitfire Fund
    (For guidance, see page 195.)

ACTIVITY

Using the information and sources on pages 165–166, how important were the Dig for Victory and the Spitfire Fund campaigns in helping to keep up the morale of British people during the war?

The importance of Churchill as wartime leader

After the outbreak of war, Prime Minister Neville Chamberlain lost more and more support, as it became obvious that appeasement had not worked. He resigned on 10 May 1940, just as Hitler launched his *Blitzkrieg* on Holland and Belgium. (*Blitzkrieg* is German for 'lightning war'. It involved the use of aeroplanes, tanks and motorised troops to achieve speed and surprise.) Britain now faced two huge issues – war had erupted in the West and its Prime Minister had resigned.

The rise of Winston Churchill

As you can see from the timeline, Winston Churchill was already a senior figure in Parliament. He detested Hitler and Nazism and had spoken out against Germany throughout the 1930s. On 10 May 1940, Winston Churchill was appointed Prime Minister of Britain, in a coalition government. This meant that it was made up of MPs from the major political parties, and its aim was to govern Britain during the war.

WINSTON CHURCHILL

Born 1874

1893	Started military career
1900	Elected Conservative and Unionist MP for Oldham
1904	Crossed the House and joined the Liberal Party
1908	President of the Board of Trade
1910	Home Secretary
1911	First Lord of the Admiralty
1916	Commander in the British army during the First World War
1921	Secretary of State for the Colonies
1924	Chancellor of the Exchequer
1935	Argued for increased defence spending
1939	Argued against Appeasement

▲ Source K: A cartoon published in the Evening Standard 14 May 1940 with the caption 'All behind you, Winston'

ACTIVITIES ?

1 Do you think that by 1940 Churchill had sufficient experience to be a wartime leader?

2 In pairs, discuss what the cartoonist is trying to say about Winston Churchill as a wartime leader in Source K. Try to work out who some of the other characters are who are 'behind Winston'.

3 As you learn more about Winston Churchill as a wartime leader, decide if you agree with the cartoonist's portrayal of Churchill as a leader.

Source L: Part of Winston Churchill's speech to the House of Commons, 13 May 1940

I would say to the House, as I said to those who have joined this government: 'I have nothing to offer but blood, toil, tears and sweat.' We have before us many, many long months of struggle and of suffering. You ask, what is our policy? It is to wage war, by sea, land and air, with all our might and with all the strength that God can give us; to wage war against a monstrous tyranny, never surpassed in the dark, lamentable catalogue of human crime. That is our policy. You ask, what is our aim? I can answer in one word: It is victory, victory at all costs, victory in spite of all terror, victory, however long and hard the road may be; for without victory, there is no survival. At this time I feel entitled to claim the aid of all, and I say, 'Come then, let us go forward together with our united strength.'

Why was Churchill appointed as Prime Minister on 10 May 1940?

There are six main reasons that Churchill was appointed as Prime Minister in May and they are summarised in Figure 5.1 below.

Reason 1

Churchill had been against the policy of Appeasement and had ultimately been proved right. He was the right person to lead the country in the fight against Hitler.

Reason 2

Churchill had improved relations with the Labour Party, as both had attacked the policy of Appeasement, so people thought he could create a cohesive wartime government.

Reason 3

Churchill's reputation as a leader had been enhanced by the varying political roles he has undertaken in his career, particularly as First Lord of the Admiralty. His speeches were admired and he was popular with the press.

Reason 4

Opinion polls suggested that the public liked and supported him.

Reason 5

Churchill was clear in his opinion that Hitler and Nazism had to be defeated, rather than lived with as Chamberlain's policy of Appeasement seemed to suggest.

Reason 6

The Nazi occupation of Denmark (8 April 1940) and the invasion of Norway (9 April 1940) effectively meant that Britain was surrounded on the eastern side, and Churchill appeared to be the only politician willing to make a stand and fight.

▲ Figure 5.1: Why Churchill was appointed as Prime Minister on 10 May 1940

The importance of Churchill as wartime leader

When Churchill was appointed Prime Minister in May 1940, he faced a difficult situation. The Germany army and air force were deep into northern France, and the British Expeditionary Force (which had been dispatched to help the French defeat Hitler) were trapped at the French port of Dunkirk on the English Channel. While the evacuation of Dunkirk led to the return of 300,000 British soldiers, the event has been seen as either a 'triumph' or 'disaster'.

The Dunkirk evacuation was quickly followed by the fall of France. Hitler now controlled most of Europe and the possible invasion of Britain seemed imminent. With the collapse of France, and with no help coming to Britain from the USA, many politicians saw negotiating with Hitler as the best way forward. However, this was not the case with Churchill.

While many thought Churchill's speeches were merely emotional, Churchill had the self-confidence to convince his Coalition cabinet and the population that Britain could stand up to Hitler. Instead of trying to negotiate a peace with Hitler, Churchill set about the following:

- organising the military
- ensuring that the air force could control the skies
- organising the war economy
- creating a command structure between the army, navy and air force
- ensuring close relations with the USA, and securing the Lend–Lease Scheme, which meant that Britain received support to fight the war.

ACTIVITIES ?

1 In groups, discuss the reasons in Figure 5.1 above and put them in order of importance. Compare your order with other groups in the class.

2 Research the Dunkirk evacuation. Was it a 'triumph or disaster'?

Ultimately, Churchill provided the strong leadership needed during this difficult period. He kept up the morale of the British people and made them believe in ultimate victory with speeches and tours of the country. His speeches were so powerful that it was said that he 'mobilised the English language' as part of the war effort. There was no talk of surrender and he rejected any idea of peace. For him the defeat of Nazism was all that mattered.

> **Source M: Extract from Churchill's speech, 18 June 1940. Quoted in Roy Jenkins** *Churchill* **published in 2001**
>
> *I expect that the Battle of Britain is about to begin. Upon this battle depends the survival of Christian civilisation. Upon it depends our own British life, and the long continuity of our institutions and our Empire. The whole fury and might of the enemy must very soon be turned on us.*
>
> *Hitler knows that he will have to break us in this island or lose the war. If we can stand up to him all Europe may be free and the life of the world may move forward into broad, sunlit uplands.*
>
> *But if we fail, then the whole world, including the United States, will sink into the abyss of a new dark age. Let us therefore brace ourselves to our duties, and so bear ourselves that, if the British Empire and its Commonwealth last for a thousand years, men will still say, 'this was their Finest Hour'.*

Practice questions

To what extent does Source M accurately explain Churchill's role as wartime leader of Britain? *(For guidance, see pages 192–193.)*

Conclusion: How important was it to maintain people's morale during the war?

In the previous chapter you considered how people in Britain coped with the experience of war, and regardless of whether you think they coped well or not, the need for morale to be maintained during war is unquestionable. If the morale of people is not maintained, it is argued by many historians that that becomes a significant factor in determining the outcome of a war. Winston Churchill convinced many in Britain that victory was possible provided people came together, and the enemy was defeated together. The morale of the British people was a combination of two things. The genuine attitude of many people that however tough the war made their lives, they would not give in, and the role of the government in doing what was necessary to maintain people's moral in support of the war effort.

On 8 May 1945, celebrations throughout Britain and Europe heralded VE Day, 'Victory in Europe'. Germany was now a defeated power and the war in Europe was over. During the first half of the twentieth century, Britain had been involved in two world wars and come out of both on the victorious side. The Second World War had lasted for almost six years, and behind the victory celebrations was a country that faced many problems. Fighting war is costly, and the Second World War was fought at enormous cost, financially as well as in terms of human life and injury. The demobilisation of military personnel, the assessment of war damage and reconstruction, and the formation of a new government were all needed. Dealing with the aftermath of war can be as demanding as dealing with the war itself.

> **Interpretation 1:** From *Popular culture in post-war Wales (1945–1995)*, written by historian Gareth Elwyn Jones, and published on the Open University website
>
> *In 1945, the people of Wales anticipated that economic recovery and the welfare state would generate a new social confidence which, in turn, would prompt a resurgence of a traditional and distinctive culture. Newly elected Labour politicians were given to describing their mission as one of 'building a new Jerusalem'. This was a generation that had experienced History: there were personal, family and collective memories of strikes, lock-outs, unemployment, neglect and then, more recently, the demands of total war. They were a people impatient to shrug off their disadvantaged condition and to commit themselves to renewal.*

▲ Source A: A Victory street party 1 September, 1945

ACTIVITIES ?

1 What can you learn from Source A about Welsh expectations at the end of the war?

2 Does Source A support Interpretation 1?

The economic position of Britain in 1945

Britain found itself in a difficult economic position by the end of the Second World War. In some ways it was in a similar position in 1945 as it was at the start of the Great Depression. Some economists suggested that Britain was in an even worse economic position.

- Britain's national debt (the total money borrowed by the government) was £3,500 million.
- Some of Britain's national wealth was held as gold, and stored at the Bank of England. When a country sells its gold reserves, it is a sign that country is in debt. In 1945, Britain's gold reserves fell from £864 million to £3 million.
- Britain had lost 30 per cent of its total wealth.
- The USA ended the Lend–Lease agreement (see page 168) and bankruptcy loomed.
- A third of Britain's housing stock had been destroyed.
- Half of Britain's factories and shops had been destroyed.
- Two-thirds (3,500 vessels) of Britain's merchant fleet had been sunk (between September 1939 to May 1940, 177 British merchant ships were sunk).
- Military deaths totalled 264,433.
- Civilian deaths totalled 60,595.
- Rationing remained in place as Britain could not afford to buy food from abroad.
- The basic rate of income tax was raised to 50 per cent to help the government raise more money to pay for the reconstruction needed after the war; however, some wealthy people felt they were being personally made to pay for the war.

However, the impact of the war had varied effects on the different regions of Britain. Many in Wales had experienced the harsh realities of war: bombing, destruction and death and injury. Some 15,000 Welshmen were killed in the war. Many others returned physically or mentally shattered by their experiences of war. Daily existence had been difficult but readjusting to peacetime and family life was going to be hard too. Nevertheless, in 1945 there was also optimism. It was suggested that the war had led to the realisation that Wales had a distinct identity, and that people from around Britain were more aware of that. Workers and troops had been moved to Wales during the bombing of other parts of Britain and this had allowed people to experience Welsh traditions and culture.

ACTIVITIES

1 Look back at Chapter 1 about Britain during the Great Depression. To what extent was Britain in a similar or different position in 1945 to that of the 1930s?

2 In groups, discuss and plan how you would go about improving the economic position Britain found itself in, in 1945. Consider how you would tackle two problems presented by the bullet points list on this page.

- What would you need to do to deal with the problem?
- Who would you involve in dealing with the problem?
- How long might it take to deal with the problem?

Present your ideas to the rest of the class.

'Victory' parties and parades

Victory in the Second World war was celebrated in many ways across the country. Some of these events were spontaneous, some were encouraged and others were planned. Many 'Victory parties' took place on VE day itself; others followed at later dates but were still called 'VE victory parties'. In many places there were 'victory' parades, involving marches of military personnel. The return of military combatants was eagerly awaited, though many women expected to lose their jobs (as they had done at the end of the First World War) once men returned.

> **Interpretation 2: From the 'Join me in the 1900s' website. Here Peter Johnson remembers events that took place in Edmonton (North London) during June 1945**
>
> *There was a military parade through Edmonton. It took place in Fore Street, starting at Noel Park and it was saluted by the mayor outside the Town Hall. My uncle, who was in the Home Guard, was involved. I remember climbing into a Bren Gun Carrier, a small tank, with lots of other children outside the town hall and speeding to the Angel Pub and back.*
>
> *We also had street parties. People put their tables and chairs out into the street. In our street these spanned nearly half the length of the street. A stage was erected in the middle of the street and there was music, lights and people singing, glad to be alive.*
>
> *In the evening we went to a dinner and dance in the ballroom above the Regal Cinema. All the street lights that were still working came on, and to walk home and see the lights on in every house blazing out, it was magic after those long years of war. Some of the shops had their windows ablaze with light.*
>
> *There was also a bonfire. Life was going to get better from now on.*
>
> *... Yet some of the houses had their curtains drawn with the residents shut inside. When these people did come out to watch they would be crying. We were told that these families had lost the man of the house or one of the grown up children while serving in the forces.*

▲ **Source B:** Cardiff City Centre Victory parade of a Home Guard contingent, June 1945

ACTIVITY ?

To what extent do the sources on pages 170–172 accurately portray Britain in 1945?

Demobilisation

In preparation for what would happen to conscripted military personnel when the war was over, in September 1944, the Minister for Labour and National Service, Ernest Bevin, designed a demobilisation plan. This was so that men and women could return to the lives that they had before being conscripted into the military. Some of these people were stationed in Britain, but many were overseas in places where key battles had taken place.

The plan was to release service men and women in an organised way:

- Servicemen and women were to be released from the army, navy and air force based on their age and service number. This calculation, made from their age and the number of months they had been in uniform, gave each person a release number. The number determined when they would be 'demobbed'.
- Some men were considered 'key men'. This was because they had a skill that was now vital in the post-war reconstruction of the country. As a consequence, these men were released ahead of their turn.
- Release priority was also given to married women, and men aged 50 or over, and these also were released ahead of their turn.

The plan was put in place on 18 June 1945. Over the next 18 months, 4.3 million men and women were released from military service and returned to the lives they had had – 'civvy street' – before the war.

While servicemen and women who were demobilised were elated and could not wait to 'get home', they nevertheless faced a number of challenges on their return. The country, cities, towns and villages were very different to the places they had left when they had joined the war.

- Food was still rationed.
- Homes and workplaces had been damaged, in many cases beyond repair.
- Returning husbands and wives had to relearn how to live together again: some had not seen each for six years.
- Some men and women returned to find that their relationship or marriage had broken down in their absence, and divorce rates increased significantly.
- Some returnees, while appearing physically fit had been psychologically affected by the war, and found ordinary life difficult to cope with and adjust to.

The plan was executed successfully but not without a few problems. Many servicemen and women felt that the process was too slow, and this led to protests and complaints.

Interpretation 3: From an author blog by historian Alan Allport. He was researching and gathering evidence for his book *Demobbed: Coming Home after World War Two* which was published in 2009

Gary Allighan of the Daily Mail reports that: 'unpleasant stories of ex-servicemen being treated harshly at work' are reaching his demobilisation help desk. 'I have been told of young foremen making 'ex' men look foolish before the rest of the workers because they were not so adept with their tools ... that kind of attitude is despicable. It is hard enough to come back from the Forces and find that their pre-Service subordinates have become foremen without having to be humiliated.' Allighan has a word of advice for the demobilised: 'Don't, for your own peace of mind, come back into civilian life with any illusions. This is still a hard world. It would have been much harder had Hitler won.'

Practice question

To what extent does Interpretation 3 accurately explain the experience of demobilisation? *(For guidance, see pages 192–193.)*

ACTIVITY ?

Why do you think that demobilisation was more commonly referred to as 'returning to civvy street'?

War damage

By 1945, most major British towns and cities had been affected by German bombing raids. The Germans made new plans in 1943 to try to restart the Blitz. In January 1944, under the command of General Peltz, a series of air raids, codenamed 'Operation Steinbock', were carried out against London and other cities. Poor training and navigation, a shortage of aircraft, and effective anti-aircraft defences made what the British called the 'Baby Blitz' relatively ineffective. By June, the attempt had been abandoned. Nevertheless, air raids continued into 1945, causing further damage, injury and loss of life, but these raids were not exactly strategic. Hitler personally ordered the use of missiles (the so-called vengeance weapons or V-weapons). These were to be fired continuously at the south-east of England. However, in most cases the weapons were inaccurate. Out of 10,492 flying bombs, only 2,419 reached London. Small air raids were still conducted through to late March 1945, when the last rocket, the last flying bomb and the last conventional air raid hit British targets. There was also extensive damage in Wales (see Chapter 4, pages 150–151).

Source C: Tonnage of bombs on British targets 1940–1945 (*includes V-weapons)

1940	1941	1942	1943	1944	1945*
36,844	21,858	3,260	2,298	9,151	761

▲ Source D: Ruined flats in Whitechapel, East London, taken in March 1945

Practice question

What can be learnt from Sources C and D about the impact of air raids on Britain up to 1945? *(For guidance, see pages 190–191.)*

The reasons for Labour's victory in the 1945 general election

The general election in 1945 was the first to be held in Britain since 1935 and several million people voted for the first time. The electorate was about 33 million and about 24 million people voted. The Labour Party had not held office since 1931 and political differences had created huge divisions within it during the Depression. It had recovered slowly during the 1930s but won only 154 seats in the 1935 election (the Conservatives won 432). There was still a fear of Labour's socialist policies and many people continued to raise the spectre of the creation of a communist state if Labour were ever to win an election and form a government.

In 1945, each of the two main parties published a manifesto indicating the policies they would follow if they were elected. Many of the policies were similar but Labour embraced the Beveridge Report and said they would implement its recommendations immediately. The Conservatives were more careful about setting time limits. The Conservatives had an aggressive election campaign that tried to smear the Labour Party but this turned out to be counterproductive. When the campaign began it was anticipated that the Conservatives would win. Their main weapon was Churchill and many people thought that his status as a war leader would be enough to guarantee that the Conservatives would easily win the election.

The radio broadcasts for each party attracted huge audiences and the public meetings were extremely well attended. Public interest in politics and international events had grown during the war and the electorate was aware of the key issues facing Britain. Voting began on 5 July and ended on 19 July – this was to permit soldiers serving overseas to vote.

▲ Source E: A Labour Party campaign poster, 1945

	Conservative Party	Labour Party
Manifesto title	*Mr Churchill's declaration of policy to the electors*	*Let us face the future*
Main policies	Comprehensive insurance scheme National Health Service Full employment Education improvements Housing improvements	Comprehensive insurance scheme National Health Service to be set up immediately Full employment Education improvements Housing improvements Nationalisation of the Bank of England, coal and power, transport, iron and steel to be carried out immediately. This policy would guarantee many jobs.
Comments	The Conservative manifesto emphasised the need for continuity under Churchill. Conservative posters also showed their reliance on Churchill. Though Churchill spoke of a clear plan, it seemed as if many policies were just hopes and not definite.	The Labour manifesto stressed planning, reconstruction and equality – all policies that people had come to recognise during the war. Labour's campaign did not mention any personalities. The Labour manifesto showed that it would implement the Beveridge Report more quickly than the Conservatives. It put forward the idea of 'Never again' – a phrase that could be interpreted in several ways – not only referring to war but also to the poverty and unemployment of the 1930s.

▲ Table 6.1: Manifestos of the Labour and Conservative parties

Results

The election results were declared on 26 July 1945. Labour had won a landslide victory (see Table 6.2). Some of the Labour leaders had not expected this and had booked their summer holidays, which then had to be cancelled.

Party	Seats	Percentage of seats in parliament	Percentage of votes cast	Percentage increase/decrease on 1935 election
Labour	395	61.7	48.1	+10.4
Conservative and Ulster Unionist	215	33.6	40.1	–13.9
Liberals	12	1.9	9.0	+0.8
Others	18	3.4	2.8	

▲ Table 6.2: A table of the 1945 general election results

Reasons why Labour won

Historians have put forward many reasons why the Labour Party won the 1945 general election:

- The Labour Party had been winning parliamentary seats before the war started, which was a sign that their popularity was improving.
- Opinion polls taken during the war years showed Labour had increasing support over the Conservatives, and by 1943 their lead was between 10–20 per cent.
- Trade unions had played a key role during the war and in doing so promoted the role and standing of the Labour Party.
- Socialism was not seen as threatening as it had been in the 1920s after the Russian revolution. The coalition wartime government had intervened and controlled people's lives and people had got used to it. People were no longer frightened of 'state planning'.
- Socialism was also seen in a good light because of the role the USSR had played in the defeat of Hitler.
- Many people blamed the Conservatives for the problems of the 1930s, and associated unemployment and social deprivation with Conservative polices. These people did not want to go back to a Conservative government.
- Many people regarded Churchill as a great wartime leader, but they did not see him as a peacetime leader. Some people simply regarded him as too old. They also associated his speech-making with war events, rather than peace and reconstruction.
- The war changed people's attitudes towards the class system, social mobility and opportunity. The Labour Party seemed to stand for a greater sense of allowing all people to access opportunity despite their background.
- In the coalition wartime government led by Winston Churchill, Labour politicians had held key posts and people thought that they would carry on the work they had done in wartime into peacetime. Attlee had been the Deputy Prime Minister, Bevin Minister for Labour and Herbet Morrison Home Secretary. In the election people associated with these Labour politicians and wanted them to lead a Labour government.

Interpretation 4: From historian Kenneth O. Morgan, in *The Oxford History of Britain*, published in 2010

The result of the 1945 election, to the general astonishment, was a political landslide. It was a striking comment on the changed atmosphere of the wars years, and no doubt a delayed verdict on the bitterness of the thirties, with its memories of Munich, Jarrow and the hunger marchers. At the same time it made people feel exhilarated and bewildered.

Practice question

Read Interpretation 4. How far do you agree with this interpretation of the Labour Party's electoral victory in 1945? (For guidance, see pages 196–197.)

ACTIVITY

Using the sources and information, what do you think was the most important reason why the Labour Party won the 1945 election?

Conclusion: How difficult were conditions in Britain in 1945?

Despite being a 'victorious' country Britain faced many problems in 1945, and most were not immediately solvable. Many people put their faith in the Labour Party to rebuild a country that had been severely damaged by the war. This meant that victory had come at a price. People's homes were destroyed or damaged, families had lost people or they had come home injured and in need of care. People who had a role in the war had to return to civilian life, and the country had to count the cost and recover.

7 Rebuilding the country after 1945

The Beveridge Report

The Labour Party's landslide electoral victory of 1945 was based on the idea that they could reconstruct Britain after the devastating effects of fighting a war. However, the desire to build a 'new' Britain did not just come as a thought at the end of the war. In 1941, the Coalition wartime government set up a Royal Commission under Sir William Beveridge to look into ways in which Britain could rebuild after the war. In 1942, Beveridge published his report, which contained a series of recommendations. The Labour Party adopted those recommendations and included them in their 1945 manifesto. As you work through this chapter you will be able to reflect upon and make judgements about whether the post-war Labour government was able to reconstruct and rebuild Britain after a six-year war, and deliver on the Beveridge recommendations and the promises the Labour Party itself made to the British people in 1945.

The Coalition wartime government portrayed the war as a 'people's war'. Therefore, when the war was over, there had to be some clear benefits for the sacrifices that were being made. Many people hoped that, in the future, the government would:

- reform existing social security system so that it covered more of the population
- reform the healthcare system, where many people had to pay for treatment and frequently could not afford to do so
- continue with the policy of free milk for all children, which had been introduced in 1940
- reform hospital treatment (it was unrealistic to expect people to pay for treatment if their houses had been bombed).

'Giant' to defeat	What Beveridge wanted to fight for
Want	The need for an adequate income for all
Disease	The need for access to health care
Ignorance	The need for access to educational opportunity
Squalor	The need for adequate housing
Idleness	The need for gainful employment

▲ Table 7.1: A summary of Beveridge's 'Five Giants'

Expectations such as the ones listed above influenced Beveridge's thinking and informed the structure of his report. Beveridge recognised that what he and his committee saw for the future was already happening, namely, greater government involvement in the lives of ordinary people to ensure a secure existence. The issue for Beveridge was to persuade politicians to accept increased peacetime government involvement. The report, entitled 'Social Insurance and Allied Services', was published on 1 December 1942 and within weeks it had sold 635,000 copies. Within two weeks of its publication, a public opinion poll said that 19 out of 20 people had heard of the report and that 9 out of 10 wanted its proposals to be carried out. The British press, with the exception of the *Daily Telegraph*, welcomed the report.

ACTIVITY

Discuss in pairs why Beveridge referred to problems in Britain in the 1940s as 'The Five Giants'.

In 1939:

- 21 million people were eligible for old age pensions.
- 15.5 million were covered by government unemployment insurance.
- 20 million were covered by national health insurance (no more than half of the population).

The Beveridge Report proposed to extend pensions and unemployment insurance, and introduce a health system for all based on the ideal that 'benefits' provided by the state should be 'universal' (available to all), and this became the cornerstone of what was now being called the 'welfare state'.

The report recommended a compulsory insurance scheme to eliminate poverty, whereby every worker would make contributions and these would be supplemented by contributions from employers and also the government. These contributions would help to build up a fund that would pay out weekly benefits to those who were sick or unemployed or who suffered industrial injury. In addition, the scheme would pay old age pensions. The scheme would support the worker and enable him and his family to survive in times of hardship. There would also be benefits for widows.

The report also proposed:

- a family allowance for the second child and subsequent children
- a marriage grant
- a maternity grant and benefit
- a death grant.

The key feature was that people were eligible to receive these benefits and grants because they had all contributed. Most importantly, the proposed system would end the hated means test of the 1930s (see pages 120–121).

The report's recommendations meant that the individual would be looked after by the state from the 'cradle to the grave' (others sarcastically said 'womb to the tomb'). If adopted, the report would create a welfare state. Beveridge argued that if his report were introduced, it would provide a minimum standard of living 'below which no one should be allowed to fall'.

▲ **Source A:** A cartoon of December 1942, shortly after the publication of the Beveridge Report. The face on the jug in the soldier's hand represents William Beveridge, the author of the report

ACTIVITIES ?

1 Why did the introduction of the Beveridge Report concern some people?

2 Look at Source A. What point is the cartoonist making about the Beveridge Report?

Attacking the Five Giants

There were some reforms before the end of the war. Most important was the 1944 Education Act, which now ensured free education during the compulsory years. Parliament also passed the Family Allowances Act in April 1945, although the first payments were not made until August 1946. The key reforms came after the Labour government took office in July 1945 and attacked the 'Five Giants' head on. In a period of just over three years the social reforms of the Labour government created a welfare state which attempted to look after all citizens, whether rich or poor.

In the 'attack on want', the Labour government introduced the National Insurance Act. Under this, all workers would pay a weekly contribution (4s 11d) and the employer and government would also contribute to the fund. The fund would then be used to pay benefits during periods of sickness or unemployment (see Figure 7.1). The act was hailed by all parties and the general public because it eliminated many of the injustices of the pre-war system. It would ensure that there would be no gaps in the welfare system and that there would be a guaranteed basic minimum income to everyone. The National Assistance Act was passed in 1948. A new National Assistance Board was set up to give benefits to those in need. By the act, all local authorities had to provide residential accommodation for the aged and people with disabilities, and ensure that there was at least temporary accommodation for the homeless. *The Times* said that 'the National Assistance Board was the citizen's last defence against destitution.'

> **Interpretation 1:** From *Britain Since 1945* written by P.J. Madgwick, 1982
>
> *Under the new Labour legislation, it was intended that the citizen would be adequately safeguarded against old age, sickness and unemployment, by an insurance-based system without the much resented means test. Poverty was not abolished, but the number of people seriously lacking in food, clothing, shelter and warmth was very substantially reduced compared with the 1930s.*

> ## Practice question
>
> How far do you agree with Interpretation 1 about the impact of the Labour government's implementation of the Beveridge Report? *(For guidance, see pages 196–197.)*

Want

1945 Family Allowances Act
- 5 shillings (25p) per week for each child after the first one
- Allowance payable to the mother
- Payable until the child was 15 or 16 if the child was in full-time education

1946 National Insurance Act
- Ministry of National Insurance set up
- Unemployment benefit
- Sickness benefit
- Maternity benefit – single payment made to a mother on birth of a child
- Death grant to cover the costs of a funeral
- Widows' benefit
- Orphans – guardians to receive an allowance
- Old age pensions – men over 65 and women over 60 – single person 25s (£1.25p) and married couple 42s (£2.10) per week

1948 National Assistance Act
- Designed to help those 'who slipped through the net' of the new system
- Abolished the Poor Law system
- Chronic sick and those whose benefits were not enough were able to use the National Assistance Board (the National Assistance Board was created to assist people whose resources were inadequate)
- Homeless, disabled and mentally ill were covered by the act

Ignorance

1944 Education Act
- Ministry of Education created
- Education divided into primary, secondary and further
- Secondary education to be divided into grammar, technical and modern, following assessment at 11
- Free education until school leaving age of 14 (raised to 15 in 1947)

Squalor

1946 Housing Production Executive set up
- One million houses built in the years 1945–51
- Thousands of pre-fabricated houses (prefabs) constructed

1946 New Towns Act
- 17 in England, 5 in Scotland, 1 in Wales. Peterborough, Crawley, Northampton and Warrington were enlarged

Attacking the Five Giants

Disease

1946 National Health Service Act (to come into operation 1948)
- Comprehensive service, with all citizens receiving all the advice, treatment and care they needed, combined with the best medical and other facilities available
- Service free to the public at the point of use

Idleness

- The wartime coalition had accepted that in peacetime it was the duty of government to maintain a high and stable level of employment. Labour, with its nationalisation of several industries, showed that it intended to manage the economy and fulfil the wartime hope. Moreover, building schemes ensured high employment for several years after the end of hostilities.

◀ Figure 7.1: The specifics of the Beveridge Report

Aneurin Bevan and the NHS

The man responsible for the introduction of the NHS was Aneurin Bevan, a staunch socialist. He was the leading figure in the development of the National Health Service (NHS) but he met stiff resistance from the medical profession, which was worried about professional independence, potential costs and loss of status.

In 1945, about half the population – the wage earners – were covered for free medical treatment under the National Insurance scheme. Families were covered only if they had private insurance and many of them did not have enough money to purchase insurance. Calling out a doctor, or going to a hospital, was often a last resort with the result that illnesses or injuries went untreated altogether, or became more serious than they might have been. During the war, an emergency medical service had come into operation and after the first four months of war, the government had provided 1,000 new operating theatres, millions of bandages and tens of thousands of extra beds. A national blood transfusion service was set up and free hospital treatment was granted to direct war casualties. By the end of the war, it was evident that a national health service could be efficiently and effectively operated.

The Beveridge Report had anticipated a national health service, and the National Health Act was passed in 1946.

National Health Act 1946

- The service was free to the public at the point of use.
- The service was comprehensive, with all citizens receiving all the advice, treatment and care they needed, combined with the best medical and other facilities available.
- Drug prescriptions, dental and optical care were included.
- Voluntary and local hospitals were co-ordinated into a single national system to be operated at local level by appointed Health Boards. The Act took into national public ownership 1,771 English and Welsh local authority hospitals and 1,334 voluntary hospitals.
- The overall administration of the system was the responsibility of the Minister of Health.
- The NHS would control hospital and specialist services, general practitioner (medical, dental, ophthalmic and pharmaceutical) services, ambulance services and community health services.

ANEURIN BEVAN

1897	Born in Tredegar, South Wales, one of ten children
1910	Left school and became a miner
1919	Won a scholarship to Central Labour College
1926	Leader of miners in Tredegar during the General Strike
1929	MP for Ebbw Vale
1945–51	Minister of Health
1951	Minister of Labour
1951	Resigned over NHS charges
1959	Elected Deputy Leader of the Labour Party

◀ Source B: Aneurin Bevan, Minister for Health, meeting Sylvia Diggory (née Beckingham), the first National Health patient at Park Hospital, Manchester, on 5 July 1948, the day the NHS began. In an interview 50 years later, Sylvia said: 'Mr Bevan asked me if I understood the significance of the occasion and told me that it was a milestone in history – the most civilised step any country had ever taken, and a day I would remember for the rest of my life – and of course, he was right.'

Opposition to the National Health Service

The British Medical Association (BMA), the doctors' professional body, opposed the introduction of the NHS. Its members believed that they would lose money as a result of the NHS because they feared there would be no private patients. Their opposition to government interference went back to the beginning of the National Insurance scheme in 1911. The BMA had no wish for its members to become merely government workers and they fought to retain their independence. They did not wish to become salaried employees of the government – they said they would just be civil servants.

In January 1948, the BMA held a ballot of all its doctors to see whether they approved of joining the NHS. Eighty-four per cent of doctors voted and the result was 40,814 against and 4,735 for joining. Despite this, Bevan specified that the new system would come into operation on 5 July of that year. Nevertheless, further talks followed and Bevan allowed the consultants to work inside the health service and at the same time still treat private patients and earn high fees. Bevan promised to amend the Act accordingly and ended fears that doctors would become salaried civil servants. Following another vote among its members, the BMA recommended that its members participate in the new system. Bevan said he had ensured the start of the service by 'stuffing the consultants' mouths with gold'.

MORITURI TE SALUTANT.

Source D: Alfred Cox, former Chairman of BMA, speaking about the National Health Service Bill, 1946

I have examined the bill and it looks to me uncommonly like the first step, and a big one, to National Socialism as practised in Germany. The medical service there was early put under the dictatorship of a 'medical fuhrer'. This bill will establish the Minister for Health in that capacity.

"ALL THAT REMAINS, GENTLEMEN, IS TO REMOVE THE NECK AND THE OPERATION WILL BE COMPLETELY SUCCESSFUL"

OPERATION SABOTAGE

▲ **Source E:** A cartoon published in the *Evening Standard*, January 1948

Source F: An extract from an article in *The Daily Sketch*, a British tabloid newspaper, February 1948, during the discussions between Bevan and the BMA

The state medical service is part of the socialist plot to convert Great Britain into a National Socialist economy. The doctors' stand is the first effective revolt of the professional classes against socialist tyranny. There is nothing that Bevan or any other socialist can do about it except in the shape of Hitlerian coercion.

ACTIVITIES ?

1 How does Source C portray the opposition to the introduction of the National Health Service?

2 In pairs, use the information and sources on pages 181–182 to create arguments for and against the introduction of the NHS. Share your ideas with other pairs in the class.

◄ **Source C:** A cartoon published for the British Medical Association in 1946 after the passing of the National Health Act. Three doctors are saluting the emperor (Aneurin Bevan). Translated, the words at the foot of the cartoon say 'Those who are about to die salute you.'

The impact of the NHS

By 5 July 1948, three-quarters of the population had signed up with doctors under the new health scheme. Two months later, 39,500,000 people, or 93 per cent of the population, were enrolled and more than 20,000 general practitioners, about 90 per cent, were participating. The new service had become immediately popular with the vast majority of Britain's population. However, the government soon encountered problems with funding the system:

- In its first year the NHS cost £248 million to run, almost £140 million more than had been originally estimated. Annual sums put aside for treatment such as dental surgery and glasses were quickly used up.
- Initially, £2 million was put aside to pay for free spectacles over the first nine months of the NHS but this was spent within weeks.
- More than 5 million people were issued with NHS spectacles in the first year and millions visited the dentist in order to have all their teeth extracted and replaced with false ones.
- The Ministry of Health assumed that around 140 million free prescriptions would be dispensed annually but this turned out to be a gross underestimate. The number of prescriptions increased each year until it reached 229 million in 1951.
- People even began to ask for free supplies of household remedies for which they had previously paid, such as aspirin, laxatives, first-aid dressings and cotton wool.
- The government had estimated that the NHS would cost £140 million a year by 1950. However, by the beginning of 1949, costs were more than double this, reaching around £400 million and, by the time Labour left office in 1951, annual costs were almost £500 million.
- In 1951, the Labour government introduced a charge for some dental treatment and for prescriptions for medicine. This led to the resignation of Bevan.
- When the Conservatives won the general election in 1951, they said they would retain the NHS, having firmly opposed the bill in 1946 and its establishment in 1948. The popularity of the NHS meant that no party now dared to threaten to dismantle it.

ACTIVITY

'The introduction of the National Health Service was too costly and unrealistic.' How far would you agree with this judgement?

Practice question

This question is about the Labour government in 1945. Explain the connections between any THREE of the following:

- The Beveridge Report 1942
- The Labour Party victory in the 1945 General Election
- The Conservative Party defeat in the 1945 General Election
- 'The Five Giants'.

(For guidance, see page 195.)

Educational opportunities following the Act of 1944

The Education Act of 1944 was in fact passed and put into operation by the wartime coalition government headed by Churchill. It created a Ministry of Education with the aim of providing a comprehensive, national system of education.

The education of children was to be split into three stages: primary, secondary and further.

These stages were to be provided for by Local Authorities, who would set up Local Education Authorities (LEAs). Education at all these stages was to be provided free to the recipient, but paid for by the state. The school leaving age was raised to 15 in 1947. The Act also made a daily act of religious worship compulsory within schools.

The Secondary stage of education was to catered for by three types of schools: grammar, technical and modern.

Which type of Secondary school a student attended was to be determined by the sitting of an examination called the '11 plus'. If passed at the higher level, a student would go to a grammar school. Passed at other levels would determine if a student went to a technical or modern school. The lower level of pass meant that a student went to a secondary modern school.

In spite of the Act's intentions, the 11-plus examination, a simple intelligence test taken once at the end of primary schooling, did little more than give those who passed at the highest level and went to a grammar school what seemed to be an advantage. The benefit being that many grammar students went on to university and better paid jobs, while those going to secondary moderns invariably left school and went straight into employment. Also, very few technical schools opened.

▲ Source G: Girls at Ruislip Bourne Secondary Modern School (Middlesex) who were among the first pupils to benefit from the new education act

ACTIVITY ?

In groups, discuss what can be learned from Source G about post-war education.

The Homes for All policy

The state of Britain's housing at the end of the war was very poor and in desperate need of repair. Damage was significant in many towns and cities, and many houses were not repairable. The immediate response by government was to build prefab (short for prefabricated) bungalows, designed to last ten years.

It was estimated by the Burt Committee (which had been formed in 1942) that approximately 200,000 prefab homes would be needed when the war ended. The aim was to build 500,000 of this type of home to cover all eventualities. The post-war Labour government agreed to deliver 300,000 units within ten years, within a budget of £150 million. In the end, of the 1.2 million new houses built from 1945 to 1951, when the programme officially ended, only 156,623 houses were prefab houses.

Council house provision was shaped by the New Towns Act 1946, and the Town and Country Planning Act 1947. Bevan, the Minister for Health and Housing, promoted a vision of new estates where 'the working man, the doctor and the clergyman will live in close proximity to each other.'

▲ Source H: A post-war council housing estate being built

▲ Source I: A post-war prefab house, which had been constructed in a redundant aircraft factory

ACTIVITY ?

How did the government help repair housing after the end of the Second World War?

Nationalisation of the key industries

During the war, the Coalition government had effectively taken control of industrial production in order to ensure that the essentials needed were produced. Some of industries had not fully recovered from the effects of the Depression in the 1930s, but the impact of the war and government control had been to their advantage. When the war ended it was realised that some of these industries were so crucial to Britain's recovery and reconstruction that the Labour government was keen to nationalise them. That would mean these industries would be owned by the state, rather than be owned by private individuals. To many people this was seen as a form of socialist control, but others realised that in order to rebuild the country, the control of these industries was a necessary pragmatic action. The Labour government had committed itself in its 1945 manifesto to a programme of nationalisation. It also pledged to financially compensate the owners of the industries it decided to nationalise, and to protect the status and jobs of the existing workers in those industries. In the ended the compensation that was paid out totalled £2,700 million.

Nationalisation was justified on the grounds of:

- Industrial efficiency
- Creating jobs to maintain full employment
- Lower prices to the consumer.

The following industries were now brought into 'public ownership' – they were 'nationalised'.

Coal

As a consequence of the Coal Industry Nationalisation Act of 1946, the coal industry was nationalised in January 1947. Even the Conservative Party accepted the need for the nationalisation of this longstanding ailing industry. A National Coal Board was set up under the Minister of Fuel and Power. Some 850 coalmine owners were compensated with £164 million.

▲ Source J: A photograph of what happened to coal mines around Britain in January 1947

Transport

In January 1948, the government bought 52,000 miles of existing railway track, heralding the birth of British Rail. This decision to effectively nationalise the rail network meant that most of Britain's railways were under public ownership. This was done to make rail transport around Britain more efficient, both for industry and commuters.

Road haulage was a more problematic issue. Hauliers carrying their own goods, and local bus services were exempt from nationalisation, but long distance hauliers were brought under the control and ownership of the British Road Services.

Electricity

In 1947, the electricity industry was nationalised. The gas industry was also nationalised a year later in 1948. Both these nationalisations were controversial and attracted opposition both outside and inside Parliament. Nevertheless, the government did not back down.

▲ Figure 7.2: The nationalised electricity industry operated by dividing Britain into area electricity boards

Reaction to the reforms of the post-war Labour governments

Reaction to the reforms introduced by post-war Labour governments between 1945 and 1951 polarised opinion at the time, and continue to this day.

The welfare state

While unemployment was lower between 1946 and 1950 (1.6 per cent) than during pre-war years, there was a mostly negative reaction to the welfare state:

- The cost of the welfare state continued to rise beyond what had been planned for.
- Expectations of what the welfare state could do grew beyond its initial aims into realms that many thought were unrealistic.
- The welfare state was an interfering state, a 'nanny state', that led to dependency and, some thought, idleness. The system of benefits meant that people were supported from the 'cradle to the grave'.

The NHS

The National Health Service (NHS) was highly regarded by the population, and very quickly seen as innovative by observers from around the world. However, by 1951, many thought the NHS had become too costly, and people's expectations of what it could do were unrealistic.

The Education Act

Many people believed that educational opportunity was fairer and available to all, and it now supported adults who had previously not had much of an education. However, some saw the Act as bringing in a system that reinforced social class and limited opportunity by categorising people based on the passing or failing of an exam taken at the age of eleven.

THE UNIVERSAL UNCLES

◀ **Source K:** 'The Universal Uncles'. A Punch cartoon published in 1946 about the work of the Labour government

ACTIVITY

What is the cartoonist who drew Source K saying about the post-war Labour government?

Homes for All

Damaged or destroyed housing was slowly replaced and people had more modern housing. Those who could not afford to buy their own house could now rent a house from the local council. These were temporary housing for people whose property had been destroyed or damaged, however, many people lived longer in the prefabs than had originally been intended, and not all local councils built sufficient housing.

Nationalisation (coal, electricity and transport)

There was a mostly positive reaction to nationalisation:

- By 1951 the nationalisation programme was complete and not only were key industries providing utilities for all people, but about one in ten men and women were employed by the newly nationalised industries.
- The state-owned sector of the economy account for about 20 per cent of the total economy.
- Nationalisation successfully rescued previously 'failing' industries. Coal production rose significantly during 1946–51.
- Nationalisation brought with it the idea of creating 'standards' and proper safely levels in work.
- Rural areas saw benefits due to the national grid, as electricity got to areas that had not had it ever before.

Criticisms included that nationalisation merely saved failing industries at the taxpayers' expense, and that nationalised industries were monopolies, and, as a consequence, became inefficient.

> **Interpretation 2:** From *The Labour Party and the Struggle for Socialism*, written by historian **D. Coates and published in 1975**
>
> *The impact of the Labour Government of 1945–51, for all its promise and its vast body of legislation, was profoundly ambiguous. There had undoubtedly been important social reforms, but power had not shifted between the classes. It had simply created a mixed economy which had only marginally altered the distribution of social power, privilege, wealth, income, opportunity and security.*

> ### Practice question
>
> Read Interpretation 2. How far would you agree with this interpretation about the impact of the post-war Labour government in the years 1945–51? *(For guidance, see pages 196–197.)*

Conclusion: How did the Labour government deal with the problems of the time?

British people voted a Labour government into power in 1945 because they wanted change. The war, despite all of its destructive effects, had made people realise that Britain could be a better country if people worked together to make change happen. The Labour government took up the challenge by adopting a programme of change that was designed to help improve all people's lives. What had been done in wartime was applied to peace time. The nation's health, its work and industries, and the care of people in need all came under the control of the government.

WJEC Examination Guidance

This section will give you step-by-step guidance on how best to approach and answer the types of questions that you will face in the exam. Below is a model exam paper with a set of exam-style questions (without the sources).

Unit one: studies in depth

<table>
<tr>
<td>

In Question 1 you have to analyse and pick out key details from two sources linked to the theme of the question

</td>
<td>

Wales and the wider perspective
1C Depression, War and Recovery, 1930–1951
Time allowed: 1 hour

1 What can be learnt from Sources A and B about the role of women during the Second World War?
[4 marks]

</td>
</tr>
<tr>
<td>

In Question 2 you have to analyse and evaluate the accuracy of a source, using your knowledge to identify strengths and weaknesses

</td>
<td>

2 To what extent does this source accurately explain the experience of evacuees who were sent to Wales during the Second World War?

[In your answer you should refer to the strengths and limitations of the source and use your own knowledge and understanding of the historical context.]
[6 marks]

</td>
</tr>
<tr>
<td>

In Question 3 you have to demonstrate knowledge and understanding to help construct a reasoned judgement upon the significance of an identified issue

</td>
<td>

3 Why was the British Government's use of propaganda significant during the Second World War?
[12 marks]

4 Explain the connections between any THREE of the following:

</td>
</tr>
<tr>
<td>

In Question 4 you have to demonstrate knowledge and understanding in order to explain relevant connections between three chosen features

</td>
<td>

■ The Beveridge Report of 1942
■ The Labour victory in the 1945 election
■ The establishment of the National Health Service
■ The nationalisation of the key industries
[12 marks]

5 How far do you agree with this interpretation of the impact of the Depression on ordinary people in Britain?
[16 marks]

</td>
</tr>
<tr>
<td>

In Question 5 you need to demonstrate knowledge and understanding of a key issue, analysing and evaluating how and why interpretations of an issue differ, before reaching a judgement about the accuracy of the interpretation based upon its authorship

</td>
<td>

[In your answer you should refer to how and why interpretations of this issue differ. Use your own knowledge and understanding of the wider historical debate over this issue to reach a well-supported judgement.]

Marks for spelling, punctuation and the accurate use of grammar and specialist language are allocated to this question.
[3 marks]

Total marks for the paper: 53

</td>
</tr>
</table>

Examination guidance

Examination guidance for Question 1

This section provides guidance on how to answer the question on what you can learn from two sources. Look at the following question:

> What can be learnt from Sources B and C about the impact of the Depression on Britain?

Source B: From *The Road to Wigan Pier* written by George Orwell, published in 1937

When you see the unemployment figures quoted at two millions, it is fatally easy to take this as meaning that two million people are out of work and the rest of the population are comparatively comfortable. I admit that till recently I was in the habit of doing so myself. I used to calculate that if you put the registered unemployed at around two millions and threw in the destitute and those who for one reason and another were not registered, you might take the number of unfed people in England as being, at the very most, five millions. This is an enormous under-estimate. I think it is nearer six millions.

Source C: From *Brynmawr* written by H. Jennings. Published in 1934

While some of the effects of unemployment are general, individual men and their families of course react in different ways, and out of some six hundred families normally dependent upon unemployment benefit probably few have precisely the same attitude to life and circumstances. One man will approach the Exchange with impatience and bitterness at his dependence and impotency to help himself; one in a mood of growing apathy; one in a growing feeling of the need for change in the economic and social system.

How to answer

- Compose an opening sentence to say that both sources provide useful information on the topic.
- Pick out several key facts/points for Source B, linking them to the question.
- Pick out several key facts/points from Source C, linking them to the question.
- Aim to write equal amounts from both sources to ensure a balanced answer.
- Make sure your answer displays a balanced use of both sources. An imbalanced answer which concentrates too much on one source will not score you top marks.

Example answer

Step 1: Opening statement which links to the question.

> The two sources provide useful information about the impact of the Depression on Britain.

Step 2: Identify two or more facts from Source B.

> Source B comments that the impact of the Depression was to make millions of people unemployed and the figure of exactly how many millions became unemployed is not clear. It also states that it is easy to consider those people who were not unemployed as comfortable and were not impacted by the Depression. The Depression also impacted on people who were already destitute and unfed.

Step 3: Identify two or more facts from Source C.

> Source C comments that while the impact of the Depression caused unemployment people reacted in different ways to that experience. It states that some unemployed people may be bitter and impatient, while others might just accept it with apathy, believing they could do nothing about it. It also states that the impact of the Depression might lead some people to want change to the social and economic system that has led to such unemployment.

Now try answering the following question:

What can be learnt from Sources A and B about the government's use of propaganda during the Second World War?

Source A: A statement issued by a government minister during a radio broadcast of May 1941

Today we are calling all women. Every woman in the country is needed to pull her weight to the utmost – to consider carefully where her services would help most and then let nothing stand in the way of giving such services. Like her, many women have made their sacrifices already and are doing their utmost to win the war. But to those thousands who have not yet come forward I would say here and now that every one of us is needed.

JUST A GOOD AFTERNOON'S WORK

▲ Source B: A government propaganda poster encouraging women to work

Examination guidance for Question 2

This section provides guidance on how to answer the question on the accuracy of a source. Look at the following question:

> To what extent does this source accurately explain the effects of the means test?
>
> In your answer you should refer to the strengths and limitations of the source and use your own knowledge and understanding of the historical context.

> **Source B:** An unemployed man describes the effects of the means test on his life in the 1930s
>
> *My wife obtained a job as a house-to-house saleswoman, and was able to earn a few shillings to supplement our dole income. This strained our relationship. It was a burden on her and constant bickerings over money matters, usually culminating in threats to leave from both of us. The final blow came when the means test was put into operation. Eventually, after the most heart-breaking period of my life, both my wife and son, who had just begun to earn a few shillings, told me to get out, as I was living on them and taking the food they needed.*

How to answer

- Identify the key points or issues raised in the source – this can be done by underlining or highlighting the most important points.
- Use your knowledge of this topic area to place the source into its historical context – you need to test the accuracy of what the source says against your knowledge of this topic area.
- Consider the attribution of the source to identify strengths and limitations:
  - ☐ Who wrote it?
  - ☐ When did they write it?
  - ☐ Why was it written?
  - ☐ What was its purpose?
- How does this impact upon the reliability and accuracy of the information?
- Make a reasoned judgement on the accuracy of the source, making clear links to the question.

Example answer

Step 1: Identifies and discusses the key points raised in the source.

> The sources shows the effects of the means test on this man and his family. He explains a number of specific issues. The means test affected his relationship with his wife as it led to arguments about money, and this then led to threats that their marriage might be over. He explains that the earnings of his wife and son were taken into account when they were means tested, and as he was unemployed he was living off them, and the means test meant they had less money, so his wife and son told him to leave the household.

Step 2: Use of own knowledge to provide historical context to test the accuracy of the source.

> The source highlights the problem with the means test. As a consequence of the means test, the amount of money (dole) an unemployed person received was dependent upon their circumstances. If an unemployed man had a wife and children that earned money that would affect the amount of dole he would get. This is explained by the man in the source when he states that the means test led to his wife and son saying that he was living off their earnings. Also the means test could mean that the earning of others in the family meant that no dole was paid to the unemployed man. The source, therefore, very accurately describes and explains this issue.

However, the source states that it was the means test that put a strain on his marriage and was ultimately responsible for his wife and son telling him to leave. This might not have been a typical impact of the means test on all families, so we have only one unemployed person's account of their experience. The means test also caused other reactions which the account does not cover, so we only have a limited view of the impact. In this personal account we have someone who might be trying to find a reason for the breakdown of his marriage and blames the means test, when there may have been other factors and reasons. Therefore, while the source accurately explains some of the effects of the means test, particularly the effect of other family earnings on the amount of dole an unemployed person might receive, it is limited in explaining other effects and may not be typical of the effect the means test had on all unemployed people.

Step 3: Reaches a substantiated judgement upon the accuracy of the statement posed in the question.

Now try answering the following question:

To what extent does Source C accurately explain the contribution made by women during the Second World War?

Source C: A young woman describes her working day in a factory in 1943

The room was about 40 yards long by 20 broad [37 metres by 18 metres]. There are three benches of small machines and a few large drilling machines on the floor. Altogether there are about 40 women and about a dozen men. My machine is a drilling one, and I am given a heap of small brass plates to drill holes in. It is quite dark when we come out – which strikes one with a curious shock of surprise, for one feels not so much tired, rather as if one has missed the day altogether.

Examination guidance for Question 3

This section provides guidance on how to answer a question on significance. Look at the following question:

> Why was rationing significant during the Second World War?

How to answer

- Use your knowledge to place the key issue in context.
- Explain what was happening at that time.
- Include specific factual detail to help construct an argument.
- Make regular links to the key issue, providing some judgement.
- Conclude with a reasoned and well-supported judgement.

Example answer

Step 1: Begin by placing the key issue into context, providing some background detail.

> Even in the late 1930s the memory of the First World War and the hardships it had caused were still in the nation's memory bank. During the war food had become scarce and the government had acted late to introduce rationing. As it looked like war might happen during 1939, the government acted quickly to introduce rationing.

Step 2: Continue to develop the context, provide specific detail and make links to the key issue, attempting some judgement.

> The introduction of rationing was significant during the Second World War as Britain imported 55 million tons of its food from abroad. The government knew that the enemy would try to disrupt this supply of food by destroying shipping carrying these supplies to British ports. As the war progressed food supplies became dangerously low, particularly in 1942, when the Germans destroyed 275 merchant ships in the Atlantic. Therefore, to plug this 55 million ton gap, the government needed food that was grown at home to be used carefully, and therefore introduced rationing of essential food items. Rationing was also significant, as it was a way that the government could ensure that the population were all getting a fair amount of food which would help maintain the basic health of civilians. Through rationing they also encouraged people to grow their own food on allotments, in their gardens and any spare land they could utilise. Rationing was also significant because it introduced many people to food types that they were not usually accustomed to or familiar with. The carrot became used in many ways including drinks and baking.

Step 3: Conclude with a reasoned and well-supported judgement upon the key issue.

> Rationing was significance during the Second World because had it not been introduced Britain civilians might not have survived the war and the national could have reached starvation levels, and that would have seriously affected the morale of people. It also showed how people were prepared to do as the government wanted, which was to pull together and make sure the nation was strong.

Now try answering the following question:

Why was the introduction of the means test so significant during the 1930s?

Examination guidance for Question 4

This section provides guidance on how to answer the question on connections between three features. Look at the following question:

> Explain the connections between any THREE of the following:
> - The introduction of conscription in Germany in 1935
> - The re-militarisation of the Rhineland, 1936
> - The Munich Crisis, 1938
> - Britain's policy of appeasement in the 1930s.

How to answer

- Select three factors which you think show clear connections.
- Use your knowledge to explain the three factors, making links between them.
- Aim to cover a number of points to illustrate how the factors are connected.
- Conclude with a final sentence demonstrating relevant connections.

Example answer

Issues chosen: The introduction of conscription in Germany in 1935, the re-militarisation of the Rhineland, 1936, and Britain's policy of appeasement in the 1930s.

As Germany had been restricted by the Treaty of Versailles (1919) to a very small army, Hitler decided that he needed a larger army. He was prepared to break the Treaty and introduce conscription, which then gave him any army with which he could re-militarise the Rhineland. Although Britain should have stopped this, they did not and let Hitler get away with it by following a policy of appeasement.

Step 1: Select three factors and introduce them, pointing out a connection.

Having an army of only 100,000 men made Germany feel weak and unable to protect itself, and it did not fit in with Hitler's plans. As he wished to break the Treaty of Versailles, and make Germany a great power again, he needed a much larger army. Also, as Hitler planned to put all Germans to work, after the effect of the Depression, putting men in the army gave them a job. With a larger and stronger army he was able to re-militarise the Rhineland. This piece of land around the River Rhine, and between Germany and France was vital to Germany's protection from future invasion. Hitler was now able to send in troops to make sure that Germany could defend its border. However, this action should have been stopped by Britain, and France. Britain, however, thought that if they allowed Hitler to undo certain parts of the Treaty of Versailles, he would soon be satisfied, and not cause a European war. Also, Britain was still recovering from the Depression and did not want to get involved in a war. So they appeased Hitler. They gave in to him and let him do what he wanted. This made him more powerful. The three are also connected because they each taught Hitler that if he broke the Treaty of Versailles he could then take an action that would be appeased by Britain, in other words he could do what he wanted and no one would stop him.

Step 2: Use your knowledge to explain and develop the connections further.

It is clear that had Hitler not conscripted an army he would not have been in a position to re-militarise the Rhineland and Britain would have not used the policy of appeasement. The connection between the three meant that Hitler became more powerful.

Step 3: Conclude with a final few sentences demonstrating clear connections.

Now try answering the following question:

Explain the connections between any three of the following:
- Competition from abroad in the 1920s
- New markets
- Obsolete methods
- The Wall Street Crash.

Examination guidance for Question 5

This section provides guidance on how to answer the interpretation question. Look at the following question:

> Read Interpretation 1. How far do you agree with this interpretation of the outcome of the Jarrow hunger march?

> **Interpretation 1:** From the memories of the Jarrow March by Kathleen Haigh who was interviewed for Radio Newcastle in 2008.
>
> *My uncle, Jimmy McCauley, was the second last of the marchers to die. He said he wore out many pairs of shoes on the march and that all of the marchers looked forward to being fed by the people in whichever town they arrived! In retrospect, he believed that the march was in vain because nothing happened afterwards to bring jobs to the town. The legacy which does remain is that Jarrow has found its place in history thanks to their brave efforts.*

How to answer

- Outline the interpretation given in the extract.
- Provide context:
  - ☐ Discuss the content of the extract linking it to your knowledge of the events.
  - ☐ What evidence can you include to support the main message of the extract?
- Consider the author:
  - ☐ How does what you are told about the author impact upon the reliability and accuracy of the information in the extract?
  - ☐ Why was the extract produced?
  - ☐ Who was the intended audience? Does this impact upon the interpretation?
- Identify other interpretations:
  - ☐ Suggest that other historians may have differing viewpoints.
  - ☐ Outline some of the arguments of other interpretations, explaining how they differ.
  - ☐ Explain why these interpretations differ.
- Conclusion:
  - ☐ Provide a substantiated judgement which addresses how and why interpretations on this issue differ.

Example answer

The interpretation clearly states that Jarrow marchers marched a long way as their boots were worn out. This suggests that they also marched for a long time. It also states that they looked forward to the food they received from people along the march, which could suggest that people were willing to support the marchers and wanted to meet them. The interpretation also states that the marcher believed that the march was in vain, and, therefore did not achieve what it set out to do, however, it did leave a legacy.

Step 1: Outline the interpretation given in the source.

It is true that the march took a long time and covered a great distance. The march was from Jarrow to London, took eight months and covered 450 kilometres. It was also true that many marchers wore out their shoes and boots. It is also true that people along the route came out of their houses to show them support, and gave them food. It is true that some people thought that the march had failed as when they reached London, they were told by the government minister to go back to Jarrow and sort out their problems themselves. It is also true that the march created a legacy, and that it did go down in history as an attempt by people to make change happen.

Step 2: Provide context – use your knowledge to expand and develop the content of the source.

Step 3: Authorship – develop the attribution to make a judgement upon the reliability and accuracy of the interpretation based upon what you know about the author.

The author of the interpretation was related to one of the marches and is retelling his account of the march. This was done for a radio interview in Newcastle, a city close to Jarrow, and a place where the Jarrow March is still keenly remembered and seen as part of their culture and heritage. She is recalling what her uncle must have told her, probably in conversation, at some point in their family relationship.

Step 4: Other interpretations – suggest other interpretations, commenting upon how and why they differ from the given interpretation.

However, there are other interpretations about the outcome of the Jarrow March. It is suggested that it did achieve some of its aims and it was not in vain. The marchers presented a petition to parliament and showed that people were prepared to make others aware of the difficulties they faced. The march raised the profile of protest, and encouraged others to take action to show the government how hard life was during the Depression. The marchers surprised some of the authorities, like the police, who were initially suspicious that the marchers just wanted to create trouble and cause disruption. In fact, the police praised the discipline of the marchers. While some people thought the march achieved little, the marchers returned to Jarrow as heroes, and were regarded highly for having done their best to make people and the government aware of how difficult life was during the depression. These types of interpretations differ somewhat from the way Kathleen Haigh recounted what her uncle said.

Step 5: Conclusion – provide a reasoned judgement upon the validity of the interpretation given, weighed up against other interpretations.

The interpretation given by Kathleen Haigh of her uncle's view of the Jarrow March is an accurate account of what she was told by her uncle, but it is based on one person's view of the march. The interpretation does support views about the march, but does not reflect some interpretations that see the march as having some success, as the interpretation sees the march as being in vain. Kathleen Haigh's interpretation should, therefore, be seen as a valid, and valuable part of the history of the Jarrow March, but not the only or complete view of it and the outcomes the march achieved.

Now try answering the following question:

Read Interpretation 1. How far do you agree with this interpretation of the experience of evacuation during the Second World War?

Interpretation 1: Peggy O'Neil Davies recalls her life as an evacuee

I was nearly ten years of age when the Second World War was declared and really didn't think it would make a difference to me. It was the grownups that were talking about it. However, life changed dramatically for us children. My mother and father decided I should be evacuated. They didn't talk to me about it, I was just told I was going. My mother came with me to see me settled and to see where I was going to live. We went by train to the nearest town, then up the valley by bus. I had always lived in a town and here I was going through these mountains and green fields. The house I went to stay at had two children, a boy and a girl. Their mother did her best to make me feel welcome before my mother left me with these strangers. However, they were so good I really didn't feel homesick. At the beginning we were 'the evacuees', but soon we were accepted in the village and in school (in the next village) to which we had to walk every day.

Glossary

The Elizabethan Age 1558–1603

Alms-house a house for the poor, paid for by charity

Ambassador the official representative of a foreign ruler

Armada Spanish word for a fleet of warships

Book of Common Prayer contained the orders of church services, including morning and evening prayer, Communion, marriage, baptism and burial

Brownist a follower of Robert Browne, separatist, *see* Separatist

Calvinist a follower of the French theologian John Calvin who carried out a Protestant Reformation in Geneva from 1541 onwards. He believed in a church structure where there were no bishops

Communion religious service that involved the offering of bread and wine to the congregation

Council of the North enforced government authority and policies in the north of England

Courtier a person who attends the Royal Court

Dissolution of the monasteries the official closure of all monasteries between 1536–39 on the order of Henry VIII

Doctrine the principles of a religious belief

Dowry money or property paid by the father of the bride on her marriage

Excommunicate to expel from the Roman Catholic Church, thereby denying the individual the right to enter heaven

Hawking the sport of causing falcons to return from flight to their trainers and to hunt under the direction of the trainer

Illegitimate a child born to parents who were not married at the time of the birth

Inflation an increase of a wide range of prices and services

Interludes a play performed by strolling players at fairs and taverns in Wales

Jesuit a member of the Society of Jesus founded in 1540 to support the pope in the fight against heretics and to carry out missionary work

Justice of the peace an official appointed by the government to keep law and order and to try minor court cases

Labouring poor those who worked with their hands, often for low wages and frequently living in poverty

Local militia part-time forces raised in each county, in times of emergency to help put down rebellions and maintain the peace

Lord Chamberlain A person who ran the Royal Household

Marches, The the name given to the borderland between wales and England

Marian debt Queen Mary had spent more money to run the country than she had received through taxation, therefore she had had to borrow money

Marian exiles those Protestants who fled abroad to Protestant cities such as Geneva and Frankfurt after the Catholic, Mary I, became queen in 1553

Marian Persecution the persecution of non-Catholics during the reign of Mary I

Mass the main service of the Roman Catholic Church in which the body and blood of Christ, in the form of bread and wine, are consumed

May Day the first day of May celebrated as a holiday

Moderate Puritan a Puritan who reluctantly accepted the Religious Settlement of 1559 but continued to call for further reforms, *see also* Puritan

Mullion a vertical stone or wooden bar between window panes, often carved or ornate

Papal Bull a document containing the Pope's instructions which all Catholics were instructed to obey

Patronage when the monarch gave out special favours such as land or positions in court to people in order to retain their support

Poor relief action taken by the government, the church or private individuals to help the poor

Prayer Book a book containing prayers used as church services

Presbyterian a Puritan who sought further reform (*see* Moderate Puritan) of the church and called for the abolition of bishops and for each church to be run by a committee of Presbyters (elders or teachers) elected by the congregation. Well established in Scotland, *see also* Puritan

Privateer a privately owned ship commissioned for war service by a government

Privy Council a committee of ministers appointed by Elizabeth to advise her

Propaganda material issued, usually by governments, to persuade people to think or behave in a particular way

Prophesyings meetings of ministers and other interested parties in which ministers practised their preaching skills

Protestant a member of the Christian Church which separated from the Roman Catholic Church in the sixteenth century

Puritan an extreme Protestant who wanted churches to be very plain, without decoration, and wanted simple services with no music, *see also* Moderate Puritan, Presbyterian and Separatist

Recusant a person who refused to attend the services of the Church of England

Regent a person who governs while the monarch is under age

Secret service government department that conducts intelligence operations such as spying

Seminary priests priests trained in Roman Catholic colleges

Separatist a member of the most radical Puritan group, who wanted to break away from the national church and for each church to be independent and run on a parish-by-parish basis by committees chosen from the congregation. Sometimes know as 'Brownists', *see also* Puritan

Smallpox an infectious disease with a high fever and eruptions on the skin

Spanish Inquisition set up in Spain in 1479 to root out heresy; those arrested were sometimes tortured and if found guilty burnt at the stake

Spanish Main term used to describe those parts of central and southern America ruled by Spain and the seas around them which they controlled

Succession the right by which one person succeeds to an office

Theology the study of the Christian faith through the teachings of the bible

Treason plotting against the monarch or government

Vagabond a homeless unemployed person

Vestments the official clothes worn by church clergy

Via media the 'middle way' between Catholicism and Protestantism

Wars of the Roses the struggle between the families of York and Lancaster for the kingship of England between 1455 and 1485

Wattle and daub the in-fill between the timbers of a timber framed house, formed from a mesh of poles and twigs woven together and coated with a layer of clay or plaster

Depression, War and Recovery, 1930–1951

Black Market   illegal buying or selling of officially controlled or scarce goods

Coalition government   a parliamentary government in which several political parties cooperate

Communist   someone who believes in the economic and social system envisioned by the nineteenth-century German scholar Karl Marx

Conscription   compulsory enlistment of people for state service, typically into the armed forces

Demilitarise   remove all military forces from an area

Demobilisation   the process of standing down a nation's armed forces from combat-ready status usually after a victorious conclusion to a war

Depression   a sustained, long-term downturn in economic activity

Deputation   a group of people appointed to undertake a mission or take part in a formal process on behalf of a larger group

Exports   goods or services sent for sale in other countries

Führer   a tyrannical leader

Hunger march   a march undertaken by a group of people in protest against unemployment or poverty, especially any of those by unemployed workers in Britain during the 1920s and 1930s

Imports   a good or service brought into one country from another

Incendiary bomb   a bomb designed to start fires when detonated

League of Nations   an international organisation established after World War I which aimed to prevent war between member nations and encourage co-operation

Lend–Lease   services supplied by the USA to its allies during World War II under an act of Congress (Lend-Lease Act) passed in 1941

Mandate   territory to be assigned to another country under the League of Nations

Manifesto   a public declaration of policy and aims, especially one issued before an election by a political party or candidate

Mass-production   the manufacture of large quantities of one product

Means Test   a determination of whether an individual or family is eligible for government assistance

National Government   a government that controls a nation

Plebiscite   the direct vote of all the members of an electorate on an important question

Polish Corridor   or Gdańsk Corridor, was a territory located in the region of Pomerelia formerly part of West Prussia

Radar   a system for detecting the presence, direction, distance, and speed of aircraft, ships, and other objects

Rations   a fixed amount of food or product officially allowed to each person during a time of shortage, as in wartime

Reparations   the compensation for war damage paid by a defeated state

Socialist   someone who believes in the collective or governmental ownership of the means of production and distribution of goods

Standard of living   the degree of wealth and material comfort available to a person

Stock Exchange   a market in which shares are bought and sold

Index

Act against Seditious Sectaries 103
Act of Exchange 60
Act of Supremacy 59–60
Act of Uniformity 59–60
actors 49, 50, 51, 53
Air Raid Precautions (ARP) 144
air raid shelters 145
air raid wardens 144
Allen, William 67
Alleyn, Edward 51
Anschluss 140
anti-aircraft guns 146
appeasement 141, 142
archery 46
Babington Plot 76–7
Baldwin, Stanley 123, 125
ball games 47, 132
Bancroft, Richard 98
barrage balloons 146
bear-baiting 44, 45
Beneš, Edvard 140
Bess of Hardwick 26
Bevan, Aneurin 181, 185
Beveridge Report 178–80
Bevin boys 147
black market 164
bombing raids 149–52, 154, 174
Boyd Orr, John 128
British Medical Association (BMA) 181
Brownists 103
bull-baiting 45
Burbage, James 49
Burbage, Richard 51
Camden, William 93
Campion, Edmund 68
Cartwright, Thomas 97
Catholics 55, 56, 66–81
Cecil, Robert 13
Cecil, William (later Lord Burghley) 10, 12, 19, 69, 73, 84
censorship 150, 155, 161, 162–3
Chamberlain, Neville 140, 141, 160, 167
Churchill, Winston 140, 142, 167–9
cinema 131, 161
cnapan 47
coal industry 24, 116, 117, 147, 186, 188
cockfighting 45
conscription 147
Conservative Party 123, 175–7, 183, 186
Cope, Anthony 100
Council of the North 72
Council of Wales and the Marches 14, 15
Court of Great Sessions 14–17

Court of the Quarter Sessions 15
Court of the Star Chamber 15
Cousins, Frank 128
Czechoslovakia Crisis 140
dancing 47
Davies, Richard 62
Davison, William 77
de Bobadilla, Francisco 92
Dekker, Thomas 51
de Mendoza, Francisco 74
demobilisation 173
Depression 116–36
    industrial decline 116–18
    light industry 133–5
    making ends meet 128–9
    self-help 129
    sports 132
Deputy Lieutenant office 16
Devereux, Robert (2nd Earl of Essex) 13
de Witt, Johannes 49, 50
'Dig for Victory' campaign 165
dole 120
Drake, Francis 84, 85, 86, 87, 88
Dudley, Robert (Earl of Leicester) 10, 12
economy 19, 171
Education Act, 1944 180, 184, 187
education systems 29, 32, 33, 35, 180, 184, 187
Edward VI, King of England 5, 55
Edward VIII, King of England 126
electricity industry 133, 186, 188
Elizabethan Poor Laws 40–2
Elizabeth I, Queen of England 5–13, 22
    coronation 7
    excommunication 72
    government legislation 40–2
    and Mary 6
    and Netherlands 84
    portraits 6, 7, 8, 93
    progresses 9, 10
    religious beliefs 57
    Tilbury speech 91
Emergency Powers (Defence) Act 160
evacuation 152, 153–4
fashion 28, 32, 35
Field, John 99
Foxe, John 57
freedom of speech 19
Gravelines, Battle of 90
Gregory XIII, Pope 74
Griffith, William 80
Grindal, Edmund 101
Gwyn, Richard 80

Hácha, Emil 142
Hardwick Hall 26–7
Harman, Thomas 38
Harrison, William 24, 25, 33, 34, 38, 40
Hatton, Christopher 10, 12, 78, 100
hawking 46
Hawkins, John 87, 88
Henry VIII, King of England 5, 55
Hentzner, Paul 45
Herbert, Henry (2nd Earl of Pembroke) 14
Hext, Edward 38
Hitler, Adolf 137, 138
Holinshed, Raphael 41, 68
Homes for All policy 185, 188
Hooker, Richard 98
housing 24–7, 30–1, 185, 188
Howard, Lord Charles (Duke of Effingham) 87, 88, 89
Huet, Thomas 62
hunger marches 121, 122–7
hunting 46
inflation 19, 37
iron and steel industry 116, 117, 175
James VI, King of Scotland 77, 78
Jarrow 116
Jarrow March 122–5
Jennings, Hilda 119
Jesuits 67, 75
justices of the peace (JPs) 15, 16, 17, 41, 59, 60, 99
Katheryn of Berain 21
Kempe, Will 51
Kyd, Thomas 51
Labour government reforms 178–87
Labour Party 123, 127, 175–7, 178
League of Nations 137, 138
Leicester, Earl of 84, 99
lifestyles, Elizabethan 24–35
    gentry and nobility 24–30, 43
    lower classes 34–5, 43
    Welsh gentry 30–3
Mainwaring, W.H. 126
Marian Persecution 5, 7
Marlowe, Christopher 51, 52
Marprelate Tracts 98, 103, 104
Mary, Queen of Scots 69–70, 73, 74, 76–7, 78
Mary Tudor, Queen of England 5, 55, 82
means test 17, 120–1
Medina Sidonia, Duke of 82, 86, 89, 92
Merrick, Rice 14
Ministry of Information 163–4
Morgan, William 62, 63

Morrison, Richard 48
Munich Agreement 140, 142
music 47, 96, 161
Nashe, Thomas 24, 52
National Government 120
National Health Act 181
National Health Service (NHS) 181–3, 187
nationalisation 186, 188
Nationalist Socialist German Workers
    (Nazi) Party 137
National Unemployed Workers' Movement
    (NUWM) 121, 123
Nazi–Soviet Pact 142
Netherlands 82, 83–4, 86, 93
night watchmen 16
Norfolk, Duke of (Thomas Howard) 71, 73
Northern Earls rebellion 71
Northumberland, Earl of (Thomas Percy)
    71
Orwell, George 119, 121
overseers of the poor 17
Owen, George 20, 47, 64
parish constables 16, 17
Parker, Matthew, Archbishop of
    Canterbury 57, 60, 97
parliament
    Elizabethan 15, 18–19, 59, 62, 67, 72,
        73, 75, 99–100
    20th-century 164, 180
Parma, Duke of (Alexander Farnese) 84,
    86, 92, 93
patronage 10, 32, 48, 52
Penry, John 104
Philip II, King of Spain 5, 57, 61, 71, 73,
    75, 78
    and Netherlands 83
    and Spanish Armada 82, 86, 92
Pius V, Pope 72
Plas Mawr townhouse, Conwy 31
Platter, Thomas 49
playwrights 51
Pope, Thomas 51
popular entertainment 44–54, 131, 161
poverty 36–7, 40, 128
Presbyterianism 97
Privy Council 11–12, 15, 99
propaganda
    Elizabethan 8, 9, 52, 81, 103
    20th-century 127, 138, 147, 155, 156,
        158, 162–3, 164
prophesyings 101
Protestants 55, 56

Puritans 52, 55, 56, 95–105
radar 146
radio 131, 161, 175
Raleigh, Walter 10
rationing 155–6, 164
recusancy 59, 60, 61, 67–8, 78
Religious Settlement 57, 61–4
reserved occupations 147
Rhodes, Hugh 32
Rhondda valley hunger march 126–7
Ridolfi Plot 73
Rowntree, Seebohm 128
Royal Court 10
Royal Injunctions 60
Saar Plebiscite 138
St Fagan's Castle, Cardiff 30
Salesbury, William 62
Scotland 69
Second World War
    aftermath 170–7
    Blitz 149–52
    coping with 148–59
    evacuation 153–4
    maintaining morale 160–9
    post-war reconstruction 178–88
    preparations for 143–7
    rationing 155–6, 164
    women's contribution 157–8
Shakespeare, William 51, 52
sheriffs 15, 16, 19
shipbuilding industry 116, 117, 122
Sidney, Henry 14
social structure, Elizabethan 23–4
Spanish Armada 82–94
    course of 88–91
    Elizabeth's Tilbury speech 91
    failure of 92
    and fireships 89, 92
    Philip's preparation for 86
    reasons for 82–5
    results of 93
    threat posed by 87
Special Areas Acts 134
Spitfire Fund 166
Stockwood, John 52
Strickland, Walter 99
strolling players 48
Stubbes, Philip 47, 53
Stubbs, John 98
taxation 19
television 132, 161
textile industry 117

theatre 48–53
    attitudes to 52–3
    theatre companies 48
    theatre buildings 49–50
Thirty-nine Articles 60, 99
Thomas, Hugh 14
Throckmorton Plot 74
transport industry 186, 188
Treason Act 72
Treforest Industrial Estate 135
Tudor dynasty 4–5
Turner, Peter 100
Ubaldini, Petruccio 89
unemployment
    Elizabethan 17, 37, 38, 43
    20th-century 117, 118–19, 120–1, 122,
        128, 129
Vagabonds Act 40, 41
vagrancy 38–9, 40
Vaughan, Edward 46
Versailles, Treaty of 137
Vestments Controversy 97
Victory parties and parades 172
Wales
    Catholic martyrs 80
    cinemas 131
    emigration from 130
    evacuation 154
    gentry 20–1
    local government 14
    post-war 170, 171
    Puritans in 104
    recusancy 78
    Rhondda valley hunger march 126–7
    Swansea, bombing of 150–1, 154
    theatre in 52
    Welsh translation of Bible 62–4
Wall Street Crash 116, 118–19
Walsingham, Francis 10, 13, 73, 75, 76, 77,
    84, 99
war damage 174
welfare state 179–80, 187
Wentworth, Peter 100
Westmoreland, Earl of (Charles Neville) 71
White, Thomas 52
Whitgift, John 102, 104
Wilcox, Thomas 99
William the Silent 84
Wyatt, Thomas 6
Wynn, John 20, 32

Acknowledgements

The Publishers would like to thank the following for permission to reproduce copyright material.

p.3 © Morphart Creation – Shutterstock; **p.5** *l* © World History Archive/Alamy Stock Photo; **p.5** *c* © World History Archive/Alamy Stock Photo; **p.5** *r* © Active MUSEUM/Alamy Stock Photo; **p.6** © GL Archive/Alamy Stock Photo; **p.7** *l* © Granger Historical Picture Archive/Alamy Stock Photo; **p.7, 12** and **13** *r* © World History Archive/Alamy Stock Photo; **p.8** © PAINTING/Alamy Stock Photo; **p.9** © DeAgostini/Getty Images; **p.12** *t* © The Print Collector/Getty Images; **p.12** *c* © ACTIVE MUSEUM/Alamy Stock Photo; **p.12** *b* © Granger, NYC./Alamy Stock Photo; **p.13** *t* © Universal History Archive/Getty Images; **p.13** *c* © Heritage Image Partnership Ltd/Alamy Stock Photo; **p.13** *b* © SPUTNIK/Alamy Stock Photo; **p.19** © FALKENSTEINFOTO/Alamy Stock Photo; **p.20** *l* Public Domain; **p.20** *r* © christopher jones/Alamy Stock Photo; **p.21** *r* © National Museum Wales/HIP/TopFoto; **p.21** *l* © watercolour by Moses Griffith, National Library of Wales; **p.26** *t* © Granger, NYC./Alamy Stock Photo; **p.26** *b* © Arcaid Images/Alamy Stock Photo; **p.27** © Corbis. All Rights Reserved; **p.29** © Granger, NYC./Alamy Stock Photo; **p.30** © Curtseyes/Alamy Stock Photo; **p.31** *t* © Rob Farrow via Wikipedia Commons (https://creativecommons.org/licenses/by-sa/2.0/deed.en); **p.31** *b* © David Lyons/Alamy Stock Photo; **p.33** © dibrova/123RF; **p.34** © Andy Harmsworth; **p.35** © Peter Horree/Alamy Stock Photo; **p.36** © A Rich Man Spurns a Ragged Beggar, from 'A Christall Glass of Christian Reformation' by Stephen Bateman, 1569 (woodcut) (b/w photo), English School, (16th century)/Private Collection/Bridgeman Images; **p.42** © Fotosearch /Stringer/Getty Images; **p.44** © The Art Archive/Alamy Stock Photo; **p.45** © SOTK2011/Alamy Stock Photo; **p.46** © Pictorial Press Ltd/Alamy Stock Photo; **p.50** © Classic Image/Alamy Stock Photo; **p.58** © TopFoto; **p.61** © Pictorial Press Ltd/Alamy Stock Photo; **p.62** © National Library of Wales; **p.63** *t* © National Library of Wales; **p.63** *b* © National Library of Wales; **p.68** *l* © World History Archive/Alamy Stock Photo; **p.68** *r* © The Trial of Edmund Campion, illustration from 'Ecclesiae Anglicane Trophea', 1584 (engraving), Cavalieri, (Cavalleriis) Giovanni Battista de' (c.1525–1601)/By permission of the Governors of Stonyhurst College/Bridgeman Images; **p.69** *l* © Pictorial Press Ltd/Alamy Stock Photo; **p.69** *r* © liszt collection/Alamy Stock Photo; **p.72** © The Pope's Bull against the Queen in 1570 (engraving) (b&w photo), Hulsen, Friedrich van (c.1580-1660)/Private Collection/Bridgeman Images; **p.74** © Chronicle/Alamy Stock Photo; **p.76** ©The National Archives, London. England/Mary Evans; **p.77** © World History Archive/Alamy Stock Photo; **p.78** and **108** © 2003 Topham Picturepoint; **p.80** © National Library of Wales; **p.82** © Heritage Images/Getty Images; **p.83** © PAINTING/Alamy Stock Photo; **p.84** © Portrait of Philip II (mounted on a cow), the Duke of Alencon, the Duke of Alba, William of Orange and Queen Elizabeth I, Moro, Philip (d.1578)/Private Collection/Bridgeman Images; **p.85** *r* © GL Archive/Alamy Stock Photo; **p.85** *l* © Mary Evans Picture Library; **p.87** © Granger, NYC./Alamy Stock Photo; **p.88** © Granger, NYC./Alamy Stock Photo; **p.89** and **107** © Hulton Archive/Getty Images; **p.90** © Hulton Archive/Stringer; **p.91** © Granger, NYC./Alamy Stock Photo; **p.92** ©Hulton Archive/Getty Images; **p.93** © Archivart/Alamy Stock Photo; **p.95** © age fotostock/Alamy Stock Photo; **p.96** *l* © Granger, NYC./Alamy Stock Photo; **p.98** © Chronicle/Alamy Stock Photo; **p.101** © Hulton Archive/2008 Getty Images; **p.102** © The Print Collector/Alamy Stock Photo; **p.115** © World History Archive/TopFoto; **p.118** © Karl Wimer/The Denver Business Journal; **p.121** © Hulton Archive/Getty Images; **p.123** © Travel Ink/Getty Images; **p.124** *l* © Fox Photos/Stringer; **p.124** *r* © Hulton Archive/Getty Images; **p.127** © Chronicle/Alamy Stock Photo; **p.129** © Popperfoto/Getty Images; **p.130** © Pictorial Press Ltd/Alamy Stock Photo; **p.131** *l* © Daily Herald Archive/SSPL/Getty Images; **p.131** *r* © Daily Herald Archive/National Museum of Science & Media/Science & Society Picture Library; **p.132** © Fox Photos/Getty Images; **p.133** © esbarchives; **p.134** © Gateshead Council; **p.135** *t* © By Permission of Rhondda Cynon Taf Libraries; **p.135** *b* © By Permission of Rhondda Cynon Taf Libraries; **p.137** © David Low/Solo Syndication; **p.138**